T0159361

The Writings of Frithjof Schuon
Series

World Wisdom
The Library of Perennial Philosophy

The Library of Perennial Philosophy is dedicated to the exposition of the timeless Truth underlying the diverse religions. This Truth, often referred to as the *Sophia Perennis*—or Perennial Wisdom—finds its expression in the revealed Scriptures as well as the writings of the great sages and the artistic creations of the traditional worlds.

Christianity/Islam: Perspectives on Esoteric Ecumenism appears as one of our selections in the Writings of Frithjof Schuon series.

The Writings of Frithjof Schuon

The Writings of Frithjof Schuon form the foundation of our library because he is the pre-eminent exponent of the Perennial Philosophy. His work illuminates this perspective in both an essential and comprehensive manner like none other.

English Language Writings of Frithjof Schuon

Original Books
The Transcendent Unity of Religions
Spiritual Perspectives and Human Facts
Gnosis: Divine Wisdom
Language of the Self
Stations of Wisdom
Understanding Islam
Light on the Ancient Worlds
Treasures of Buddhism (In the Tracks of Buddhism)
Logic and Transcendence
Esoterism as Principle and as Way
Castes and Races
Sufism: Veil and Quintessence
From the Divine to the Human
Christianity/Islam: Essays on Esoteric Ecumenicism
Survey of Metaphysics and Esoterism
In the Face of the Absolute
The Feathered Sun: Plains Indians in Art and Philosophy
To Have a Center
Roots of the Human Condition
Images of Primordial and Mystic Beauty: Paintings by Frithjof Schuon
Echoes of Perennial Wisdom
The Play of Masks
Road to the Heart: Poems
The Transfiguration of Man
The Eye of the Heart
Form and Substance in the Religions
Adastra & Stella Maris: Poems by Frithjof Schuon (bilingual edition)
Songs without Names, Volumes I-VI: Poems by Frithjof Schuon
Songs without Names, Volumes VII-XII: Poems by Frithjof Schuon
World Wheel, Volumes I-III: Poems by Frithjof Schuon
World Wheel, Volumes IV-VII: Poems by Frithjof Schuon
Primordial Meditation: Contemplating the Real

Original Books Not Yet Published in English
Autumn Leaves & The Ring: Poems by Frithjof Schuon

Edited Writings
The Essential Frithjof Schuon, ed. Seyyed Hossein Nasr
Songs for a Spiritual Traveler: Selected Poems (bilingual edition)
René Guénon: Some Observations, ed. William Stoddart
The Fullness of God: Frithjof Schuon on Christianity,
ed. James S. Cutsinger
Prayer Fashions Man: Frithjof Schuon on the Spiritual Life,
ed. James S. Cutsinger
Art from the Sacred to the Profane: East and West,
ed. Catherine Schuon

Christianity/Islam
Perspectives on Esoteric Ecumenism

A New Translation with
Selected Letters

by

Frithjof Schuon

Includes Other Previously
Unpublished Writings

Edited by
James S. Cutsinger

World Wisdom

Translated by Mark Perry, Jean-Pierre Lafouge,
and James S. Cutsinger

Published in French as
Christianisme/Islam: Visions d'œcuménisme ésotérique
Archè, 1981.

Library of Congress Cataloging-in-Publication Data

Schuon, Frithjof, 1907-1998.
  [Christianisme/islam. English]
  Christianity/Islam : perspectives on esoteric ecumenism : a new translation with
selected letters / by Frithjof Schuon ; edited by James S. Cutsinger.
      p. cm. -- (The writings of Frithjof Schuon) (The library of perennial philoso-
phy)
  Translated by Mark Perry, Jean-Pierre Lafouge, and James S. Cutsinger.
  "Includes other previously unpublished writings."
  Includes bibliographical references (p.   ) and index.
  ISBN 978-1-933316-49-9 (pbk. : alk. paper) 1. Christianity. 2. Islam. I.
Cutsinger, James S., 1953- II. Perry, Mark. III. Lafouge, Jean-Pierre, 1944- IV. Title.
  BR121.3.S3713 2008
  261.2'7--dc22

                                                                        2008003696

Cover Art:
The Church of St. Mary Magdalene and
the Dome of the Rock, Jerusalem

Printed on acid-free paper in Canada.

For information address World Wisdom, Inc.
P.O. Box 2682, Bloomington, Indiana 47402-2682
www.worldwisdom.com

CONTENTS

EDITOR'S PREFACE

We are pleased to present this new edition of Frithjof Schuon's *Christianity/Islam: Perspectives on Esoteric Ecumenism.*

Widely regarded as one of the greatest spiritual writers of the twentieth century, Frithjof Schuon (1907-1998) was an authority on an extraordinary range of religious and philosophical topics, and his books have been praised by scholars and spiritual teachers from many different traditions. He was also the leading representative of the perennialist school of comparative religious thought. Deeply rooted in the *sophia perennis, philosophia perennis,* or *religio perennis*—that is, the perennial wisdom, perennial philosophy, or perennial religion, as he variously called it—Schuon's perspective embodies the timeless and universal principles underlying the doctrines, symbols, sacred art, and spiritual practices of the world's religions.

Christianity/Islam, Schuon's fourteenth major work, was published in Milan in 1981 by Archè Milano under the title *Christianisme/Islam: Visions d'œcuménisme ésotérique;* an English translation by Gustavo Polit appeared with World Wisdom Books in 1985. The present edition is based on a fully revised translation of the original French.

Among the special features of this new edition is an appendix containing previously unpublished selections from the author's letters and other private writings. Throughout his life Schuon carried on an extensive correspondence, much of it in response to questions posed by the many inquirers and visitors, from a variety of religious backgrounds, who looked to him for advice; nearly two thousand of his letters have been preserved. He also composed nearly twelve hundred short spiritual texts for close friends and associates, compiled in his later years as "The Book of Keys". These and other private writings often contained the seeds of ideas that were later developed into published articles and chapters, and it is hoped that the selections included here will afford the reader a glimpse into a new and very rich dimension of this perennial philosopher's message.

The breadth of Schuon's erudition can be somewhat daunting, especially for those not accustomed to reading philosophical and religious works. The pages of his books contain numerous allusions to traditional theological doctrines, important philosophers or spiritual authorities, and the sacred Scriptures of the world's religions, but a citation or other reference is not often provided. A series of editor's notes, organized by chapter and tagged to the relevant page numbers, has therefore been added to this new edition. Dates are provided for historical figures together with brief explanations regarding the significance of their teachings for Schuon, and citations are given for his frequent quotations from the Bible, Koran, and other sacred texts. The Authorized Version of the Bible has been used throughout; since the author made his own translations from the Koran, we have chosen to render his French for these passages directly into English, though the Pickthall interpretation of the Arabic has been given a certain preference when Koranic quotations appear in our editorial notes.

It is customary for Schuon to employ a number of technical terms in his writings, drawn from a multitude of traditions and involving several languages, including Arabic, Latin, Greek, and Sanskrit. A glossary has therefore been provided as well; here one will find foreign terms and phrases appearing both in Schuon's text and in our notes, together with translations and definitions.

James S. Cutsinger

Frithjof Schuon in 1965

Part One

CHRISTIANITY

On the Margin of Liturgical Improvisations

The liturgy can be regarded in two different ways: one may assume either that the primitive simplicity of the rites should be preserved from any cumbersome additions or on the contrary that liturgical embellishment contributes to the radiation of the rites, if not to their efficacy, and is therefore a gift of God. From the point of view of simplicity one can assert—not without pertinence—that the Rabbinical tradition added an enormous number of practices and prayers to the religion of Moses and that Christ, the spokesman of inwardness, suppressed all these observances and rejected long and complicated vocal prayers, for he intended that man make his way to God "in spirit and in truth". The Apostles continued along this way, as did the Desert Fathers, but little by little worshiping "in spirit and in truth" gave way to increasingly numerous observances, though without one possibility precluding the other;[1] thus the liturgy was born. In early times liturgy was comparatively simple and was performed only in cathedrals around the bishop and only on the eve of great festivals, "because it was necessary to occupy the faithful who came to spend long hours in church but no longer knew how to pray", as we were told by a religious who seemed to know something about this. It was then taken up by the monks, who out of zeal performed it daily; even so the liturgy used by Saint Benedict remained rather simple, though it grew more complicated and ever more laden over time with continual additions.

In order to understand the liturgy in a way that is at once precise and nuanced, one must take into account the following essential facts: if liturgical development is in part the result of negative factors, such as the spiritual deterioration of an ever more numerous collectivity, it is determined above all by an entirely unavoidable concern for adapting

---

[1] This principle "in spirit and in truth", combined with a rejection of the "commandments of men", is nonetheless a two-edged sword; Protestantism availed itself of this principle, and it cannot be denied that everything worthwhile and Biblical in the piety of the best Protestants comes from its validity; this also explains why Protestantism was able to provide asylum to certain esoteric currents. Be that as it may, in order to forestall the Lutheran paradox, it would have been necessary for medieval Catholicism to be much more realistic, complex, and flexible in its mentality and structure; we shall speak of this again in another chapter of this book.

to new conditions; and this adaptation—or this flowering of a tangible symbolism—is in itself something altogether positive and in no way opposed to the purest contemplativity. There are two elements, however, that must be distinguished: on the one hand the symbolism of forms and actions and on the other hand certain verbal developments; no doubt both are useful, but it is in the nature of formal symbolism to express the concurrence of the Holy Spirit in a more direct and incontestable manner, for the teaching of a pure symbol is not subject to the limitations of verbal expression in general or pious prolixity in particular.[2] As for the appropriateness of textual additions, one must also take into account the growing need to counter or prevent heresies, ever more numerous and more likely.

The first Christians called themselves "saints", and with good reason: in the early Church there was an atmosphere of sanctity, which doubtless could not prevent certain disorders but which in any case was dominant among the majority; the sense of the sacred was in the air, so to speak. This quasi-collective sanctity disappeared fairly rapidly—and quite naturally, men of the "dark age" being what they are—chiefly because of an increase in the number of the faithful; it then became necessary to make the presence of the sacred more tangible so men of an increasingly profane mentality would not lose sight of the majesty of the rites and access to these rites would not be too abstract, if one may put it this way. We should note in this context that there is nothing of this kind in Islam, where the element of mystery does not penetrate in a quasi-material fashion into the exoteric domain;[3] *Mahāyāna* Buddhism, on the other hand, shows a liturgical

---

[2] There is in particular the extreme complication of the rubrics. These are derived from the Roman Ritual, the Ceremonial of the Bishops, and the decrees of the Sacred Congregation of Rites; they regulate what must be done during the Mass and what must be done outside it, and the casuistry connected to this cannot be forgotten. Combined with the liturgical calendar, these rubrics give rise to an extremely complicated and finely shaded science, which can make one lose sight of the essential or reduce its importance, which amounts to the same thing; for there is no common measure between the intrinsic reality of the Eucharist and the numerous categories of Masses—"low", "solemn", "pontifical", and so forth—to say nothing of the particular and sometimes trivial intentions attached to this holiest of sacraments.

[3] In other words the liturgical element, which is exceedingly sober, is contained within the *Sunnah* itself and is not added on; its principal content is the chanting of the Koran. In Judaism the *Torah* provides us with the example of a liturgy that is at once very rich

development similar to that of Christianity; in neither case, however, is the liturgy merely a concession to human weakness, for it possesses at the same time, and by the very nature of things, the intrinsic value of a tangible crystallization of the supernatural.

The first of the viewpoints we have been comparing, that of original simplicity, is legitimate in the sense that the contemplative and the ascetic, although not always desiring to do so, are able to manage without any liturgical framework—and they would obviously prefer the sanctity of men over that of ritual forms to the extent such an alternative presents itself—whereas the second point of view, that of liturgical elaboration, is legitimate because symbolism is legitimate and also because of the demands of new situations.

One of the major errors of our time, at least on the religious plane, is to believe that a liturgy can be invented—that the ancient liturgies were inventions or that elements added in a spirit of piety are such; this is to confuse inspiration with invention,[4] the sacred with the profane, saintly souls with bureaus and committees. Another no less pernicious error is to believe that one can leap across a millennium or two and retrace one's steps to the simplicity—and sanctity—of the early Church; there is a principle of growth or structure to be observed here, for a branch cannot become the root again. One must strive toward primitive simplicity by recognizing its incomparability and without imagining that it can be recaptured by external measures and superficial attitudes; one must seek to realize primordial purity on the basis of the providentially elaborated forms and not on the basis of an ignorant and impious iconoclasm; and above all one must give up trying to introduce a pedantic and vulgar sort of intelligibility into the rites, for this is an affront to the intelligence of the faithful.

and fully revealed, but no longer possible after the destruction of the Temple.

[4] One theologian has dared to write that Saint Paul was "obliged to invent" in order to put the celestial message into practice; this is the most flagrant as well as the most ruinous error imaginable in this realm.

The following remarks should be made regarding the question of liturgical languages. The value of such languages is objective and not a subjective question of appreciation, and this means that there are languages of a sacred character and that they possess this character either by their nature or by adoption: the first case is that of languages in which Heaven has spoken and of forms of writing—alphabets or ideograms—inspired or confirmed by it; the second case is that of still noble languages that have been consecrated to the service of God, such as Armenian or Slavonic. In our day one is led to believe that the liturgical languages are obsolete and that they should be replaced by profane and modern languages because—so it would seem—people no longer understand liturgical language and therefore no longer want it; now aside from the fact that this conclusion is false—and moreover the people have never been consulted—the least that can be asked of believers is the minimum of interest and respect needed for learning the common liturgical formulas and for bearing with those they do not understand; a religious affiliation that requires vulgarization, excessive easiness, and thereby platitude is in any case worthless.[5]

All ancient languages are noble or aristocratic in their very nature: there could be nothing trivial about them,[6] triviality being the result of individualism, worldliness, and the democratic mindset. Modern languages are not incapable of expressing higher truths, of course, but they are unsuited for sacred use because of their excessively analytical

---

[5] In many cases vernacular languages run the risk of becoming the instruments of alienation and cultural tyranny: oppressed populations must henceforth have the Mass in the language of the oppressor, which is supposed to be theirs, and tribes speaking archaic languages—languages that are therefore capable in principle of liturgical use, though not in fact widely prevalent—find Latin replaced by another foreign language linguistically inferior to their own and moreover charged for them with associations of ideas far removed from the sacred. The Sioux will have Mass not in their noble Lakota but in modern English; doubtless it is impossible to translate the Mass into all the American Indian languages, but this is not the point since the Mass in Latin does exist.

[6] In ancient times the "people" possessed to a great extent the naturally aristocratic character that comes from religion; as for the "plebeians"—made up of men who do not seek to control themselves or *a fortiori* to rise above themselves—they could not determine the language as a whole. It is only democracy that seeks on the one hand to equate the plebeians with the people and on the other hand to reduce the people to the plebeians; it ennobles what is base and debases what is noble.

character and because they possess a quality that is in some respects too chatty and sentimental;[7] sacred use requires a more synthetic and impersonal idiom. In order to forestall certain objections, let us observe that Low Latin, although no longer the language of Caesar, is nonetheless not a vulgar tongue like the different languages derived from it; even if it was not entirely transformed by the mold of Christianity, it was at least adapted to it and stabilized by it, and perhaps also influenced by the Germanic soul, more imaginative and less cold than the Roman. Furthermore, the classical Latin of Cicero is not free from arbitrary restrictions as compared with the archaic language, certain values of which persisted in popular speech, so that Low Latin, derived from the fusion of the two languages, is not simply a privative phenomenon.

In the Middle Ages European intellectuality flourished within the framework of Latin;[8] with the abandonment of Latin, intellectual activity made its imprint more and more on the dialects in such a way that the modern languages derived from them are on the one hand more supple and intellectualist and on the other hand more blunted and profaned than the medieval languages. Now from the point of view of sacred usage the decisive quality is neither philosophical suppleness nor psychological complexity—altogether relative factors in any case—but the character of simplicity and sobriety, which is proper to every nonmodern idiom; it takes all the insensitivity and

---

[7] It should be noted that these shades of meaning also seem to escape many Orthodox, who appear to reason thus: since Slavonic, which is not Greek, is worthy of liturgical use, modern French, which is neither more nor less Greek, is also worthy of such use. When one is sensitive to spiritual undertones and the mystical vibrations of forms, one cannot but regret these false concessions, which moreover are not limited to the realm of language and which impoverish and disfigure the expressive splendor of the sacerdotal genius of the Eastern Church.

[8] Latin does not possess every kind of superiority, however. The Italian of Dante has many more musical and imaginative qualities; the German of a Meister Eckhart has more plasticity, more intuitive and evocative power, and more symbolic quality than Latin. Nonetheless, Latin exhibits an obvious overall pre-eminence in relation to its derivatives and the later Germanic dialects; it is also the language of the Roman Empire and is the compelling choice for this reason, especially since there is no reason for considering a plurality of liturgical languages in this linguistically and culturally over-divided sector.

narcissism of the twentieth century to conclude that the present languages of the West, or any one of them, could be substantially and spiritually superior to the more ancient languages or that a liturgical text could amount practically to a dissertation or novel.

This does not mean that only the modern languages of Europe are unsuited to sacred use: the general degeneration of humanity, which has been accelerating for several centuries, has had the particular effect outside the West of bringing about a deterioration of certain tongues existing on the margin of the sacred languages they accompany; the cause is not a fundamentally ideological and literary trivialization, as is the case in Western countries, but simply a naive materialism at the level of fact, not philosophical but nonetheless favoring dullness and flatness, and at times even vulgarity. Doubtless this phenomenon is not universal, but it does exist, and it was necessary to note it in the present context; as for oral languages, which have not been subject to this kind of deterioration, they too have lost at least much of their ancient richness, but without necessarily becoming unsuitable for liturgical use.

Liturgical elaboration depends on the genius of the religion and on the ethnic groups destined to receive it; it is providential, like the disposition and shape of the branches of a tree, and it is disproportionate—to say the least—to criticize this elaboration with a short-sighted retrospective logic[9] and to wish to correct it as if it amounted merely to an accidental succession of events. If the Latin Church has a right to exist, the Latin language is an irremovable aspect of its nature or genius.

---

[9] It goes without saying that logic is valid only if it possesses sufficient data and draws genuine conclusions from those data. But in this case it is also a question of imagination and not solely of logic: an imagination that is completely at ease in a world of din and vulgarity, to the point of finding everything that does not belong to this world abnormal and ludicrous, forfeits all right to pronounce on sacred matters.

In connection with liturgy as with everything else, people today readily refer to the rather problematical rights of "our time": this taboo notion means that things with the misfortune of being situated in what appears to us as the "past" are *ipso facto* "antiquated" and "out of date" and that things situated in what seems to us subjectively as the "present"—or, more precisely speaking, things arbitrarily selected for identification with "our time", as if other contemporary phenomena did not exist or belonged to a different period—are presented as a "categorical imperative" imbued with an "irreversible" motion. In reality what gives our time its significance are the following factors: first, the progressive decadence of the human species in conformity with cyclic law; second, the progressive adaptation of religion to the collectivity as such; third, an adaptation to the different ethnic groups concerned; fourth, the qualitative oscillations of the traditional collectivity in the grip of the temporal flux. Everything one can say to explain "our age" refers to one of these factors or their various combinations.

As for the adaptation of a young religion to a total society, what we are referring to is the transition from the "catacomb" stage to that of a state religion; it is altogether false to assert that only the first stage is normal and that the second stage—the "Constantinian", if one prefers—represents merely an illegitimate, hypocritical, and unfaithful petrifaction, for a religion cannot remain forever in the cradle but is by definition destined to become a state religion and therefore to undergo the adaptations—not at all hypocritical but simply realistic—this new situation demands. It cannot but ally itself with the ruling power, provided of course that this power submits to it; in such a case one must distinguish between two Churches: the institutional Church, immutable by virtue of its divine institution, and the human Church, necessarily political in being linked with a total collectivity, apart from which it would have no earthly existence as a great religion. While admitting that this state Church may be bad—and it is necessarily so to the extent men are bad—the holy Church nonetheless needs it in order to survive in space and time: it is from the human and imperial Church that there springs the qualitative prolongation of the early Church, that is, the Church of the saints. And there is a liturgical and theological re-adaptation that necessarily corresponds to this transition from the "catacomb" Church to the "Constantinian" Church, for it is impossible to speak to an entire society as one would speak to a handful of mystics.

We have also mentioned an adaptation to providential ethnic groups, which in the case of Christianity are *grosso modo*—after the Jews—the Greeks, Romans, Germans, Celts, Slavs, and a minority of Near-Easterners. Here again it is wrong to speak of "our time" when dealing with factors that do not depend on a particular period but on a natural unfolding, which can take place over various periods. Theological and liturgical forms clearly depend upon ethnic mentalities insofar as the question of diversity can arise in this domain.

Then there is the paradoxical problem of what one might call the progressive manifestation of religious genius. On the one hand religion displays its greatest sanctity at its origin; on the other hand it requires time to implant itself solidly in the human soil, where it needs to create a humanity in its own image if it is to bring about a maximal flowering of intellectual and artistic values coinciding with a further flowering of sanctity; this might cause one to assume an evolution, and unquestionably a kind of evolution does take place, though only in a specific human respect and not at the level of intrinsic spirituality. In every religious cycle four periods are to be distinguished: first the "apostolic" period, then the period of full development, after which comes the period of decadence, and last the final period of corruption; in Catholicism there has been an anomaly in that the period of development was brutally cut short by an influence wholly foreign to the Christian genius, namely, the Renaissance, so that in this case the period of decadence existed in a completely new dimension.

For the innovators the word "time" is in practice identified with the relativistic idea of evolution, and everything belonging to the "past" is viewed according to this false perspective, which finally reduces all phenomena to evolutionary or temporal fatalities, whereas in fact the essential lies entirely in the eternal present and in the quality of absoluteness whenever it is a question of values of the spirit.

—— ∴ ——

Beginning with the idea that the liturgy is the garment of the spiritual order and that in a religious, hence normal, civilization nothing is wholly independent of the sacred, it will be admitted that liturgy in its broadest sense embraces all forms related to the arts and crafts—insofar as they are connected to the sacred—and that for this very reason these forms cannot be just anything. Now what has to be noted here is that artistic liturgy—or liturgical art—has been radically false for several centuries, as if there were no longer any relationship between the visible and the Invisible; it would be absurd to think this state of affairs has no bearing on the spiritual order in regard to the general conditions governing ambience and development. As we have said, a particular saint may have no need for imaginative and aesthetic symbolism, but the collectivity needs it, and the collectivity must be able to produce saints; whether one likes it or not the great things in this world are bound up with little things, at least extrinsically, and it would be absurd to see nothing more than a question of ornamentation in the outward expressions of a tradition.

But let us return to the liturgy properly so called, or more exactly to the problem of its possible re-adaptation. There is no sort of charity that permits or demands degradation: to place oneself at the level of childhood or naiveté is one thing; to sink to the level of vulgarity or pride is another. The faithful have had the idea of the "people of God" or even of the "holy people" imposed upon them, and a sacerdotal function they have never even dreamed of has been suggested to them—this in an age when the people are as far removed as can be from sanctity, so far indeed that the need is felt to lower the level of the liturgy, and even the whole of religion, for their use. This is all the more absurd in that the people are still worth much more than the leveling down that is imposed upon them in the name of a perfectly unrealistic ideology; under the pretense of introducing a liturgy the people can relate to, one means to force them to lower themselves to the level of this pale imitation of liturgy. Be that as it may, it would be well to be reminded of this saying of Saint Irenaeus: "One never triumphs over error by sacrificing any of the rights of truth."

To claim that the ancient and normal, or sacerdotal and hence aristocratic, liturgy simply expresses a "time" is radically false for two reasons: first because a time amounts to nothing and explains nothing, at least in the order of values at issue here, and second because the message of the liturgy, or its sufficient reason, lies precisely outside and beyond temporal contingencies. If one enters a sanctuary, it is to escape from time; it is to find an atmosphere of the "heavenly Jerusalem", which delivers us from our earthly epoch. The merit of the ancient liturgies is not that they expressed their historical moment, but that they expressed something transcending it; and if this something gave its imprint to an epoch, this means the epoch had the quality of possessing a nontemporal side, so much so that we have every reason for loving it to the extent it possessed this quality. If "nostalgia for the past" coincides with nostalgia for the sacred, it is a virtue, not because it is directed toward the past as such, which would be totally devoid of meaning, but because it is directed toward the sacred, which transforms all duration into an eternal present and which is located nowhere else than in the liberating "now" of God.

The Enigma of the *Epiclesis*

The word *epiclesis*, which entered only gradually into the Christian vocabulary and is not found in the Bible, means an invocation (*epiklēsis*) of the Holy Spirit, specifically in connection with the Eucharistic prayers. According to the Greeks the *epiclesis* is necessary for transubstantiation[1]—the words of institution being simply a part of the Gospel narrative—whereas according to the Latins it is the words of Christ that effect the sacrament, in keeping with the theses of Saint Ambrose, Saint John Chrysostom, and Saint Augustine. For the Western Church the words of Christ—and of the priest speaking *in persona Christi*—bring about the consecration because God created by His word; for the Eastern Church, on the other hand, it is the Holy Spirit who effects the consecration because it is the Spirit who brought about the Incarnation in the Virgin.[2] It is true that certain Orthodox now recognize the validity of the Latin Mass since in principle they accept intercommunion; the reason for this is doubtless that in the Roman canon, in which the collection of prayers dates back to the fifth century but which does not include an *epiclesis*, they discern an element that in their eyes replaces it. For Catholics the Orthodox liturgy scarcely presents a problem since it includes the words of institution, whatever might be taught regarding the formula of consecration; there are even theologians, Catholic as well as Orthodox, who think that the exact delimitation of the consecration is not certain, which is rather paradoxical considering the gravity of the issue. Be that as it may, the Eastern Churches concerned themselves with the question of the moment of the consecration much later than did the Latin Church; for a long time they remained vague on this subject: the

---

[1] Let us note that for the Orthodox this term (*metousiosis* in Greek) does not have the precise meaning—the quasi-magical meaning, if you will—it has for Catholics.

[2] The first Eastern theologian to assert that the consecration is effected by the *epiclesis* and not the words of institution was Theodore, Bishop of Andide, in the twelfth century; the same position was held in the fourteenth century by Theodore of Melitene and above all by Nicholas Cabasilas. It was then that a controversy over this matter began in the Greek Church, but the doctrine of Cabasilas gained ground and little by little was generally accepted in the East in the sixteenth century, except in the Russian Church, which did not accept it until the eighteenth century.

bread and the wine become the body and blood of Christ "during the course of the *anaphora*", that is, during the general Eucharistic prayer, which corresponds to the Roman canon in the West.[3]

It is imperative to specify here that by the "Roman canon" we mean the Tridentine canon, promulgated—but not created—by Saint Pius V. He took what was in use in the Church of Rome of his time while at the same time allowing some other liturgies consecrated by custom to remain; he would never have dreamed of disallowing a Eucharistic prayer of confirmed tradition or making redundant use of a similar text having a more precise or ample import. The work of Saint Pius V was therefore solely retrospective and conservative, and it is precisely this that enabled him to be definitive; even supposing this Pope had no knowledge of all the existing manuscripts, those he did have at his disposal were clearly sufficient both theologically and liturgically, or else there would be no reason to speak of Providence or the Holy Spirit in connection with the Church.

Through the *epiclesis* the priest "prays" and "implores" God the Father to cause His Holy Spirit to descend upon the Eucharistic species and change them—"by the favor of Thy goodness", says Saint Basil—into the body and blood of Christ. Saint John Chrysostom, author of one of the most widely used *epicleses*, rightly specifies that it is the words of institution that bring about the sacramental change, but he adds that it is accomplished through the Holy Spirit since it is by its action that the body of Jesus was formed in Mary's womb; he has in any case given his *epiclesis* a consecrating form that anticipates a later Orthodox interpretation.

One of two things if we wish to be logical: either transubstantiation is certain *ex opere operato* and by virtue of the divine command

---

[3] The liturgy in Syriac seems to prove—although this strikes us as self-evident—that the ancient Easterners attached more importance to the words of institution than to the *epiclesis*: the entire *anaphora* was translated from Greek into Syriac, including the *epiclesis*, but the words of institution were left in Greek in view of their consecratory importance.

(*hoc facite in meam commemorationem*), in which case the supplication is unnecessary; or else the supplication is necessary, in which case tran-substantiation is uncertain; it is then merely possible or probable, for there is no point in praying for something whose realization is not in doubt, since it results from a divine promise, except in order to pre-pare for it and thank Heaven for it. "This is my body, this is my blood" (*calix sanguis mei*), said Christ, and not: this may be my body and my blood if you ask for it, or if you ask for it with sufficient fervor—*quod absit*; moreover, he did not entreat the Father to send the Holy Spirit in order to bring about the miracle, and therefore his order to "do this in remembrance of me" could not have implied any consecrating sup-plication; or again, in instituting the Eucharist he was not complying with any supplication on the part of the Apostles. The gift was free; nothing had been requested.[4]

Taken literally the consecratory *epiclesis* is a kind of tautology, but it is necessary to understand its underlying intention, which is above all a moral one and which is to indicate our awareness of the immense disproportion between divine grace and human impotence. To entreat God to grant us a favor already promised amounts to recognizing that the gift is undeserved, that the distance between the gift and ourselves exceeds every measure; in other words there are two elements in the *epiclesis* or Eucharistic prayer, namely, the attestation of our unwor-thiness and the invocation of the Holy Spirit so that it might prepare us for receiving the gift. For according to Saint Paul the Eucharistic gift is fatal for the unworthy, and the *epicleses* of Saint Basil and Saint John Chrysostom do not fail to take this fact into account.[5]

To this general explanation may be added another more particular one. We have noted above that the *epiclesis* is unnecessary from the standpoint of consecratory efficacy since it asks for something that has already been granted, not as a response to a prayer but by command;

---

[4] Catholicism also possesses a Eucharistic prayer by which the priest implores God to accept the sacrifice he is going to offer Him; now the priest acts *in persona Christi*, and besides it is impossible for God not to accept a sacrifice He Himself has instituted, provided the sacrifice is accomplished according to the rules.

[5] Let us note that although the Roman canon has no *epiclesis*, most of the other Latin canons—the Gallican and the Mozarabic for example—do have one. But these *epicle-ses* have never been consecratory: they ask the Father to send the Holy Spirit into the hearts of the faithful.

this in short is the objection of the Latins against the Greeks. Nicholas Cabasilas notes this objection in his "Commentary on the Divine Liturgy" and attempts to refute it, but the arguments he brings to bear are so weak that it seems to us unnecessary to analyze them.[6] On the other hand we have no difficulty in seeing the function of the *epiclesis* for Orthodox sensibility: since this sensibility is reluctant to accept the idea of a consecration *ex opere operato*, which seems to confer upon the priest, hence upon man, a kind of magical power that obliges God to bring about the miracle, the supplication—however tautological in itself—eliminates this feeling and gives man the awareness of being perfectly humble and depending solely on God. Since the Latin mentality has no such scruples—or not to the same degree—the accompanying prayers of the Catholic consecration do not have the same function as the *epiclesis;* nonetheless they play a similar role, that of actualizing in man the feeling of his unworthiness.

If the reason for the existence of the *epiclesis* is the "active cooperation of the Eucharistic community"—as an Orthodox theologian explained to us—then it is impossible to explain its specific wording, for in principle this cooperation could express itself in an entirely different manner. It could take the form of a *Domine non sum dignus*, or it could consist in giving thanks or in a prayer for the officiating priest or the entire community, and all this without being accompanied by a supplication logically bound up with the efficacy of the rite; since this is not the case, we have a right to assume that a psychological or mystical element is attached to this precise function of cooperation, an element more or less independent of the function even while coloring it in its own fashion. We have seen that the Catholic Mass also includes one such element of piety in its Eucharistic prayers, but without intending any quasi-sacerdotal communal cooperation, which is foreign to authentic Catholicism—so foreign in fact that the priest

---

[6] In saying "be fruitful and multiply" God created sexual union and the productive efficacy it involves; now the Latins would take this divine saying as an example of the consecratory words of Christ, given precisely that the word of God in Genesis was creative and not legislative, for otherwise chastity would be disobedience. An error, objects Cabasilas: for just as man must add the sexual act to the divine injunction in order to make it effective, so too the priest must add the *epiclesis* to Christ's words—as if it were the *epiclesis* rather than the accomplishment of the rite instituted by Jesus that corresponds analogically to man's sexual initiative.

can celebrate a Mass without the presence of the community, contrary to what is done in the Eastern Church.

One could argue that the supplication addressed to the Holy Spirit does not express a request that is thought to be necessary to the sacrament, but that it is simply a desire, an aspiration, a hope: a desire to see the saving miracle accomplished, an aspiration to receive the grace of the Holy Spirit, a hope for mercy and salvation. In this case the content of the prayer would be more subjective than objective; it would not be a participation in the rite as such but in the attitude of the priest before God, and it is this that would confer upon the supplication an indirectly sacerdotal function.

As to the problematic character of the *epiclesis*—in connection with the logical relationship we have indicated—some will doubtless call attention to the inadequacy of logic in theological and sacramental matters. But in our judgment the rights of logic extend to all that is expressible: a logical objection would never deserve the insult implicit in a condemnation of logic as such; on the contrary it calls for a response that resolves the objection on its own level; such a response may be difficult in fact, but it is always possible in principle. We would add—and this indeed is what matters most—that the laws of logic are rooted in the divine nature: they manifest ontological relationships within the human spirit; the delimitation of logic is itself extrinsically logical, for otherwise it would be merely arbitrary. It is obvious that logic is inoperative in the absence of indispensable objective data and of subjective qualifications that are equally necessary, and this fact renders null and void the luciferian constructions of the rationalists as well as—on another plane—the sentimental and expeditious speculations of certain theologians, no matter how formally logical those speculations might be.[7]

---

[7] The "wisdom of the world" or "according to the flesh" may encompass an arrogant and scientistic Aristotelianism, which promotes worldliness and leads to a luciferian adventure; but clearly it cannot include the Platonic current, which according to Saint Justin Martyr attests to the *Logos* and thus to Christ.

Until the third century there was no fixed Eucharistic prayer: each bishop composed or improvised his own, which shows how improbable it is that the *epiclesis* possessed an exclusively consecratory virtue; in fact it is quite implausible that the efficacy of a rite, hence its very validity, depends on an improvised prayer or on a second or third degree of inspiration.[8]

Be that as it may, the fact that the ancient bishops created prayers in no way means one can do the same in our day, for the possibilities of inspiration in the early Church cannot be transposed to a later age, an age even further removed from the origin. The temporal or historical Church is like a tree, whose phases of growth are irreversible; one phase cannot be replaced by another on the pretext of returning to the origin—that is, by referring to the possibilities of the early Church—any more than the branch of a tree can again become the trunk or the trunk the root. There is an inspiration at the apostolic level, then one at the patristic level; there is also the inspiration of saints in varying degrees, but there is assuredly no inspiration of commissions and committees, to say the least. It is true that the "spirit bloweth where it listeth", but this does not mean it wishes to blow everywhere nor in the same manner everywhere.

To put this question of an appeal to the Holy Spirit in its proper context, it is important to remember that every sacrament contains three elements: its matter, its form, and its intention. In the case of the Eucharist, the bread and wine constitute the matter, that is, the sensible supports; the consecratory words constitute the form, which "determines the matter in producing the effect and in signifying it

---

[8] There appears to have existed a Syrian liturgy in the seventh century that included neither a consecratory *epiclesis* nor words of institution; this latter point seems to us unverifiable, for this liturgy could perfectly well have contained consecratory elements not included in the written documents: the officiant could very well have uttered the words of institution "in the heart" in a manner valid in God's eyes and in conformity with certain conditions, objective as well as subjective, pertaining to the time and place; in any case an inaudible or mental utterance of the consecratory words could refer to the principle *nolite dare sanctum canibus*.

clearly"; the canon—the *anaphora* of the Greeks—conveys the intention, the *epiclesis* being part of the *anaphora*, essential for the Greeks and without importance for the Latins. Now the content of the intention is obviously not just the Eucharistic doctrine with its indispensable context of piety, but also the concern—or obligation—to do what the Church does, for otherwise there would be no guarantee of orthodoxy or of homogeneity.

To do what the Church does: for the Orthodox the Church is wherever there is a bishop in communion with all other Orthodox bishops; in another respect it could be said that it is wherever there is one of the faithful in communion with all the other faithful, but in this case the notion of the Church is both wider and more restricted in the sense that it then refers solely to the "ecclesial" condition while setting aside the "ecclesiastical" power. For the Catholic Church the first relationship is expressed by saying that the Church is where the Pope is, which essentially presupposes that the Pope is the spokesman and instrument of what has been taught always and everywhere in Western Christianity and that none of his initiatives runs counter to this orthodoxy; indeed doctrinal orthodoxy is institutional and not subject to the Pope, who on the contrary is himself subject to this orthodoxy on pain of not answering to the description of his function. If the Church is where the Pope is, it is because the Pope—or the papacy in principle—is where there is Catholic orthodoxy; one does not believe in the catechism because the Pope wishes it, but rather one believes in the Pope because the catechism requires it and to the extent it requires it. Obedience to the Pope strictly depends upon obedience to the tradition just as the quality of the papacy depends on the conformity of the Pope to traditional constants.[9]

These considerations call to mind the divergence between the Latins and Greeks on the subject of the papacy: whereas for the Latins the Pope is the sole and absolute head of the Church, invested with a power that is not merely sacerdotal but also in fact imperial and prophetic, for the Greeks he is the bishop of Rome and president of

---

[9] It seems to be forgotten in our day that by the sixteenth century a Cajetan had already deemed it useful to specify that if the Church is where the Pope is, it is on express condition that the Pope behaves in accordance with his function, for otherwise "neither is the Church in him, nor is he in the Church".

the assembly of all the bishops, hence *primus inter pares*, that is, the spokesman for his companions, as in the Gospel; that he is inspired by the Holy Spirit when he speaks *ex cathedra* is for this reason evident and requires no particular charism. The words of Christ to Peter do not consecrate either a monarch or a legislating prophet, and they are to be understood in the context of Christ's words to the other apostles and especially in the context of the immense role played by Saint Paul; if the Catholic thesis were altogether true and the Orthodox thesis altogether false, there would have been no need for Paul since there was Peter, and it is he who would have accomplished Paul's mission. The papacy is one of those traditional institutions that are problematical but inevitable; in other words they are providential with regard to both their legitimacy and their ambiguity, for the destiny of the world must be accomplished with the aid of imperfections and uncertainties as well as perfections and clarities.

Even if the words of institution are the only consecratory element, their efficacy nonetheless depends upon a sufficient formulation of intention, given that intention is one of the three elements *sine qua non* of a sacrament. It may therefore be said that the canon, or the *anaphora*, is directly indispensable for the sacrament as such and indirectly indispensable for the efficacy of the consecration *ex opere operato*, in much the same way as the priestly quality is an essential condition for this consecration, though it is nonetheless extrinsic as to its "form"; without priesthood the "form" would remain inoperative in practice. In their doctrine of the *epiclesis* the Greeks seem to have related the obligatory character of the "intention" to a particular element of it, namely, the invocation of the Holy Spirit, and then to have attributed the obligatory or even fundamental character of the "form" itself to the Spirit; thus the intention—or a part of the intention felt to be especially salient—has become the very "form" of the rite. The canon may assuredly contain a purificatory and preparatory—not operatively consecratory—invocation of the Holy Spirit; but such an invocation with its consecratory form can have only an indirect and as it were symbolical meaning, even though this meaning remains spiritually concrete, as we have indicated above.

According to Saint Basil, "We do not content ourselves with the words that have been reported by the Apostle and the Gospel, but we add to them others before and after, as having much force for the mysteries." The significance of these added words can be of concern to the human receptacle alone and has no bearing on the divine content—except as an extrinsic condition—for it goes without saying that the human and more or less variable words, although inspired at a second or third degree, can add nothing to the sacramental efficacy of the divine words; the same remark is even truer when one considers the intensity of human prayer as expressed by such words as "entreat" and "beseech".

There is an element that is logically part of the form of the sacrament, but in a secondary and not a consecratory manner, and this concerns the introductory prayers uttered by Christ, the precise wording of which is unknown: Christ expressed thanks for the bread and wine, and then he blessed them. These two elements, thanksgiving and blessing, should therefore be found in the canon as an immediate context conditioning the consecrating supplication; and it may be said that the *epiclesis*—with its tone of intense and sacramentally paradoxical supplication—translates what Christ said in the words of the God-man into the words of a sinner, thus introducing part of the element "intention" into the element "form".

It should be noted that according to the older theologians—among them the Popes Innocent III and Innocent IV—Christ consecrated the two species by the blessing mentioned in the Gospels, hence before uttering the words having the form of a consecration; the Council of Trent debated this but then postponed the matter indefinitely. It may be argued against this opinion that the writers of the Gospels—who after all were inspired by the Holy Spirit—did not deem it necessary to record the literal wording of the blessing, that there is no reason for thinking that the benediction was something other than what the word or notion implies, and that it is impossible for the essence of a sacrament to be something uncertain and thereby conjectural.

Meister Eckhart, with his usual audacity, does not hesitate to assert, "If someone were as well prepared for ordinary nourishment as he is for the holy sacrament, he would receive God in this nourishment just as fully as in the sacrament itself." What he means is that sacraments and other rites are necessary only because of our fallen state; they actualize a receptivity in us that primordial man possessed in a "supernaturally natural" manner; certainly they confer positive graces while removing obstacles, but these graces precisely are always present in our existential and as it were transpersonal substance.

But let us return to the question of intention as the introduction *sine qua non* of the sacrament. The intention must contain—hence express—the following parts: first an awareness of the objective mystery; and then, subjectively, faith in the mystery, with the crucial virtues of humility and hope. Humility—whose opposite is pride—is the awareness of our impotence and unworthiness resulting from the fall; and hope—whose opposite is despair—is trust in saving mercy, hence in the will of God to save us, which is manifested precisely in the Eucharistic mystery. In the canon the Church makes these diverse notions and attitudes its own in order that it might be able to testify before God—and that all the officiants might testify by and in the Church: We do this fully in remembrance of Thee.

The Question of Protestantism

Christianity is divided into three great denominations: Catholicism, Orthodoxy, and Protestantism, not to mention the Copts and other ancient groups close to Orthodoxy. This classification may surprise some of our regular readers since it seems to place Protestantism on the same level as the ancient Churches; what we have in mind here, however, is not liberal Protestantism or just any sect but Lutheranism, which incontestably manifests a Christian possibility—a limited one, no doubt, and excessive through certain of its features, but not intrinsically illegitimate and therefore representative of certain theological, moral, and even mystical values. If Evangelicalism—to use the term favored by Luther—were located in a world such as that of Hinduism, it would appear as a possible way and would no doubt be considered a secondary *darshana* among others; in Buddhism it would be no more heterodox than Amidism or the school of Nichiren, both of which, however, are quite independent with regard to the main tradition surrounding them.

To grasp our point of view, it is necessary to understand that religions are determined by archetypes, which are so many spiritual possibilities: on the one hand every religion *a priori* manifests an archetype, but on the other hand any archetype can manifest itself *a posteriori* within every religion. Thus Shiism, for example, is obviously not the result of a Christian influence but is instead a manifestation within Islam of the religious possibility—or the spiritual archetype—that affirmed itself in a direct and plenary fashion in Christianity; and this same possibility gave rise to Amidist mysticism within Buddhism, though in a way that accentuates another dimension of the archetype, namely, as a cosmic prodigy of Mercy—a prodigy requiring and at the same time conferring the quasi-charism of saving Faith; in the case of Shiism, on the other hand, the accent is upon the Superman, who opens Heaven to earth. It could be said in a similar way that the Germanic soul—treated by Rome in too Latin a manner, though this is another question—which is neither Greek nor Roman, felt the need of a simpler and more inward religious archetype, one less formalistic and therefore more "popular" in the best sense of the word; this in certain respects is the archetype of Islam, a religion based on a Book and conferring priesthood upon every believer. At the same time and from another point of view, the Germanic soul had a nostalgia for a perspective that integrates the natural into the supernatural, that is, a perspective tending toward God without being against nature, a piety that is not monastic but accessible to every man of good will in the midst of earthly preoccupations, a way founded upon Grace and trust, not upon Justice and works; and this way incontestably has its premises in the Gospel itself.

Here it is once again appropriate—for we have done so on other occasions—to clarify the difference between a heresy that is extrinsic, hence relative to a given orthodoxy, and another that is intrinsic, hence false in itself as well as with regard to all orthodoxy or to truth as such. To simplify the matter we could limit ourselves to pointing out that the first kind of heresy manifests a spiritual archetype—in a limited manner, no doubt, but nonetheless efficaciously—whereas the second is merely a human contrivance and therefore based solely on man's own productions;[1] and this settles the entire issue. To claim that a "pious" spiritualist is assured of salvation is meaningless, for in total heresies there is no element that can guarantee posthumous beatitude, even though—apart from all question of belief—a man can always be saved for reasons that elude us; but he is certainly not saved by his heresy.

On the subject of Arianism, which was an especially pervasive heresy, the following remark ought to be made: Arianism is unquestionably heterodox in that it takes Jesus to be a mere creature; this idea can have a meaning in the perspective of Islam, but it is incompatible with Christianity. Nonetheless, the lightning-like expansion of Arianism shows that it satisfied a spiritual need—a need corresponding to the archetype of which Islam is the most characteristic manifestation—and it is precisely to this need or expectation that Protestantism finally responded,[2] not by humanizing Christ, of course,

---

[1] Such as Mormonism, Bahaism, the Ahmadism of Kadyan, and all the "new religions" and other pseudo-spiritualities that proliferate in the world today.

[2] Arius of Alexandria was not a German, but his doctrine fulfilled a certain desire of

but in simplifying the religion and Germanizing it in a certain fashion. Another well-known heresy was Nestorianism, which rigorously separated the two natures of Christ, the divine and the human, and in this way saw in Mary the mother of Christ but not of God; this perspective corresponds to a possible theological point of view, and it is thus a question of an extrinsic, not a total, heresy.

Strictly speaking, all religious exoterism is an extrinsic heresy, clearly so in relation to other religions, but above all in relation to the *sophia perennis*; it is precisely this perennial wisdom that constitutes an esoterism when combined with a religious symbolism. An extrinsic heresy is a partial or relative truth—in its formal articulation—that presents itself as complete or absolute, whether it is a question of religions or, within these, of denominations; but the starting point is always a truth, hence also a spiritual archetype. An intrinsic heresy is entirely different: its starting point is either an objective error or a subjective illusion; in the first case the heresy lies more in the doctrine, and in the second it is *a priori* in the pretension of a false prophet; but it goes without saying that both can be combined and indeed are necessarily so in the second case. Even though no error is possible without a particle of truth, intrinsic heresy can have neither doctrinal nor methodic value, and it is impossible to justify it in relation to some extenuating circumstance, precisely because it projects no celestial model.

It is not difficult to argue—against the Reformation—that the traditional authorities and Councils, by definition inspired by the Holy Spirit, could not have been mistaken; this is true, but it does not exclude paradoxes that mitigate an otherwise virtually self-evident claim. First of all—and this is what gave wings to the Reformers, starting with Wycliffe and Huss—Christ himself repudiated many "traditional" elements supported by the "authorities" in calling them "commandments of men"; furthermore, the excesses of "papism" at

the German mentality, whence its success with Visigoths, Ostrogoths, Vandals, Burgundians, and Langobards.

the time of Luther and well before prove at the very least that the papacy contains certain excesses, which the Byzantine Church is the first to note and stigmatize, if not that the papacy in itself is illegitimate. What we mean is that the Pope, instead of being *primus inter pares* as Saint Peter had been, has the exorbitant privilege of being at once prophet and emperor: as prophet he places himself above the Councils, and as emperor he possesses a temporal power surpassing that of all the princes, including the emperor himself; and it is precisely these unheard-of prerogatives that permitted the entry of modernism into the Church in our time, in the fashion of a Trojan horse and despite the warnings of preceding Popes; that Popes may personally have been saints does not at all weaken the valid arguments of the Eastern Church. In a word, if the Western Church had been such as to avoid casting the Eastern Church into the "outer darkness"—and with what a manifestation of barbarism!—it would not have had to undergo the counterblow of the Reformation.

Be that as it may, to say that the Roman Church is intrinsically orthodox and integrally traditional does not mean that it conveys all the aspects of the world of the Gospel in a direct, compelling, and exhaustive manner, even though it necessarily contains them and manifests them occasionally or sporadically; for the world of the Gospel was Oriental and Semitic and immersed in a climate of holy poverty, whereas the world of Catholicism is European, Roman, and imperial, which means that the religion was Romanized inasmuch as the characteristic traits of the Roman mentality determined its formal elaboration. Suffice it to mention in this regard its legalism and its administrative and even military spirit; these traits can be seen, among other places, in the disproportionate complication of rubrics, the prolixity of the missal, the dispersing complexity of the sacramental economy, and the pedantic manipulation of indulgences, as well as in a certain administrative centralization, indeed militarization, of monastic spirituality; nor is this to forget, on the level of forms— which is far from negligible—the Titanic paganism of the Renaissance and the nightmare of Baroque art. The following remark could also be made, again from the point of view of formal outwardness: in the Catholic world the difference between religious and secular dress is often abrupt to the point of incompatibility, and this was already the case even by the end of the Middle Ages; when the essentially worldly and vain, even erotic, trappings of the princes are compared to the majestic garments of the priests, it is difficult to believe that the first, like the second, are Christians, whereas in Oriental civilizations the style of dress is in general homogeneous. In Islam there is no dividing line between religious personages and the rest of society; there is no lay society opposed at the level of appearances to a priestly one. This being said, let us close this parenthesis, the point of which was simply to show that the Catholic world presents certain traits—on its surface as well as in its depths—which certainly do not express the climate of the Gospels.[3]

Too often people have argued that it is sacred institutions that count and not the human accidents that disfigure them; this is obvious, and yet the very degree of this disfiguration indicates that some of the imperfection was due to a certain human zeal within the institutions themselves; Dante and Savonarola saw this clearly in their own way, and the very phenomenon of the Renaissance proves it. If we are told that the papacy—such as it was throughout the centuries—represents the only possible solution for the West, we readily agree, but the risks this unavoidable adaptation so unavoidably included should therefore have been foreseen, and everything should have been done to diminish, not increase, them; if a strongly marked hierarchy was indispensable, the priestly aspect of every Christian should have been insisted upon all the more.

Be that as it may, what permitted Luther to separate from Rome[4] was his awareness of the principle of "orthodox decadence", that is,

---

[3] For someone like Joseph de Maistre, whose intelligence otherwise had great merits, the Reformers could not be other than "nobodies", who dared to set their personal opinions against the traditional and unanimous certitudes of the Catholic Church; he was far from suspecting that these "nobodies" spoke under the pressure of an archetypal perspective, which as such could not help but reveal itself in appropriate circumstances. The same author accused Protestantism of having done an immense evil in breaking up Christianity, but he readily loses sight of the fact that Catholicism did as much in rashly excommunicating all the Patriarchs of the East; and this is without forgetting the Renaissance, whose evil was—to say the least—just as "immense" as that of the political and other effects of the Reformation.

[4] He separated from the Roman Church only after his condemnation, by burning the bull of excommunication; one should not lose sight of the fact that at the time of the Reformation there was no unanimity on the question of the Pope and the Councils, and even the question of the divine origin of papal authority was not free from all controversy.

the possibility of decadence within the immutable framework of a traditional orthodoxy, an awareness inspired by the example of the scribes and Pharisees in the Gospel with their "commandments of men"; objectively, these are the specifications, developments, elaborations, clarifications, and stylizations that may be required by a given temperament though not by another.[5] Another association of ideas that was useful to Luther and to Protestantism in general is the Augustinian opposition between a *civitas Dei* and a *civitas terrena* or *diaboli*: in witnessing the disorders of the Roman Church, he was easily led to identify Rome with the "earthly city" of Saint Augustine. There is also a fundamental tendency in the Gospel that responds with particular force to the needs of the Germanic soul: namely, a tendency toward simplicity and inwardness, hence away from theological and liturgical complication, formalism, dispersion of worship, and the too often comfortable tyranny of the clergy. On the other hand the Germans were sensitive to the nobly and robustly popular appeal of the Bible; this has no relationship with democracy, for Luther was a supporter of a theocratic regime upheld by the emperor and the princes.

Without question, the perspective of Protestantism is typically Pauline; it is founded on what might be called the Gnostic dualism of the following elements: flesh and spirit, death and life, servitude and freedom, Law and Grace, justice through works and justice through faith, Adam and Christ. On the other hand Protestantism is founded, like Christianity as such, on the Pauline idea that the universality of salvation answers to the universality of sin or of the state of the sinner; only the redemptive death of Christ could deliver man from this curse; through the Redemption Christ became the luminous head of all humanity. But the typically Pauline accentuation of this Message is the doctrine of justification through faith, which Luther made the pivot of the religion, or more precisely of his mysticism.

---

[5] Hinduism—without mentioning the Mediterranean paganisms—furnishes another example of this kind, with the heavy and endless pedantry of the Brahmans, which it was not too difficult to escape, however, given the plasticity of the Hindu spirit and the suppleness of its corresponding institutions.

After the failure of Wycliffe and Huss—the tendencies of whose doctrine, if not the doctrine itself, it would have been good to retain—the Popes contributed to the Lutheran explosion by their impenitence;[6] after the failure—within the very framework of Catholic orthodoxy—of Dante, Savonarola, and other admonishers, Luther caused the Catholic renovation by his virulence; Providence willed both outcomes, the Protestant Church as well as the Tridentine Church. After the Council of Trent, the ideal situation would have been for Catholicism to assimilate the essence of Protestantism without disavowing itself, just as Protestantism should have rediscovered the essence of the Catholic reality; instead both parties hardened in their respective positions, and in fact it could not have been otherwise, if only for the same reason that there are different religions; for it is necessary that spiritual perspectives be entirely themselves before being modified, all the more so in that their over-accentuation responds to racial or ethnic needs.[7]

Each denomination expresses the Gospel in a certain manner; now this expression seems to us to be the most direct, the most ample, and the most realistic in the Orthodox Church, and this can already be seen in its outward forms, whereas the Catholic Church offers an image that is more Roman and less Oriental, and in a certain sense even more worldly since the Renaissance and the Baroque epoch, as we have pointed out above. Latin "civilizationism" has nothing to do with the world and spirit of the Gospel; in the final analysis, however, the Roman West is Christian, and therefore Christianity has the right to be Roman. As for the Protestant Church, the question of its forms of worship does not arise since in this respect it participates in Catholic culture, though it introduces into this culture a principle

---

[6] This is something Cardinal Newman and others have acknowledged from within the Catholic camp.

[7] In saying this we do not lose sight of the fact that the Germans of the South—the Allamanis (the Germans of Baden, the Alsatians, the German Swiss, the Swabians) and the Bavarians (including the Austrians)—have a rather different temperament from that of the Germans of the North and that everywhere there are mixtures; racial and ethnic frontiers in Europe are in any case somewhat fluctuating. We do not say every German is made for Lutheran Protestantism, for Germanic tendencies can obviously appear within Catholicism, just as conversely Protestant Calvinism expresses above all a Latin possibility.

of somewhat iconoclastic sobriety, while having the advantage of not accepting the Renaissance and its prolongations; what this means is that Protestantism retained the forms of the Middle Ages, artistically speaking and according to the intention of Luther, while at the same time simplifying them, and thus it escaped the unspeakable aberration of Baroque art. From the spiritual point of view Protestantism retains a spirit of simplicity and inwardness from the Gospel while accentuating the mystery of faith, and it presents these aspects with a vigor whose moral and mystical value cannot be denied; this accentuation was necessary in the West, and since Rome would not take it upon itself, it is Wittenberg that did so.

In connection with Protestant quasi-iconoclasm, we would point out that Saint Bernard also wished that chapels be empty, bare, and sober—in short, that "sensible consolations" be reduced to a minimum; but he wished this for monasteries and not cathedrals; in this case the sense of the sacred was concentrated on the essential element of the rites. We meet with this perspective in Zen as well as Islam, and above all we meet with it repeatedly in Christ, so much so that it would be unjust to deny any precedent in the Scriptures for the Lutheran attitude; Christ wanted one to worship God "in spirit and in truth" and to pray without using "vain repetitions, as the heathen do"; it is an emphasis on faith, with sincerity and intensity being pre-eminent.

The celibacy of priests, which was imposed by Gregory VII after a thousand years of the contrary practice—the ancient practice being maintained to this day in the Eastern Church—presents several serious drawbacks. In the first place, it needlessly repeats the celibacy of monks and separates priests more radically from lay society, which in this way becomes all the more laic; in other words this measure reinforces a feeling of dependence and lower moral value in the laity, marriage being in practice belittled by yet another ukase. Furthermore, when celibacy is imposed upon an enormous number of priests—for society has all the more need of priests as it grows increasingly numerous, and Christianity embraces all the West—it inevitably creates moral disorders and contributes to a loosening of morals, whereas it would have been better to have good married priests than bad celibate priests; the only alternative is to reduce the number of priests, which is impossible since society is large and needs them. Finally, the celibacy of the clergy is an obstacle to the procreation of men of religious vocation and thus impoverishes society; if only men without a religious vocation have children, society will become more and more worldly and "horizontal" and less and less spiritual and "vertical".

Be that as it may, Luther in turn lacked realism: he was astonished that during his absence from Wittenberg—this was the year of Wartburg—the promoters of the Reformation gave themselves up to all kinds of excesses; at the end of his life he even went so far as to regret that the mediocre masses had not remained under the rod of the Pope. Not much concerned with collective psychology, he believed the simple principle of piety could replace the material supports that contribute so powerfully to regulate the behavior of the crowds; it not only keeps this behavior in equilibrium in space but stabilizes it in time. In his mystical subjectivism he did not realize that a religion needs symbolism in order to survive, that the inward cannot live within a collective consciousness without outward signs;[8] but as a prophet of inwardness he scarcely had a choice.

The Latin West has too often lacked realism and moderation, whereas the Greek Church, like the East in general, has better understood how to reconcile the demands of spiritual idealism with those of the everyday human world. Adopting a particular point of view, we would like to make the following remark: it is very unlikely that Christ, who washed the feet of his disciples and taught them that the "first shall be last", would have appreciated the imperial pomp of the Vatican court: the kissing of the foot, the triple crown, the *flabella*, the *sedia gestatoria*; on the other hand there is no reason to think he would have disapproved of the ceremonies surrounding an Orthodox Patriarch, these being of a priestly and not imperial style; he would no doubt have disapproved of the cardinalate, which further raises the princely throne of the Pope and constitutes a dignity that is not sacerdotal and is more worldly than religious.[9]

---

[8] This, let it be said in passing, is what is forgotten even by most of the impeccable *gurus* of contemporary India, beginning with Ramakrishna.

[9] "But be not ye called Rabbi: for one is your Master, even Christ; and all ye are breth-

We have spoken above of the celibacy of priests imposed by Gregory VII, and we must add a word concerning the Evangelical counsels and monastic vows. When one reads in the Gospel, "There is no man that hath left house, or brethren, or sisters, or father, or mother, or wife, or children, or lands, for my sake, and the gospel's, but he shall receive an hundredfold," one immediately thinks of monks and nuns; now Luther thought it was solely a question of persecutions, in the sense of this saying from the Sermon on the Mount: "Blessed are they which are persecuted for righteousness' sake: for theirs is the kingdom of Heaven";[10] and he is all the more sure of his interpretation in that there were neither anchorites nor monks before the fourth century.

Viewed in its totality, Protestantism has something ambiguous about it: on the one hand it is inspired sincerely and concretely by the Bible, but on the other hand it is bound up with humanism and the Renaissance. Luther incarnates the first aspect: his perspective is medieval and so to speak retrospective, and it gives rise to a conservative and at times esoterizing pietism. In Calvin, on the contrary, the tendencies of humanism, hence of the Renaissance, mingle with the movement rather strongly, if indeed they do not determine it; no doubt he is greatly inspired in his doctrine by Luther and the Swiss Reformers, but he is a republican in his own way—on a theocratic basis, of course—and not a monarchist like the German Reformer; and it can be said on the whole that in a certain manner he was more opposed to Catholicism than Luther was.[11]

ren." "Neither be ye called masters: for one is your Master, even Christ" (Matthew 23:8, 10).

[10] He says so in a marginal note of his translation: "Whosoever believes must suffer persecution and risk all" (*alles dran setzen*). And he repeats it in his hymn *Ein feste Burg ist unser Gott*: "Even if they [the persecutors] take body, goods, honor, child, and wife, let them go (*lass fahren dahin*); they shall receive no benefit; the Kingdom [of God] shall be ours" (*das Reich muss uns doch bleiben*).

[11] As for Protestant liberalism, Luther eventually foresaw its abuses, and he would in any case be horrified to see this liberalism as it appears in our time—he who could

The fundamental ideas of the Reformation had already been "in the air" for some time, but it is Luther who lived them and made of them a personal drama. His Protestantism—like other particular perspectives contained within a general perspective—is an over-accentuated partitioning, but one that is nonetheless sufficient and efficacious, hence "nonillegitimate".[12]

One cannot study the question of Protestantism without taking into consideration the powerful personality of its real, or at least its most notable, founder. First of all, and this follows from what we have just said, there are no grounds for asserting that Luther was a modernist ahead of his time, for he was in no way worldly and sought to please no one; his innovations were assuredly of the most audacious kind, to say the least, but they were Christian and nothing else; they owed nothing to any philosophy or scientism.[13] He did not reject Rome because it was too spiritual, but on the contrary because it seemed to him too worldly—too "after the flesh" and not "after the Spirit", from his particular point of view.

The mystic of Wittenberg[14] was a German semiticized by Christianity, and he was representative in both respects: fundamentally German, he loved what is sincere and inward, not clever and formalistic; Semitic in spirit, he admitted only Revelation and faith and did not wish to hear of Aristotle or the Scholastics.[15] On the one hand

---

bear neither self-sufficient mediocrity nor iconoclastic fanaticism.

[12] Evangelical Protestantism, properly so called, which is at the antipodes from liberal Protestantism, was perpetuated in pietism, whose father was de Labadie, a mystic converted to the Reformation in the seventeenth century, and whose most notable representatives were no doubt Spener and Tersteegen; this pietism, or piety, always exists in various places in either a diminished or a quite honorable form.

[13] As is the case on the contrary with Catholic modernism. The fact that this modernism is open not only to Protestantism but also to Islam and other religions gets us nowhere since this same modernism is just as open to no matter what—to everything except Tradition.

[14] For he was a mystic rather than a theologian, which explains many things.

[15] It might be objected that the Semites adopted the Greek philosophers, but this is not the question, for the adoption was varied and unequal, not to mention undertaken with numerous hesitations. And in any case Luther—a cultivated man—was also a logician and could not be otherwise; in certain respects he was Latinized of necessity—as was an Albert the Great or an Eckhart—but this was only on the surface.

there was something robust and powerful (*gewaltig*) in his nature, with a complement of poetry and gentleness (*Innigkeit*); on the other hand he was a voluntarist and an individualist, who expected nothing from either intellectuality or metaphysics. No doubt his impetuous genius was capable of being crude—to say the least—but he lacked neither patience nor generosity; he could be vehement but no more so than a Saint Jerome or other saints who reviled their adversaries, "devoured" as they were by "zeal for the house of the Lord"; and no one can deny that they found precedents for this in both Testaments.[16]

The message of Luther is expressed essentially in two legacies, which attest to the personality of the author and to which it is impossible to deny grandeur and efficaciousness: the German Bible and the hymns. His translation of the Scriptures, while conditioned in certain places by his doctrinal perspective, is a jewel of both language and piety; as for the hymns—most of which are not from his hand, although he composed their models and thus gave the impulse to all this flowering—they became a fundamental element of worship, and they were a powerful factor in the expansion of Protestantism.[17] The Catholic Church itself could not resist this magic; it ended by adopting several Lutheran hymns that had become so popular they seemed as essential as the air one breathes. In summary, the whole personality of Luther is in his translation of the Psalms and in his famous hymn, "A Mighty Fortress Is Our God" (*Ein feste Burg ist unser Gott*), which became the "war song" (*Trutzlied*) of Protestantism and whose qualities of power and grandeur cannot be denied. But more gently, this personality is also seen in his commentary on the *Magnificat*, which attests to an inner devotion to the Holy Virgin, whom Luther never rejected; having read this commentary without knowing its author, Pope Leo X remarked, "Blessed be the hands that wrote this!" Clearly

---

[16] When the Reformer calls the "papist mass" an "abomination", we are made to think of the bonze Nichiren, who claimed that it sufficed to invoke Amida only once to fall into Hell, not to mention the Buddha, who rejected the *Veda*, the castes, and the gods.

[17] Among composers of hymns, there were notably the pastor Johann Valentin Andrea, author of the "Chemical Wedding of Christian Rosenkreutz", and later Paul Gerhardt, Tersteegen, and Novalis, whose hymns are among the jewels of German poetry; and let us add that the religious music of Bach testifies to the same spirit of powerful piety.

the German Reformer was not able to maintain public devotion to the Virgin, but this was because of the general reaction against the dispersion of religious sentiment, hence in favor of worship concentrated on Christ alone, which had to become absolute and therefore exclusive, as is the worship of Allah for Muslims. And in any case Scripture treats the Virgin with a somewhat surprising parsimony—a fact that played a certain role here—though there are also the crucial, and doctrinally inexhaustible, declarations that Mary is "full of grace" and that "all generations shall call me blessed".[18]

The German Reformer was a mystic in the sense that his way was purely experimental and not conceptual; the pertinent demonstrations of a Staupitz were of no help to him. To discover the efficacy of Mercy he needed first the "event of the tower": having meditated in vain on the "Justice" of God, he had the grace of understanding in a flash that this Justice is merciful and that it liberates us in and by faith.

The great themes of Luther are Scripture, Christ, the Inward, Faith; the first two elements belong to the divine side and the second two to the human side. By emphasizing Scripture—at the expense of Tradition—Protestantism is close to Islam, where the Koran is everything; by emphasizing Christ—at the expense of the Pope, hierarchy, clergy—Protestantism recalls devotional Buddhism, which places everything in the hands of Amitabha; the liturgical and ritual expression of this Christic primacy is Communion, which is as real and as important for Luther as it is for Catholics. The Lutheran tendency toward the "inward", the "heart" if one will, is incontestably founded on the perspective of Christ, as is the emphasis on faith, which moreover evokes—we repeat—Amidist mysticism as well as Muslim piety. We would not dream of making these seemingly needless comparisons if they did not serve to illustrate the principle of the archetypes we mentioned above, which is of crucial importance.

---

[18] As Dante said: "Lady, thou art so great and possesseth such power that whosoever desireth grace and has not recourse to thee, it is as if his desire wished to fly without wings" (*Paradiso*, 33:13-15).

As for Christ made tangible in Communion, it is not true that Luther reduced the Eucharistic rite to a simple ceremony of remembrance, as did his adversary Zwingli;[19] on the contrary he admitted the Real Presence, but neither transubstantiation—which the Greeks also do not accept as such, although they ended up accepting the word—nor the bloodless renewal of the historical sacrifice; nonetheless these sacramental realities as perceived by Catholics are implied—objectively though not subjectively—in the Lutheran definition of the Eucharist, so much so that this definition could be said to be acceptable even from the Catholic point of view, provided one is conscious of the implication. For Catholics this implication constitutes the very definition of the mystery, which is perhaps disproportionate if one takes into account the somewhat dispersing and "casual" usage Catholicism makes of its Mass;[20] certain psychological facts—human nature being what it is—would no doubt have required the mystery to be presented in a more veiled fashion and handled with more discretion. Lutheran Communion is certainly not the equivalent of Catholic Communion, but we have reasons for believing—given its overall context—that it nonetheless communicates the graces Luther expected of it to a sufficient degree;[21] this assumes that the intention of the ritual change was fundamentally Christian and free from all ulterior motives of a rationalist, let alone political, kind—as was in fact the case.

If Lutheran Communion is not the equivalent of Catholic Communion, it is because its spiritual virtualities are not as extensive; but this is as it should be, for these initiatic virtualities are in fact too lofty

---

[19] Whose thesis has been retained by liberal Protestantism; Calvin attempted to restore more or less the position of Luther. The idea of a commemorative rite pure and simple is intrinsically heretical, since "to do in memory of" is meaningless from the standpoint of sacramental efficacy.

[20] For one must not "cast pearls before swine" nor "give what is holy unto the dogs". For the Orthodox the Mass is the center and has priests at its disposal, whereas it could be said that for Catholics it is in practice the priest who is the center and who has Masses at his disposal.

[21] With perhaps certain reservations that are difficult to specify, the same could be said for Calvinist and Anglican Communions, but not for those of the Zwinglians or liberal Protestants, nor again—and at first sight this will seem quite paradoxical—for the "conciliar" or "post-conciliar" masses, which are not covered by a valid archetype and which, with their ambiguous intentions, are merely the result of human arbitrariness.

for the average man, and to impose them on him is to expose him to sacrilege. From another point of view, if the Mass were always equal to the historic Sacrifice of Christ, it would become a sacrilege because of its profanation by the more or less trivial manner of its usage: hurried low Masses, Masses attributed to this or that, including the most contingent and profane occasions. No doubt the Mass coincides potentially with the event of Golgotha, and this potentiality or virtuality can always give rise to an effective coincidence;[22] but if the Mass itself had the character of its bloody prototype, at each Mass the earth would tremble and be covered by darkness.

One of the most absurd arguments with which Zwingli, Karlstadt, Oekolampad, and others opposed both the Catholic Church and Luther was the following: if the bread is really the body of Christ, do we not eat human flesh when communing?[23] To this there are four responses. First, Christ said what he said, and one must take it or leave it; there is nothing to change in it, unless one wishes to leave the Christian religion. Second, Christ in fact offers neither flesh nor blood, but bread and wine, so why the complaint? Third, the crucial point is the question of knowing what is signified by this body that one must eat and by this blood that one must drink; now this meaning or content is the remission of sins, Redemption, the restitution of man's glorious nature, innocence at once primordial and celestial; man eats and drinks what he must become because this is what he is in his immortal essence; and to eat is to become united. Fourth, the fact that bread is not flesh and that wine is not blood can be seen without difficulty; why then ask in what manner bread is the body and wine is the blood? This does not concern us and has no interest for us; it is God's concern. What alone is important for us is the transforming and deifying power of the sacrament—its capacity to grant us salvific impeccability, that of Christ.[24]

---

[22] And this is independent of the intrinsic efficacy of the sacrament, though this efficacy is realized only in proportion to the holiness, hence receptivity, of the communicant.

[23] This argument is supposed to allow us to conclude that the bread "signifies"—hence "is not"— the body of Christ; the weakness of the argument is at the level of its intention.

[24] In the mysteries of Eleusis, too, bread and wine were used "eucharistically" and

— ∴ —

The Lutheran doctrine is founded mainly on the anthropological pessimism and predestinationism of Saint Augustine: man is fundamentally a sinner, and he is totally determined by the Will of God.

What then does Saint Augustine mean by the idea that man is irremediably a sinner—that he is powerless as long as he is left to rely on his own strength? It means that the "fall" has the effect of destroying the equilibrium between the inward and outward, the vertical or ascending and the horizontal or earthly; that the exteriorizing and worldly tendencies prevail over the interiorizing and spiritual tendencies; and that when left to itself the horizontal tendency leads *ipso facto* to the descending tendency. Now works are not enough to rectify the situation; faith alone can accomplish this marvel, which does not mean that faith can suffice without works—that it can be perfectly itself in their absence.

As in Amidism, the first condition of salvation—according to Luther—is an awareness of abysmal and invincible sin, hence of the impossibility of vanquishing sin by our own strength. Man is practically the same thing as sin for Luther, as is the case for Christianity in general;[25] on God's side there is Grace—which Luther identifies with the "Justice" of a redeeming God—and between these two extremes there is faith, where the sinner and Grace meet. In a lecture on the Epistle to the Romans, Luther declares that Christ "made his Justice mine, and my sin his", and he adds: "For him who throws himself body and soul into God's Will it is impossible to remain outside of God." Likewise, in speaking about Justice he says that "faith raises the human heart so high that it becomes one spirit with God (*dass er ein Geist mit Gott wird*) and acquires the very Justice of God".

The mysticism of Luther—tormented and yet in its own way finally victorious—evokes all the tension between knowing and believing or between knowledge and faith. For Luther there is nothing

---

communicated a divine power.

[25] In a similar manner Islam views every man as a "slave", and Asharism practically concludes from this that every man is capable only of fear and obedience—that he is intellectually a "villain", or a *shūdra* as Hindus would say.

but faith; but he could not deny that a faith united with Grace to the point of being "one spirit with God" is a manner of knowing God through God or that it is the divine Knowledge in us; for all certainty is knowledge, and there is no faith without certainty. To deny this would be to deny the Holy Spirit and along with it our deiformity.

"Blessed are they that have not seen, and yet have believed": this is the very definition of faith; faith is the key—or the anticipation—of knowledge; it is a kind of "sympathetic magic" with regard to transcendent realities. But faith may also be viewed in another manner: when the starting point is metaphysical certainty or intellection—and this is a "naturally supernatural" mystery—faith is the life of knowledge in the sense that it causes knowledge to penetrate into all our being; for it is necessary to "love God with all our strength", hence with all we are.

A very important aspect of the question of faith that we have alluded to already is the relationship between faith and works: for Luther works contribute nothing to salvation; to believe they do would be to doubt the Redemption—to imagine that our actions, intrinsically sinful, could take the place of the saving work of Christ or could add anything whatsoever to it. It is therefore faith alone that saves, and this is acceptable if we specify—and Melanchthon did not fail to do so—that works prolong faith and are an integral part of it, proportionate to its sincerity; in short they prove faith. Without works faith would not quite be faith, and without faith works would be eschatologically inoperative.

If Luther, who despite his occasional violence was a virtuous man, underestimated the role of works, this could also have been because he included works in virtue and virtue in faith; virtue is in fact situated between these two poles, for it is a dimension of sincere faith and at the same time is expressed by works; but virtue is independent of works, and needless to say it is better to be virtuous without works than to accomplish works without virtue. Moreover, it is fitting to distinguish between works that are obligatory and those that are optional, and it follows that the man of little virtue ought to insist all the more upon meritorious actions in order to compensate for his moral indigence and remedy this indigence gradually.

For Luther faith ennobles even insignificant actions, except for sins of course; faith for him is a kind of sanctity, and indeed it is the only sanctity possible. But what his mystical subjectivity seemed unable to realize, at least *a priori*, is that this mystery of faith cannot constitute a rule of life for the masses; in this the German reformer was as unrealistic as the Popes, who wished to impose a kind of monastic perfection on the clergy—or even, practically speaking, on the whole of Christianity, though to a lesser degree.

All this brings us to the crucial question of asceticism and permits us to insert some parenthetical remarks on this subject. There is an *ascesis* that simply consists of sobriety, and this is sufficient for the naturally spiritual man; there is another that consists of fighting against the passions, and the degree of this *ascesis* depends upon the demands of the individual nature; finally there is the *ascesis* of those who mistakenly believe themselves to be burdened with every sin or who identify themselves with sin through a mystical subjectivism, without forgetting those who practice an extreme asceticism in order to expiate the faults of others or even simply to give a good example in a world that needs it. Of these modes of asceticism, Protestantism retains only the first, and this is for two reasons: first because it is faith that saves, and not works; second—and this reason coincides on the whole with the first—because it is not for us to add our insignificant merits to the infinite merits of Christ.

In summary: according to Luther the grace obtained by and in faith regenerates the soul and permits it to become united with the divine Life; it enables man to resist and combat evil and to exercise charity toward others. Works are useful when we do not consider them meritorious; in this case they become integrated into faith.

In the Lutheran perspective the awareness of being a sinner is everything since strength of faith depends upon this awareness; according to Luther it is better to sin and be aware of one's misery than not to sin and not have this awareness.

But in connection with the crucial idea of sin there is also the fear of damnation and the scruple of not burdening oneself with yet another sin by rashly yielding to the contrary certitude; the tensions and complexities resulting from this attitude are altogether characteristic of voluntaristic and sentimental individualism, which is not to be found in other forms of piety; it is a fact, however, that this attitude determines the entire perspective with Semitic peoples. Be that as it may, the solution to the problem is the following, and it is furnished by esoterism, which always considers the simple nature of things: it is true that the individualistic sentiment of being saved can easily—though not necessarily—give rise to a quasi-narcissistic and morally paralyzing satisfaction, which is liable to compromise the tension toward God and above all the virtue of fear; now the healthy attitude here—the virtue of hope, if one prefers—consists of a conditional and nearly unarticulated certainty; that is, certainty of salvation is included in an eminent and sufficient manner in the certainty of God. One should say: thanks to the knowledge and love of God, no fear of damnation; and not: thanks to good works, certainty of salvation; for by its very nature, or rather by reason of the mechanism of the human soul, the latter conviction risks drawing us away from God insofar as it becomes rooted in consciousness; it draws one away from God because it practically takes the place of God.

It follows from all of this that the terrors and despairs of Luther were logically unnecessary, although mystically fruitful and necessary in fact; if Scripture must contain threats of hell, it is because most men are wild beasts, and subtle considerations regarding the relationship between cause and effect would be ineffectual, to say the least. On the one hand a great number of souls have been saved thanks to the image of eternal suffering; on the other hand this image has not sufficed to prevent innumerable crimes; if we wish to take pity on men, let us also take pity on Scripture.

As for the scruple we mentioned above, it is appropriate to add the following precisions: when our starting point is intellectual certainty concerning absolute Reality and its hypostatic dimensions, we would say that this certainty has as its consequence, and also in a certain manner as its condition: first, that we abstain from everything that takes us away from the supreme Reality in principle or in fact; and second, that we practice what brings us closer or what leads us to it; these two consequences are an integral part of metaphysical certainty to the extent it is really ours. It is in certainty concerning the Sovereign Good, and nowhere else, that we have certainty of salvation—of salvation as such and not of our own salvation only—and we have it to the very extent the second certainty is absorbed in the first.

Gnostically speaking, there are "psychics", who can be saved or damned; then the "pneumatics", who by their nature cannot but be saved; and finally the "hylics", who cannot but be damned. Now for all practical purposes Luther conceived only of this third category, though theoretically—with reservations and conditions—he also conceived of the "psychics"; but in no way did he consider "pneumatics", hence all the tormentedness of his doctrine. In reality all three seeds are found in every man, the "pneumatic", the "psychic", and the "hylic"; it remains to be seen which predominates. In practice it is enough to know that saying "yes" to God while abstaining from what takes one away from Him and accomplishing what brings one closer to Him pertains to the "pneumatic" nature and assures salvation, every question of "original sin" and "predestination" aside; thus in practice there is no problem, except what we imagine and impose on ourselves.

The "pneumatic" is the man who incarnates as it were the "faith that saves" and thus also its content, the "grace of Christ"; strictly speaking, he cannot sin—except perhaps at the level of form—because all he touches turns to gold, his substance being "faith" and therefore "justification by faith". Being "avataric" above all, this possibility is extremely rare, and yet it exists, and cannot but exist.

Be that as it may, Luther does not seem to know what to do with a good conscience, the one Catholics obtain through confession and works; he confuses it with self-satisfaction and laziness, whereas it is the normal and healthy basis for the requirements of loving God and neighbor. But the essential here is not the fact of this confusion, but the consequence Luther draws from it and the stimulation he obtains from it.

The question of knowing whether we are good or bad may be asked approximately, for we possess intelligence, but it cannot be asked in all strictness, for God's measures are not at our disposal; now to say we cannot answer a question means we do not need to ask it.

On the subject of faith and works, let us insert the following parenthetical remarks. Just as Luther puts faith in place of moral works, so Shinran—well before him and on the other side of the globe—puts faith in place of spiritual means: it is not necessary to invoke Amida in order to obtain birth in the "Pure Land"—for this would be to rely on "self-power" to the detriment of "other-power"—but it is necessary to do so out of gratitude to Amida, who has saved us *a priori* by granting us faith; Shinran has but one concern, which is to avoid—or circumvent—the idea that we save ourselves thanks to our own merit. The notion of "gratitude" is here a euphemism intended to veil the fact that it is impossible to deprive ourselves of a realizing initiative; and in any case, if faith is not ours, whose is it, and if it is Amida's, what proof is there that it belongs to us or that we benefit from it? One of two things: either the act of gratitude is optional, in which case one may do without it, it being sufficient to believe instead of invoking Amida; or else the act of gratitude is obligatory, in which case there is no longer a question of gratitude, and the argument is merely a ruse masking "self-power", which determines every act and which we, as free and responsible creatures, cannot escape.

Neither Luther nor Shinran can change the nature of man, which in fact entails a certain liberty and thus a possibility of "self-power", hence of merit; but like the Japanese mystic, the German Reformer is in love with the experience of faith and with the Scripture that nourishes it, and perish all the rest. There is also in Luther a share of Asharism: like the Arab theologian, Luther sacrifices intelligence to faith and freedom to the Foreknowledge and Omnipotence of God. And if an Ashari and a Shinran are "orthodox" in their fashion, as their respective traditions acknowledge, we do not see why we cannot grant Luther the same extenuating circumstances or the same approving evaluations, *mutatis mutandis.*

Like Shinran, Luther believes that in putting faith in place of works he brings a certain consolation and liberation, but this is solely a question of spiritual temperament. It is much more reassuring for some men to base themselves upon works, which are something objective, concrete, tangible, and definable, whereas one can always torment oneself with the question of whether one really has faith or whether one has understood what faith is.

Be that as it may, in the thought of Luther as in that of Shinran—and this follows from certain of our preceding demonstrations—there are compensatory arguments that re-establish equilibrium in such a way that our objection has a merely relative import, except for minds that abuse the formulations in question. One thing is certain, and it is the essential element here: faith sometimes saves in the absence of outward works, but works never save without faith.

Man cannot escape the duty of having to do good; it is in fact impossible under normal conditions not to do good; but what matters is that he knows it is God who acts. A meritorious work belongs to God, though we participate in it; our works are good—or better—to the extent we are penetrated by this awareness.

As for predestination, which is so important in Augustinian and then in Lutheran thought, it is fundamentally none other than ontological necessity insofar as it refers to a determined possibility. Now God may displace or change the mode of a possibility, but He cannot make a possibility become impossible.

Predestination as such is situated in Relativity—in *Māyā*, if one prefers—since it concerns the relative or contingent; but its root in the Absolute is reducible to Necessity. Absolute Being comprises both Necessity and Freedom, and the same therefore holds true for relative or contingent Being, the world; thus it is false to deny the possibility of freedom in the world, just as it is false to deny predestination. A work freely accomplished by man always contains predestination as a different dimension; but with a change of emphasis it could also be said that a freely done work is located within predestination as in an invisible mold pertaining precisely to another dimension; the difference is like that between space and time inasmuch as time is totally different from the three spatial dimensions and yet is always present. Space then corresponds to necessity in the sense that the things within it are what they are and are found where they are found, whereas time corresponds to freedom in the sense that things can change or move; all this is a purely symbolic, hence indirect and partial, analogy, for in reality necessity and freedom are found everywhere.

Be that as it may, it follows from all we have said that it is an error to reduce works to predestination, thereby denying their freedom, and that it is no less an error to deny all predestination in works, thereby lending them an absolute freedom belonging only to God. For the principle is this: freedom as such is always freedom, and necessity as such is always necessity, but whereas Necessity and Freedom are absolute in God, they are relative in the world, for there is no manifested necessity that does not include an element of freedom because of contingency any more than there is a manifested freedom that does not include an element of necessity because of predestination. To reduce our actions to predestination is to attribute absoluteness to them; to believe they are free in relation to the Absolute is to attribute its Liberty to them. Ontologically our actions are predestined, and we must know this in order not to believe we are as sovereign as God or could be situated outside His Will; but practically our actions are free, hence meritorious, and we must know this in order to be able to act and merit.

In theology there is an opposition, however, not only between predestination and freedom but between faith and knowledge; just as some believe freedom must be denied in the name of predestination, or conversely, so others believe knowledge must be rejected in the name of faith, or on the contrary—as is the case with rationalists—that faith must be rejected in the name of what they believe to be knowledge. In reality there is no incompatibility here, any more than there is between freedom and predestination; for if these latter two principles are complementary dimensions of one and the same possibility of manifestation, the same holds true for knowledge and faith in the sense that there is no faith without knowledge and no knowledge without faith. Nonetheless knowledge takes precedence: faith is an indirect and volitive mode of knowledge, whereas knowledge suffices unto itself and is not a mode of faith; on the other hand, when knowledge is situated within Relativity it requires an element of faith to the extent it is *a priori* intellectual and not existential, mental and not cardiac, partial and not total; otherwise all metaphysical understanding would imply sanctity *ipso facto*. Be that as it may, all transcendent certainty has something divine about it, though as certainty only and not necessarily as the acquisition of a particular man.

In other words, in a Semitic climate much is made of the incompatibility between knowledge and faith and of the pre-eminence of the second—to the point of holding the first in contempt and forgetting that within Relativity the one goes hand in hand with the other. Knowledge is the adequate perception of the real, and faith is the conformity of will and sentiment to a truth imperfectly perceived by the intelligence; if the perception were perfect it would be impossible for the believer to lose his faith.

Even when theoretical knowledge is perfect and hence unshakable, however, it always requires a volitive element, which contributes to the process of assimilation or integration, for we must "become what we are"; and this operative element or element of intensity stems from faith. Conversely, in religious faith there is always an element of knowledge that determines it, for in order to believe it is necessary to know what one must believe; moreover, in plenary faith there is an element of certainty, which is not volitive and the presence of which we cannot prevent, regardless of our efforts to reject all knowledge in order to benefit from the "obscure merit of faith".

In God alone is knowledge excused from an element of realizational intensity or totalizing will; as for faith, its prototype *in divinis* is Life or Love; and in God alone are Life and Love independent of every motive justifying or determining them *ab extra*. It is by participation in this mystery that Saint Bernard could say, "I love because I love", which is like a paraphrase of the Saying of the Burning Bush, "I am that I am": "That which is".

It is knowledge, or the element truth, that gives faith all its value; otherwise we could believe no matter what as long as we believed; it is only as a function of truth that the intensity of our faith has meaning. And quite paradoxically it is predestination that makes us freely choose truth and goodness; without freedom there is no choice. In the final analysis Predestination is all we are.

But divine Freedom requires a predestination that is paradoxically relative and relates to modes and degrees together with the Predestination that is absolute. Likewise divine Necessity requires a relative freedom together with the Freedom that as such is absolute; this relative freedom is ours, and while it cannot be anything other than freedom it nonetheless falls within the framework of a necessity that surpasses it.

Just as the early Churches conceive a hierarchy that places monks and priests above the laity and the worldly, so also Luther—who had nothing of the revolutionary or even of the democrat in him—conceives a hierarchy that places those who truly live by faith above those who have not yet reached this point or are simply incapable of it. He intended to appeal to those who "willingly do what they know and are capable of acting with firm faith in the beneficence and favor of God" and "whom others ought to emulate"; but not to those who "make ill use of this freedom and rashly trust in it, so that they must be driven with laws, teachings, and warnings", and other formulations of this kind. What this means is that there was a kind of esoterism in his intention at least in practice: "Faith does not suffice," he declares, "except the faith that takes shelter under the wings of Christ"; now Christ is love.

"Though I speak with the tongues of men and of angels . . . though I have all faith, so that I could remove mountains, and have not love (*caritas, agapē*), I am nothing. . . . And now abideth faith, hope, love, these three; but the greatest of these is love." This crucial passage of the First Epistle to the Corinthians seems to contradict all the Apostle taught concerning justification by faith in his Epistle to the Romans; how to explain this paradox? The answer on the one hand is that love is the greatest thing since "God is Love" and the noblest of the Commandments is the love of God and neighbor; but on the other hand faith has primacy since it is the key to everything and it is faith that saves. The mystic of Wittenberg would even say that in practice—not in principle—faith is greater because love, being too great, is impracticable and cannot be attained except by and in Christ and through faith; that love is too great follows precisely from the passage in the Epistle to the Corinthians, in which the Apostle believes he must call upon the intercession of the "tongues of angels", the "gift of prophecy", the understanding of "all mysteries, and all knowledge", and the faith that "removes mountains". Basing himself on the doctrine of the Epistle to the Romans, Luther not unreasonably deduces that love is realizable only indirectly or virtually by and in faith, except for the level that is accessible to us naturally, namely, charity toward our neighbor. In a word, to affirm that love is the greatest thing is not the same as saying it is the most immediately essential; it is often necessary to interpret a particular passage of Scripture in light of another given passage, which, though seeming to contradict it, in reality defines it and renders it concrete.

Furthermore, there is an element of Semitic stylization in this famous verse to the Corinthians in the sense that exaggeration, taken to the point of absurdity, serves to underscore the grandeur of the thing spoken of; it is what one might call a "henotheistic" logic, that is, a logic that lends an absolute character to the thing whose excellence one wishes to demonstrate to the detriment of another thing, which is nonetheless presented in a quasi-absolute light at another moment. Taken literally, however, it is clearly absurd to maintain that someone whose faith can move mountains, *et cetera*, is nothing if he does not have love, for a faith of such strength could lack nothing, or else it would not be so strong; Luther rightly noticed this in his own way.[26]

We could also say that the Apostle has slipped from one perspective to another, namely, from that of faith to that of love, or rather that both points of view forced themselves upon his mind successively, independently of each other. Now a choice must be made: Catholicism and Orthodoxy—which were united for more than a thousand years—accorded the pre-eminence to love, whereas Protestantism wished to emphasize faith; love with faith in the first case, faith with love in the second. In all justice both accentuations should have always co-existed, and indeed they often did before the Reformation; but in fact the Abrahamic and moreover somewhat "Quietistic" idea of the faith that saves had lain dormant during that period of mystical heroism and superstitious abuse we call the Middle Ages.

The proof of the primacy of love is that the supreme Commandment is the love of God and neighbor; and the proof of the primacy of faith is that the creed is in practice more essential than charity since it is better to believe in God without charity than to exercise charity without believing in God. Catholicism starts with the idea of the primacy of love and with the fact of our freedom, and it demands ascetic zeal; Protestantism for its part starts with the primacy of faith and with the fact of our powerlessness, and it demands steadfastness in trust.

We might mention an analogy here that brings us back to our considerations of religious archetypes: Vishnuism distinguishes

---

[26] Nonetheless, not all his arguments are conclusive. Let us note at this point that in all interdenominational controversies one meets with purely "functional" arguments, which are inadequate in themselves; for example, the Epistle to the Romans attributes all vices to the pagans, whereas they cannot be attributed to the best of the Stoics or Neoplatonists. Some arguments are meant to clear the ground and not to serve the truth as such; these are necessarily two-edged.

between *bhakti*, love properly so called and heroic when necessary, and *prapatti*, confident abandonment to divine Mercy; these are the two ways it offers the faithful. Now the way of love corresponds analogically to the priestly and monastic perspective of early and Patristic Christianity, whereas the way of trust or faith is found in Protestantism; analogy is not identity, but in the final analysis the fundamental attitudes and celestial archetypes from which they derive are the same on both sides.

Love is on the one hand our tendency toward God—the tendency of the accident toward the Substance—and on the other hand our consciousness of "myself" in the "other" and of the "other" in "me"; it is also the sense of beauty, above us and around us as well as in our own soul. Faith is saying "yes" to the truth of God and immortality—the truth we carry in the depths of our heart—and seeing concretely what appears as abstract; to speak in Islamic terms, it is "serving God as if thou sawest Him, and if thou seest Him not, He nonetheless seeth thee"; and it is also the sense of the goodness of God and trust in Mercy. He who has faith has goodness, and he who has love has beauty; but at the same time each of these poles contains the other. We are the accidents, and the Substance is Beauty, Goodness, and Beatitude.

Love and faith: the one like the other is a door to knowledge; and knowledge in turn gives rise to both faith and love. Love opens to *gnosis* because it tends toward union; faith opens to it because it is founded on truth; to love is to want to be united, and to believe is to acknowledge what is true and to become what one acknowledges.

———— ·:· ————

In plucking the ears of corn, the Apostles violated the Sabbath; it is the inward Sabbath that counts and that takes priority over the outward. Saint Paul suppressed "circumcision in the flesh" in the name of "circumcision in the spirit"; Meister Eckhart teaches that if we knew God is everywhere we would receive Communion even when eating ordinary bread. All this becomes clear in the light of this principle: outward means are necessary only because—or to the extent that—we have lost access to their inward archetypes; a sacrament is the exteriorization of an immanent source of grace—the "living water" of

Christ—just as Revelation is an outward and macrocosmic manifestation of Intellection. Luther was certainly unaware of this principle or mystery; nonetheless his exclusive recourse to faith, his tendency to interiorize everything for the sake of the "spirit" and against the "flesh", hence also his reduction of the sacraments with regard to their form and number, all refer logically and mystically to the principle of inwardness or immanence we have just spoken of.[27]

The Koran gives more than one example of the principle of abrogation (*naskh*): certain verses annul other verses, and in most cases the meaning of one—whether the "nullifying" (*nāsikh*) or the "annulled" (*mansūkh*)—is more universal than that of the other. The profound significance of this phenomenon is that every form can be abrogated by a more essential form, and with all the more reason by their common essence; a form is never a pure absolute, although it may be "relatively absolute", as is the case precisely with sacred forms. In a Hindu and Buddhist climate this transition from the formal to the essential—whether gradual or abrupt—is an acknowledged possibility, whereas in the Semitic West it is excluded; the notion of heresy does not allow for relativizing, or even justifying, reservations; this is the spirit of alternativism, which in many cases is justified—in the East as well as in the West—but not in all cases. As for the principle of abrogation, we had to mention it in the context of Lutheran audacities in order to demonstrate at least indirectly that if a spiritual perspective is indeed possible it may well draw conclusions exceeding what one would normally expect or undermining the usual bases of a given traditional criteriology.

If Luther rejects all that Catholicism understands by "tradition", it is because of an association of ideas connected with the "commandments of men" mentioned in the Gospel, as we pointed out earlier;

---

[27] If this perspective, which could not but appear at a given moment of the Christian cycle, were intrinsically false and ineffectual, one could not explain how an esoterist such as Jakob Boehme could flower in such a climate, not to mention other Rosicrucian and Hermetic Lutheran theosophists. Moreover, it is known that Luther's coat-of-arms features a rose with a heart and cross in the center, which perhaps is more than chance. Let us also mention in this context such Anglican esoterists as John Smith the Platonist and William Law, the mystical theologian, without forgetting the isolated mystic of the first half of the twentieth century who was the anonymous author (Lilian Staveley) of *The Golden Fountain*, *The Prodigal Returns*, and *The Romance of the Soul*.

he allows only "Scripture" to remain, and it becomes everything; bibliolatry is the pivot of his religion, as is also the case in Judaism and Islam.

Scholastic theology teaches that man can—and therefore must— obtain grace not only through a supernatural gift of God but also by natural means, such as virtues and works. Luther was well aware that we cannot produce the grace of God—and in fact no one has ever said the contrary—but he seems to have been unaware that we can remove the obstacles separating us from grace, just as it is enough to open a shutter in order to let in sunlight; one does not attract light by magic any more than one creates it, but one removes what renders it invisible.

The mystic of Wittenberg is "more Catholic than the Pope" in feeling that it is pretension on the part of man to believe in the quasi-theurgical virtue of certain actions—to believe a good act can *ipso facto* precipitate a concordant grace, as if man had the power to determine the divine Will; and this feeling furnishes Luther with a reason, perhaps the main one, for rejecting the Mass. In fact to believe we can determine the divine Will by our comportment—*Deo juvante*—is in no way pretentious, given that God created us for precisely this; it is a normal or "supernaturally natural" consequence of our theomorphism; thus there is no harm in the idea that our actions can be meritorious before God, and no one obliges us to become proud of them. A good conscience is a normal phenomenon; it is the normal climate within which a man runs toward God; there is nothing in a good conscience that attracts us to the world, it being perfectly neutral in this respect, unless we are hypocrites. On the contrary, it draws us toward Heaven since by its very nature it is a taste of Heaven.

What constitutes the Lutheran message fundamentally is an emphasis on faith within an awareness of our misery, or by this very awareness, though also in spite of it. All the limitations of this point of departure have indirectly the function of a key or symbol and are compensated for, beyond words, by the ineffable response of Mercy; in the final analysis the initial torment is resolved in a quasi-mystical experience of the faith that appeases, vivifies, liberates.

The idea that no work can be "justice" before God because all human work is tainted with sin—first with concupiscence and then with pride as a result of the sin of Adam and Eve—has its logical basis in the limitation of the human "I" in the face of the divine "Self" and in the impossibility for the "I" to liberate itself without the decisive concurrence of the "Self". Analogy is certainly not identity, and theology is not metaphysics in spite of points where they meet; but where there is analogy there can always be identity by way of exception and to some degree, as the spark can always flash forth from the flint. The Christian denominations as such can never be of the same order as *gnosis*, any more than can any other exoterism; and yet a Meister Eckhart and a Jacob Boehme manifest this perspective in their own way, the first within the framework of Catholicism and the second within that of Protestantism.[28] Both saw the "immanent transcendence" of the pure Intellect, Eckhart in recognizing the *increatum et increabile* character of the kernel of human intelligence and Boehme in referring to "inward illuminations" (*innere Erleuchtungen*) of a sapiential, hence intellective, nature. Similarly each was able to account for *Māyā*, the principle of universal Relativity, Eckhart in establishing the distinction between hypostatic differentiation and the "ineffable Depth" (*der Ungrund*) and Boehme in posing the principle of opposition or contrasts, rooted in God and operating in the world in order to make God knowable in an objective and distinctive mode.[29]

---

[28] It is true that certain convictions of Boehme stray from Lutheran—or post-Lutheran—orthodoxy, but even so he did not become a Catholic; he lived and died in the Protestant Church, and his death was that of a saint. We could also mention Paracelsus—by whom Boehme was moreover inspired—who was at once Rosicrucian theosophist, mystic, and physician and to whom is owed a "spagyric medicine", that is, one akin to Hermeticism and based upon the *solve et coagula* of the alchemists. It would be inexplicable for so eminent a mind to have chosen Protestantism if it were intrinsically heretical. As for Boehme, let us note in passing that his anthropology, like that of certain Fathers of the Church, was not immune to an anti-sexual and moralizing angelism, which sees the original fall in the form of the body and not in matter alone, whereas Hindu doctrine, for example, takes seriously the sexual aspect of human theomorphism.

[29] In theology the pure Intellect is prefigured by the objectifying notion of the Holy

One finds certain tendencies in Luther that are very similar to those of the "friends of God" (*die Gottesfreunde*), a mystical society that flourished in the fourteenth century in the Rhineland, Swabia, and Switzerland, whose most eminent representatives were Tauler and the blessed Suso. The former—known to Luther—made himself the spokesman of the Eckhartian doctrine of "quietude" (*Gelassenheit*) and fought against "justice through works" (*Werkgerechtigkeit*) and against outward religiosity.

According to Tersteegen[30]—one of the saintly men of the Protestant Church—"The true theosophers, of whom we know very few after the time of the Apostles, were all mystics, but it is very far from the case that all mystics are theosophers, not one among thousands. The theosophers are those whose spirit [not reason] has explored the depths of the Divinity under divine guidance and has known such marvels thanks to an infallible vision."[31]

What exoterism does not and cannot say—neither Catholic nor Orthodox any more than Protestant—is that the Pauline or Biblical mystery of faith is none other at its root than the mystery of *gnosis*, which is to say that *gnosis* is the prototype and underlying essence of faith. If faith can save, it is because intellective knowledge delivers—a knowledge that is immanent while being transcendent, and conversely. The Lutheran theosophers were gnostics within the framework of faith, and the most metaphysical Sufis emphasized faith on the basis of knowledge; no doubt there is a faith without *gnosis*, but there is no *gnosis* without faith. The soul can go to God without direct assistance from the pure Intellect, but the Intellect cannot manifest itself

---

Spirit and *Māyā* by the temporalizing notion of predestination; the Holy Spirit enlightens, strengthens, and kindles, and predestination makes creatures and things to be what they are, and what they cannot not be.

[30] In an epistle entitled *Kurzer Bericht von der Mystik.*

[31] The theosopher Angelus Silesius would not perhaps have left the Lutheran Church had he not been expelled for his esoterism; in any case Bernardine mysticism seemed to correspond best to his spiritual vocation. This makes us think somewhat of Sri Chaitanya, who as an Advaitin threw out all his books one fine day so as to think only of Krishna; and let us note at this point that this *bhakta*, while accepted as orthodox, rejected the ritual of the Brahmans and the castes in order to put the entire accent on faith and love, not on works.

without giving the soul peace and life and without requiring from it all the faith of which it is capable.

Part Two

INTERMEDIARY QUESTIONS

The Problem of Moral Divergences

Divergences in traditional morals may result from outward conditions of life combined with profound differences of temperament; they may also come about because of differing levels of application and differences of perspective. The discrepancy between the Law of Moses and that of Christ offers an obvious example.

In speaking of divorce Christ points out that Moses—but a Moses commissioned by God—permitted divorce because of "the hardness of your heart", and he adds, "What therefore God hath joined together, let not man put asunder." The question that arises here has to do with knowing whether the human reality that determined the prescription of Moses ceased to exist at the time of Christ; to say the least, there is no reason for supposing it did; we therefore have the right to conclude that in promulgating his ban on divorce Christ is concerned with a different human fact from the one considered by Moses, namely, a particular and not a general fact, one created in a sense by the Christic Message itself. If Islam returns to the Mosaic Law, it is because it refers to the same human facts as that law; it does not presuppose a climate of sacrificial *bhakti* but the psychological and social possibilities common to all men. From the Judeo-Islamic point of view, divorce is certainly not good in itself—a *hadīth* terms it "hateful"—but it is acceptable according to circumstances, and it then becomes something neutral; this proves that these legislations take account of conditions that are independent of "hardness of heart" while admitting that not every matrimonial union is the work of God, the sole condition that would render it indissoluble. If one wishes to claim a quasi-direct divine will for marriage, one must exclude every economical and political motivation and all petty bargaining; in any case the fact that marriage is indissoluble in principle, since it refers metaphysically to the paradisiacal prototype or to an ecclesiastical symbolism, does not mean it is something absolute from the standpoint of human facts or contingencies—a standpoint that unquestionably has a right to existence, for otherwise the Sinaitic and Koranic prescriptions would not exist.[1]

---

[1] Moreover, hardness of heart does not necessarily reside in the complaining spouse; it

To situate properly what we have just said, it is necessary to understand that by "hardness of heart" Christ does not mean blatant malice so much as basic egoism, the egoism that makes the average man attach himself to the here-below more than to the hereafter or to the outward more than to the inward. If the Sinaitic and Koranic Laws authorize divorce—and thus seem to accept a certain "hardness of heart"—it is because there is a form of egoism that is legitimate, fundamental, and perhaps even healthy; one could also say that Christ considers the principle of individual interest only in its worldly or passional aspect, whereas these Laws take account of conditions, modalities, or degrees that are able to neutralize this aspect or tendency. Both points of view—the Christian and the Judeo-Islamic—are of divine origin since they give rise to sacred prescriptions; each must appear in its providential context as a result of the divine play of possibilities. Christ, who is concerned solely with the hereafter—"My Kingdom is not of this world"—expects one to submit to destiny; Judeo-Islamic Law admits, however, that a man has a right to shape his life in the interest of his own equilibrium, hence also for the sake of the goods of the next world; this assumes on the one hand that the good things of the here-below contain an indirect spiritual value in principle and by their nature—because of their participation in the celestial prototypes[2]—and on the other hand that our choice of these goods or manner of dealing with them does not run counter to objective Law or our subjective interest. For Christians whatever is of this world *ipso facto* takes one away from God; for Abrahamic Semites whatever *de facto* takes one away from God is of this lower world alone; this *distinguo* is more than a truism, despite its schematic and apparently simplistic form.

---

certainly does reside in the oppressing spouse, and above all in parents who impose on their children partners who are contrary to their natures. If divorce violates the sacrament of marriage, forced marriage is also a profanation of the sacrament.

[2] This is expressed by the following verse of the Koran: "Each time that a fruit shall be offered them [in Paradise] they shall say: This used to be offered unto us beforehand [on earth]. . . . And in this place they shall be offered pure spouses" (*Sūrah* "The Cow" [2]:25). The good of heavenly rewards does not lie in the fact that they imitate earthly pleasures; on the contrary the good of earthly pleasures—objectively conditioned and subjectively precarious—resides in the fact that they imitate heavenly pleasures by ontological participation.

"My Kingdom is not of this world": this saying implies that the things of this world must be lived in relation to the other world in a moral, separative, and limitative manner, not in a manner that is contemplative and unitive; it is not the cosmologically "vertical" contents that count but the "horizontal" containers, the superimposed levels, earth and heaven, "flesh" and "spirit"; and "no man can serve two masters". On the Muslim side it is said that the Prophet intended to bring "not only the goods of the other world but also the goods of this world", which means that there is an alternative only in a certain respect, but that in another respect there is compatibility and interaction, for both positions, the spiritual and the moral, are relative and conditional. The Christian point of view is founded upon an axiomatic and quasi-exclusive consideration of the humanly irremediable fall of the soul, which is hopelessly given to concupiscence, passional attachment, and even pride; the Judeo-Islamic point of view begins on the contrary by considering not only human nature as such, which is deiform and in this respect incorruptible, but also the positive symbolism of natural things, since neither our fall nor that of the surrounding world can be substantial, hence absolute. According to Islam either there is no "original sin" or else this sin is not absolute and not able to impair the soul's capacity for salvation, a capacity conditioned objectively by Law and Grace and subjectively by faith and effort.

—— .:. ——

Since Christianity sees a maximum of concupiscence in sexuality—it is almost the "ontological sin", the sin *par excellence*—and for this reason exalts chastity and recommends celibacy, it is logical in wishing to combine a maximum amount of penance with marriage and therefore in being opposed to all eroticism and forbidding divorce and polygamy; in short it eliminates all chance of escaping from the pitfalls of an unhappy marriage, and it endeavors as far as possible to attach a kind of punishment or reproach to marriage. Be that as it may, from the Judeo-Islamic point of view it can be said that Christianity does not take into account certain legitimate facts of human nature while nonetheless attributing an absolute value to the requirements of its perspective, even though they are relative like the perspective itself; and it can also be said that this is because Christianity is not *a priori* a religion but a mystical brotherhood that has become religion. Now a religion, Muslims say, is composed of a *sharī'ah* and a *tarīqah*—an exoterism and an esoterism—whereas the Christian system is an esoterism lacking the corresponding exoterism and conferring therefore an exoteric significance upon its institutions.[3]

The ambiguity of earthly pleasure, above all sexual pleasure, comes from the fact that it combines concupiscence or animality—insofar as it involves a desire for what we do not have—with an angelic and quasi-divine awareness of what we are in our ontological and paradisiacal substance. All moral and mystical oscillations and tensions are explained in this way, and the ambiguity is not just in the experience but in the subject as well as in the object. Man oscillates between sacraments and idols, objectively and subjectively: he is himself either angel or animal, but he can also be both at different times according to his disposition or circumstances. For primordial man every natural pleasure was a sacrament, hence a unitive rite, which is what caused Meister Eckhart to say that to eat is in principle to take Communion—in principle, that is, in an eminently conditional manner. Be that as it may, noble joy is the encounter, at once concrete and Platonic, with what we are in our depths; if the *Upanishad* says that "man is made of desire", it could as well have said—and more ontologically—that man is made of beatitude.

This saying is entirely characteristic of the Christian perspective: "But those things which proceed out of the mouth come forth from the heart; and they defile the man"; this is said in order to emphasize the "commandment of God", which concerns purity of heart, in contrast to the "tradition of men", which concerns legal purity and includes physical purifications. What Christ means is that purifications of the body and utensils are worthless without purity of heart; he goes even further by asserting that inward purity does away with the necessity of

---

[3] The social framework of Christianity is *grosso modo* a combination of Jewish tradition, Roman Law, and Germanic custom, the result being stylized where necessary by Christian sensibility.

outward purifications, which is undeniably an esoteric attitude. Quite paradoxically—though this is a possibility, which as such could not but be realized—Christ instituted a religion, hence a *de facto* exoterism, based on the very negation of exoterism, but without including, at least not explicitly, what we might call an "absolute esoterism", that is, a form of spirituality based on intellective and unitive contemplation of metaphysical truths.

"A new commandment I give unto you," said Christ, "that ye love one another": this message is an innovation only insofar as it is superimposed upon the old traditional order or the morally polyvalent Law; in any case it in fact abolishes prescriptions that do not enter directly into its perspective, and it provides the key for all the new things presented by Christianity. This "new commandment" sets forth a climate of ascetic perfection for the sake of a mystical love that rejects the "world", but even so it could not abolish the positive virtualities that are present in human nature as such.

Judeo-Islamic morality, or Abrahamic morality if one prefers, is "equilibrium for the sake of ascension" or "the horizontal for the sake of the vertical", not equilibrium or the horizontal for its own sake. As for Christian morality it is "ascension alone", equilibrium appearing as a betrayal; and in this lie the strength and the weakness of this perspective.[4] The juxtaposition we have just presented is doubtless schematic, but it must be so in order to characterize the divergent principles of the theologies and moralities in question; certain objections are easy to foresee, though it is impossible to do justice to all the nuances and compensatory factors. Nonetheless we would add the following clarifications: the Christian tradition relativizes the quasi-absoluteness of the first sin and its consequences—and in this way comes closer to the other two Semitic monotheisms—when it asserts that original sin "wounded" but did not "destroy" deiform human nature, which as such continues to be capable of goodness.

As for the Jewish perspective, it cannot simply be combined with the perspective of Islam as if to constitute what we have termed a "Judeo-Islamic morality": in fact Judaism gives much more weight to

---

[4] The separation between clergy and laity or between men of religion and men of the world is quite revealing in this regard; conflicts between these two groups eventually gave rise to scissions and inversions, which are only too well known.

the idea of original sin than does Islam, although this idea is brought out in the Koran as well. Obviously Judaism is at the very origin of this idea since it has its revealed basis in Genesis, or the first chapter— *Bereshit*—of the *Torah;* starting here the Jewish tradition taught that the sin committed in Eden has repercussions for all human generations; every man has inherited the guilt incurred by his first ancestors, and through it he is corrupted in his very nature and destined to suffering and death. Christian exegesis of Genesis merely follows and elaborates this doctrine, carrying it to its ultimate penitential conclusions, whence arises a "Judeo-Christian" morality of an ascetic kind, prefigured among others by the morality of the Essenes and perpetuated as one of the currents within Judaism itself; but it is in fact merely one current in the midst of an overall ethical system much more closely related to that of Islam than to that of Christianity.

The entire Christian paradox, whose legitimacy results from the positive spiritual possibility it manifests, becomes clear when one considers the fact that Christianity is a sacrificial *bhakti*—not a musical and dancing *bhakti* like Krishnaism—which was predestined to become a complete, hence "world", religion and which by its very particularity, presented as absolute, fatally provoked a reaction from the Semitic and Biblical world, a reaction that took the form of Islam precisely; this is a providential sequence independent of the intrinsic content of these religions, for each is situated in its fashion at the center and origin.

—— ·:· ——

Karma, bhakti, jnāna: ways of action, love, knowledge. Christianity is a personalist *bhakti* founded upon a fact, namely, the salvific Redemption brought about by the historical Christ; this fact, since it requires the quality of absoluteness, is necessarily unique in the strict sense of the word, and this is why Jesus was born of a virgin and raised the dead. But whatever a given fact might be, it cannot of itself take the place of total Truth; the "Christic" fact, for entirely material and all the more paradoxical reasons, therefore neglects all men whom it cannot reach in space and time, and this is a sign of its limitation. But this does not prevent this perspective-framework from being able to convey every metaphysical truth; Christianity in fact possesses its *gnosis*, its theosophy, its esoteric dimensions.

Islam on the other hand presents itself as a *karma-mārga* insofar as it insists upon works and as a *jnāna-mārga* insofar as it identifies itself with an idea, that of principial Unity; upon this double basis it conveys a theocentric, not personalist, *bhakti*. What this means is that Islam is a *karma-bhakti-jnāna*, and this synthesis or equilibrium is in any case characteristic of its nature—a synthesis founded not upon a fact but upon a principle, that of absolute Reality. Thus the prophetic fact becomes in turn a principle, and it does so in the form of the succession of "Messengers", the last of them, Muhammad, necessarily being conceived as their synthesis. Contrary to what takes place with a historical fact, which is accessible only to those who could have been informed of it, principial truth is by its very nature accessible to all, for it can appear everywhere: there can be a prophet who proclaims it everywhere, and in principle nothing prevents it from revealing itself to every well-disposed intelligence since it is inscribed in the very substance of the human spirit. It is true that at the exoteric level of Islam this universalist perspective becomes in turn a simple confessional fact, a fact that can be transcended only by an integral esoterism; we insist upon the epithet "integral", for in every religion there are semi-esoterisms, which release us only partially, if at all, from the limitations of the "saving mirage".

A remark is called for here in order to forestall—or rather dispel— certain misunderstandings that are as common as they are unfortunate. Formerly, the prince of darkness fought against religions above all from without and apart from the sinful nature of man; in our age he adds a new stratagem to this struggle, with regard to emphasis at least, which consists in seizing religions from within, and he has largely succeeded, in the world of Islam as well as in the worlds of Judaism and Christianity. This is not even very difficult for him—ruse would be almost a needless luxury—given the prodigious lack of discernment that characterizes the humanity of our epoch, a humanity that more and more tends to replace intelligence with psychology, the objective with the subjective, even the truth with "our time".

Alternations in Semitic Monotheism

In order to understand the antagonism between Christianity and Judaism on the one hand and between Christianity and Islam on the other, it is necessary above all to give due weight to the fact that every religion is a form. This means two things: first, each religion has a specific character that is destined to lay claim to a given set of mental tendencies and develop what is best in them; second, the dogmatic premises and sacramental means of each religion—insofar as the characteristics of the particular form or *upāya* are emphasized—have a relative and not an absolute significance at the level of their literal interpretation, even though they reflect in their own way absolute, and not relative, realities. Dogmas and sacraments are keys to the divine Reality, but they do not represent it in an exclusive and irreplaceable fashion.

As for Christianity, it is distinguished by the fact that it constitutes a *mārga*, or specific way, of *bhakti*,[1] and operates within a perspective of sacrificial love, whence its dramatic and ascetic character. Notwithstanding its purely metaphysical implications, the Christian message is a truth expressed in terms of *bhakti* and not the Truth as such, and this is already apparent in the fact that it presents itself as something new; now the quality of newness is proof of particularity, not of general significance. The "new law" of love and other innovations in relation to Mosaism can be explained by the particularism of *bhakti* as opposed to the general scope of the Mosaic Law and also by the relative esoterism represented by *bhakti*, with its insistence on inwardness, as compared to the exoterism clearly represented by the practical prescriptions of Moses. In retrospect it seems more than likely that the interiorization and sentimentalization—not using the last term in any pejorative sense—brought about by Christianity were the only means of spiritually regenerating the Western world, but this

---

[1] Let us recall that Buddhists use the word *upāya* to mean a "divine stratagem" or "saving mirage": it is not intrinsic truth that is of primary importance but saving efficacy. As for the Hindu term *bhakti*, it designates a way of love, not of knowledge or obediential works. Hinduism is even less reducible than Buddhism to a single *upāya* or—with all the more reason—to a single *mārga*, for it includes several of these, and this is at once its strength and weakness.

does not mean that this "divine stratagem" constitutes the unique, exclusive, and total Truth and that everything else is only error and barbarism. Theology is intellectual insofar as it expresses the intrinsic, hence essential and universal, truth of dogmatic formulations, and it is sentimental insofar as it defends the "letter"—which nonetheless "killeth", according to Saint Paul—against other possible formulations of the truth; it is no doubt obliged to do so, but this does not make it true in an absolute sense.

If Christianity appears as something new, it could be argued that the same is true of every other religion; but the issue here is obviously not the simple fact that every beginning is new, for in this case we would never think of attributing novelty to Christianity alone. Sinai clearly marks a new stage in Judaism, and yet there was no intention of abolishing the religion of the Patriarchs; its spirit is such that it neither invites nor encourages innovation in any way; the orthodox Messianism of the Jews—this should be emphasized—is opposed to the idea of progress. The same is true of Islam: far from presenting itself as something new, Islam wishes only to restore—not "reform"—what existed from the beginning; the Prophet is simply the last in a succession of Prophets, known and unknown, and he brings nothing that was not brought by his predecessors in one form or another; according to the Koran "there is no change in the words of God". The situation is just the same in Hinduism and Buddhism: each cosmic cycle has its *Avatāra* or *Buddha*; even the historical Buddha had no intention of innovating; he manifested *Bodhi*, Enlightenment, just as numberless Buddhas did before him and will do after him; his Enlightenment is not in itself something new but rather the actualization of an eternal reality, that of *Nirvāna*, which bursts forth whenever the human cycles permit or demand it.

—— ·:· ——

The *Magna Carta* of Christianity is not only the superhumanness of Christ but the unique nature of this superhumanness; otherwise Christ would lack the quality of absoluteness that provides the Christian Revelation with its reason for being as a religious form. This quality, at once superhuman and unique, is therefore required by the Christian *upāya* itself; in other words a personalist *bhakti*—such as Krishnaism—requires a divinity in human form, hence a "divine form" that can provide love with the supreme and irreplaceable object it needs, an object without which it would have no content. Religious personalism is a spiritual possibility that must necessarily appear in certain circumstances and in a certain environment, taking these notions in their broadest sense.

Now saying that the Christian *upāya* requires the intervention of an *Avatāra*, a "God-man", amounts to saying that it is founded, doctrinally and emotionally, not on the divine Nature as such—as is Islam in particular—but on the divine Manifestation in the world and that this emphasis determines the very way in which the divine Nature is conceived, whence the Trinity, which is fundamentally nothing other than the "Christification" of God, if one may use such an expression.[2] What this means is that the divine Manifestation is emphasized in an intense and exclusive fashion, even in its principial prefiguration, at the expense of a metaphysically adequate definition of the supreme Principle.[3]

No doubt God permits this *upāya* for the sake of its efficacy—otherwise Christianity would not exist—but He does not thereby exclude other possible perspectives, to say the least; on the contrary God limits the expansion of the Christian *upāya*—and re-establishes equilibrium within the context of Monotheism—precisely by means of Islam, which places its stress on Substance and not Manifestation. The very notion of *upāya* enables one to understand the following: the fact that Christ appeared in a superhuman form does not mean that

---

[2] One might speak in a similar way of an "Israelization" of God in the sense that God is as it were the property of Israel in the Judaic *upāya*.

[3] Christ said, "Whatsoever ye shall ask the Father in my name, He will give it you"; this causes no difficulty if we take "Father" to mean God and if as Christ said the Father is "greater than the Son". But if like the Father Christ is also God, why ask something of the Father rather than of the Son, who is present and who speaks? Why does Christ not say: "I will refuse you nothing" since he is just as much God as is his Father? If Christ is God, why ask something of God in the name of Christ, hence in the name of God; or again, why not address oneself to the Trinity, given that the divine Persons are considered equal? In formulating these questions we do not mean to enter into a theological imbroglio; we simply wish to give an idea—indirectly and with the help of a single example—of the problematic nature of a dogmatism that is too intent upon dotting every "i" in a context where holy indetermination would do no harm and would in any case be more appropriate.

Christianity is superior to religions that emphasize the element Truth rather than the element Phenomenon, but simply that the personalist *bhakti* of Christianity requires a divine Manifestation and cannot be satisfied with a metaphysical message of Truth, a message therefore unsuited to support the form of worship in question.

Certainly Christ is a summit, but he is so in his superhumanness and as savior, not as a doctor of metaphysics; Christians acknowledge this, but they conclude that metaphysics has no salvific value, Christ being the sole dispenser of salvation. This disdain of sapience appears indirectly in the way Christians treat Solomon: in their opinion it is not even certain that he is saved nor that he will not have to remain in purgatory until the Last Judgment, and they insist all the more readily upon the incomparability of his wisdom since his fall from grace proves in their eyes the vanity of sapience.[4] It is perhaps not improper to conclude that this is the verdict of a perspective that gives primacy to love: it is the verdict of a systematic *bhakti*, comparable to a certain type of devotional Vishnuism. It is quite natural that Islam, where the perspective opens to *gnosis*, should have rehabilitated Solomon by including him in the family of Prophets and accusing the Biblical account of duplicity, this being an indirect and in turn exoteric way of demonstrating the *a priori* narrowly legalistic character of the Book of Kings.

Before proceeding we must emphasize the following point: even though Christianity is a *bhakti* by virtue of the general form that defines it,[5] it nonetheless possesses a dimension of *jnāna* or *gnosis*, and this is necessarily so since it is an integral and autonomous tradi-

---

[4] Jesus refers to Solomon in praising the Queen of Sheba and in speaking about the lilies of the field, which in our eyes is a mark of approval for him who was the first "Son of David". Christ was a second Solomon in the sense that he built a new Temple and included the Gentiles in the Nation of God.

[5] "I thank thee, O Father, Lord of heaven and earth, because thou hast hid these things from the wise and the prudent, and hast revealed them unto babes." This statement can also be taken as a sign of *bhakti*, although its immediate meaning relates to the "doctors of the Law" and profane philosophers.

tion. This Christian esoterism is founded upon the idea of the immanent Christ, that is, the Intellect—or the "Heart"—which is at once
"Light" and "Love": for "I am the Light of the world", and "God is
Love". Now the intellect is essentially identified with the Self; it is
aliquid increatum et increabile.

The Virgin Mother embodies supra-formal Wisdom; it is from
her milk that all the Prophets have drunk; in this respect she is greater
than the Child, who here represents formal wisdom, hence a particular revelation.[6] Next to the adult Jesus, however, Mary is not the
nonformal and primordial essence but his feminine prolongation, the
shakti: in this case she is not the *Logos* in its feminine and maternal
aspect but the virginal and passive complement of the masculine and
active *Logos*, its mirror, made of purity and mercy. Christic *gnosis*
approaches the Essence through different aspects of divine Manifestation:[7] to enter into the mold of this Manifestation is to realize union
with the Self, *Ātmā*, which "became man that man might become
God". The sacrificial aspect of this union is not located merely on
the moral or ascetic level, which is outward, but also—or even above
all—on the level of the soul as such to the extent it is substance.

The great supports of the Christic way are prayer, fasting, vigil,
poverty, chastity; the first is positive and essential, being in principle
sufficient unto itself, whereas the others are negative or privative
and are meaningful only in connection with the first. Furthermore,
fasting and vigil are more directly essential than poverty and chastity;
these are voluntary, though they do possess a mystical significance
that concerns everyone and that coincides with the spiritual virtue
of detachment and purity, as well as with that of childlikeness—in

---

[6] We could also say that the Child is the formal and determinate Intellect, which
drinks the milk of the nonformal and indeterminate Intellect. It is thus that a crystal
absorbs the undifferentiated light, which it must bring into focus through its own
form; the form is perfect because it is a divine reflection, but it is a form nonetheless.
On the one hand Christ is the rigorous center, and the Virgin is the gentle ray that
prolongs it; on the other the Mother is the ray that infuses itself into the circle, which
represents the Child; limitlessness infuses itself into perfection.

[7] Outward or inward, Eucharistic or onomatological: the *Logos* is Jesus, but it is also
the Heart-Intellect, just as it can be the Eucharist or the very Name of Jesus; in the
macrocosm the *Logos* is the "Spirit of God" with its archangelic functions, and as such
it prolongs or projects the *Logos* inherent in the divine Nature.

short, with nonconcupiscence, victory over the Fall; this is prefigured in Baptism.

Since it is founded upon divine Manifestation, the Christian perspective is a doctrine of the Intermediary: the Intermediary, "Door", or *Logos* is any metaphysical or cosmic reality that simultaneously separates and unites two hierarchically different levels and thus relates to both levels without being reducible to either; and this is the case within the Principle as well as in its Manifestation and in the human microcosm as well as in the macrocosm.

It is understandable that exoterists should hate *gnosis* since on the one hand it threatens the Trinitarian dogma by contemplating an undifferentiated Absolute and on the other hand universalizes and thus depersonalizes Christ by reducing him to a *Logos* that is at once impersonal and multi-personal. Nonetheless this *gnosis* no more denies the uniqueness of Christ than knowledge of the fixed stars negates the sun: the literal truth remains intact, though it becomes relative even while remaining absolute in its essence, which—in the last analysis—is its reason for being.[8]

According to Shankara it is necessary to distinguish between absolute truth, which is founded on the idea of Beyond-Being (*Paramātmā* or *Brahma nirguna*), and relative truth, which is founded on the idea of creative Being (*Īshvara* or *Brahma saguna*), the first point of view corresponding to *jnāna*, the way of knowledge, and the second to *bhakti*, the way of love; now within the framework of Semitic monotheism, Islam represents the first of these perspectives whereas Christianity represents the second. It is from this distinction that Islam draws its conviction of superiority, notwithstanding the fact that in its general

---

[8] By a crowning paradox, modernism—which stands at the antipodes of *gnosis*—accepts certain of its extrinsic theses, whereas traditionalists not only reject *gnosis*, for which they cannot be criticized, but place it in the same category as any and all modern errors, and this is proof of blind prejudice. It is because of this same prejudice that some people confuse modernism with Arianism or Sabellianism, inexcusably losing sight of the fact that the intellectual, moral, and other tendencies of the ancient heresies are diametrically opposed to those of modernism.

form—and leaving aside Sufic *gnosis*—it too is derived from the perspective of creationist ontologism; but this is not the point, for what matters here is that Islam, on the very level of what Shankara calls relative truth, reflects absolute truth as directly as possible and thus *a priori* opens the way to it.

From another point of view, Hinduism distinguishes between major and minor *Avatāra*s, that is, complete and partial incarnations;[9] now Christ, who identifies the divine Message with himself, belongs to the first of these two categories whereas the Prophet, who passively receives the Message that God "causes to descend", belongs to the second; it is because of his avataric plenitude that Christ is "before Abraham", and it is from this pre-eminence that Christianity draws its conviction of superiority. Islam does not consider this aspect of things since it is founded on the pre-eminence of essential truth and opens to *gnosis*, and this is why it views the Prophet solely in light of the pre-eminence of the Message; for its part Christianity takes no account of this pre-eminence and claims for its doctrine the pre-eminence of Christ. For one, the theophanic excellence of the Messenger is that of the Message; for the other, the metaphysical excellence of the Message is that of the Messenger.[10]

When God declared on Mount Sinai, "Thy God is One", it was neither to promulgate an incomplete truth nor to conceal an essential truth; and when Jesus commanded the Apostles, "Baptize them in the name of the Father, and of the Son, and of the Holy Spirit", it was not in order to declare that this triad constitutes the Absolute, that there is no Absolute outside of it, and that God is therefore One through it alone. The Sinaitic definition of God being essential, complete, and definitive, a complement added to it can have only a relative significance—in the metaphysical, not the current, sense of this adjective or in the sense of the "relatively absolute", if one prefers. For what is at stake here is principial relativity, which means a degree of reality that represents the Absolute in relation to the world and man while nonetheless being relative in relation to the Absolute as such.

---

[9] This distinction pertains to the level of the great *Avatāra*s and has nothing to do with the distinction between greater and lesser *Avatāra*s.

[10] The *Logos* is one, but its modes of human manifestation may differ without in any way detracting from its quality as *Logos*.

Compared with the perspective of knowledge, the perspective of love is relative in rather the same way that the Trinity or other hypostatic constellations are relative in relation to the Absolute properly so called; the perspective of knowledge could not determine the Christian Message, which must be what it is, and yet this perspective—that is, *gnosis*—is necessarily included as a virtuality within the Message and is thus rightly called "Christic". Of course *gnosis* is not a virtuality of the perspective of love as such, but it is contained virtually in the divine Message considered in relation to its universality and sacramentality.

Christian doctrine teaches that Christ has two natures, one divine and one human, but only one Person, which is divine—so divine as to require that Mary be called the "Mother of God"; now this unipersonalist theory, while theologically useful, is problematical to say the least, and in failing to give sufficient weight to the incommensurability between the divine and human orders, it cannot avoid certain contradictions; but this is the price one pays for a perspective that absolutizes the divine Manifestation and in this way weakens the very notion of the Absolute. Integral Christian esoterism—apart from the question of its historical actualizations—restores the neglected or missing dimension by drawing it from Scripture itself; this at least is a principial possibility within Christianity, one that results in fact from all intrinsic orthodoxy.

"There is none good but God", said Christ; and also, "I ascend unto my Father and your Father; and to my God and your God." These words imply shades of meaning that have been providentially disregarded by Christian theologians—though this is unrelated to the question of integral truth—but strongly emphasized by Islam in order to "restore equilibrium", if one may so express it. In other words the extreme stylization of the Christian *upāya* has inevitably lost sight of the complete situation by accentuating the mystery of divine Manifestation—which can be only "this Manifestation" once it has assumed human form—to the detriment of what is required by the divine Nature considered as such and therefore from the standpoint of its Essence. Arianism is not an intrinsic heresy—although it was bound to disappear because of its incompatibility with the fullness of the Christian *upāya*—but it was like a presentiment of the divine corrective that was to appear later as the Islamic Revelation.

In Islam God does not appear in a human form; He simply makes known what He is and what He wishes. Now it is the divine content of the Message that matters and not its mode; the mode is the means and cannot take precedence over the question of truth. The purpose of the Muhammadan phenomenon is first of all to be messenger rather than message, hence perfect man rather than human God, and second to provide a demonstration of clearly differentiated virtues applied to the most diverse situations. Here analysis is the key to synthesis, whereas in the case of Christ synthesis is the key to analysis.

"The stone which the builders rejected is become the head of the corner": though this saying of David concerns Christ above all, it can also be applied to Ishmael, or more precisely to his progeny: Ishmael was driven from his father's house only to return at the end of the prophetic cycle in the person of Muhammad, his distant descendant, in whom and in whose community the promises made by God to Abraham and Hagar were fulfilled.[11]

To use anthropomorphic language—examples of which are furnished moreover by the Bible—one could say that God the Father "regretted" having established an *upāya* upon the earth that took the form of an extension of Himself, of the "Father", and that He corrected or compensated for this form—though without retracting it—by means of another, which was obliged to stress that God alone is God and that man is always man. The word "regret" may be offensive, but it is Biblical: in the Bible God "regretted" on a number of occasions having done this or that; this is simply a very human way of expressing necessary, hence inevitable, fluctuations in the cosmic unfolding or the interplay of compensations proper to divine *Māyā*.

—— ·:· ——

[11] Another Biblical figure that incarnates the same symbolism of the rejected stone is the Patriarch Joseph. "The last shall be first, and the first last": this formula encapsulates a particular order of possibilities connected with the reversal of relationships that takes place—in a way that is parallel to direct analogy—between the divine Principle and its cosmic projection.

We saw earlier that Christianity presents itself as something new, and this moreover by force of circumstance;[12] though legitimate on its own level, this quality of innovation nonetheless contains a danger of disequilibrium and infidelity,[13] which in fact has been actualized in the Christian world in the form of an increasingly pronounced progressivism;[14] this has been true above all since the Renaissance—a worldly, exteriorizing, and individualistic movement if there ever was one—with its abuse of intelligence on the plane of the arts as well as that of the sciences, notwithstanding the interest aroused at that time in certain circles by Platonic thought. From then on religion readily made common cause with an obviously worldly and ultimately titanic civilization; in the twentieth century the Catholic Church is reaping the poisoned fruits of this amalgam. Here too Islam appears as a divine corrective or a way of re-establishing equilibrium, for it excludes *a priori* the cult of the new; like Mosaism, and even more explicitly,[15]

---

[12] Jesus stresses that he has come "not to destroy the Law" but "to fulfill it", which indicates that Christic "newness" has nothing to do with human innovations but has the meaning on the contrary of a return to the transcendent origin; it goes without saying that this *distinguo* eludes the innovating psychology of Western humanity in just the same way that the true significance of Israelite Messianism eludes modernistic Jews.

[13] Men are quick to burn what they have worshipped and to worship what they have burned. The Celts had a reputation for loving novelty whereas the Germans were notorious lovers of adventure; these characteristics, combined with Catholic innovationism, contributed to shaping the Western mentality, which ended up spreading—whether willingly or by force—to Eastern Europeans of the Orthodox faith.

[14] Apart from problematical innovations such as the *filioque* and the obligatory celibacy of the priesthood, there is the disproportionate complication of the rubrics and a kind of *de facto* profanation of the Mass: there are greater and lesser Masses, Masses for this or for that; instead of everything being subordinated to the one and only Mass and as if annihilated before it, the Mass is in practice subordinated to this or that more or less trivial intention, to this or that occasion, and this or that category of men; in the long run this can only undermine the credibility of the Mystery. As for the celibacy of the priesthood, its imposition was a particularly unrealistic innovation—a thousand years after Saint Paul—when Saint Paul had not even found it necessary to forbid the marriage of bishops.

[15] For in Mosaism there were "innovations" of crucial importance from the human point of view, though they were contingent and not dogmatic, namely, the institution of kingship and the construction of the Temple, not to mention the Talmudic or rabbinical innovations, which Christ rejected but which for the rabbis are applications of principles and not novelties.

it reduces civilization to religion and thus in a sense reduces human time to religious space.

Our reference to Catholic civilizationism permits us to make the following digression: the amalgam in question can be defended on the grounds that the Church was born into the Greco-Roman world, which lent it its ethnic and cultural substance; this is true, but one should also take into consideration the Germanic world, which instilled itself in this Mediterranean world and exerted considerable influence, a fact to which the role of Charlemagne, the Holy Roman Empire, and the founding of France by the Franks bear witness. The Catholic Church is not only Greco-Latin but also Latino-Germanic; as for the Celtic element, which ultimately is of less importance, it does not differ fundamentally from the Germanic, being simply another branch of the Nordic element.[16]

It is significant that in the artistic order—the importance of which cannot be overestimated—Christianity gave birth *grosso modo* to three styles: Byzantine, Roman, and Gothic, which express respectively the Greek, Latin, and Germanic geniuses combined with Semitic and Christian Monotheism.[17] There are the Greek and Latin

---

[16] The prejudice that seeks to reduce the ethnic and cultural substance of the Catholic Church to the Mediterranean world alone is at the root of a number of fatal errors: from the very beginning the needs and rights of the Germanic soul were not taken seriously enough in Rome—Protestantism was the reaction to this—and later on Catholic nationalists and racists of Latin culture obstinately refused to understand that there is no Western Christianity without the Germanic world and that to exclude this world from Christianity or from Western civilization is to destroy the one as well as the other, or the one along with the other; indeed this has already come about to a large extent. Moreover it should not be forgotten that the Renaissance, and later the French Revolution, were Latin and not Germanic misdeeds: to each his role, for good and for ill.

[17] The cathedrals called Gothic are not the expressions of a specifically "French" genius but of the Germanic or Celto-Germanic genius, or of a genius both Frankish and Gallic, if one prefers; this is proven on the one hand by their sometimes exuberant imaginativeness and on the other hand by a certain grandiose heaviness, which is nonetheless never cold; none of this has anything Latin about it, and the disdain the men of the Renaissance affected toward cathedrals is a further proof. Though the specifically French spirit did not appear in the cathedrals as such, it did appear in particular cathedrals and churches, notably in Sainte Chapelle, where it asserts itself in the lightness and joyousness of forms and colors; here no doubt is the Celtic side of the French mentality.

Churches, which should co-exist without schism; but there should also be another branch of the one Church, namely, the German or Germano-Celtic Church, which would be an extension of the Latin Church in the same manner that the Slavonic and Oriental Churches are extensions of the Greek Church.

— ∴ —

Fundamentally, Muslims criticize Christians for veiling metaphysical truth with a historical phenomenon, or in other words for divinizing Jesus at the cost of humanizing God; for advocating a social and mystical morality that goes against nature; and for having betrayed and in a way destroyed the Biblical world—the world of all the Prophets and of Christ himself—by replacing it with an increasingly profane "civilization"; this final criticism is implicit and the others explicit. Like every religious community Christianity is "triumphalist" by nature, and while it is doubtless human for it to lay claim to the glories of this "civilization", in the end it is suicide; for one can Christianize pagans but not the sins of paganism.

The excessive number of victims of the Inquisition does not prove the guilt of the condemned as much as it does that of the theologians; for one does not needlessly dot "i's" if it means the suffering and death of tens of thousands of men. We certainly do not condemn the principle of a legislation designed to protect a religion; what we condemn are the theological subtleties that fed the jails and pyres, and we obviously disapprove of the immoderation and baseness of the methods of repression. In Islam the simplicity of the dogmas corresponds to the intellectual capacity of the average man, and this is both realistic and charitable, without forgetting the essentiality of the Islamic perspective, whence its formal simplicity, which coincides precisely with the mental capacity of the masses. Of course Islam also had its inquisition (*mihnah*), but its principles were less intolerant and its victims less numerous than was the case in Catholicism, and this is because a certain tolerance results from Islamic dogma itself or, to be more exact, from Islamic legislation.

As for real or apparent heresies in the Christian world, we shall call attention by way of example to the antagonism between dyotheletism and monotheletism; the first distinguishes between two wills in

Christ, the divine and the human, whereas the second acknowledges only one, the divine.

Dyotheletism, which is the official doctrine of the Catholic and Orthodox Churches, is right in the sense that both wills are evident, that they result from the two natures, and that the Gospel testifies to this; even so monotheletists are not inexcusable in upholding a unity of will, for a conflict between the two dimensions of Christ is inconceivable, so much so that for all practical purposes there is only one will, which emanates from God, and the strictly human will is only an appearance. No doubt the Church had the right to decide in favor of the dyotheletist solution, but it erred in misunderstanding the pious intention of monotheletism and in anathematizing its partisans—Pope Honorius I at their head—as if they were enemies of Christ and religion, when metaphysically the idea of one will is neither more extraordinary nor more harmful than that of a "Mother of God"; just as with this latter idea, monotheletism is at once an ellipsis and a hyperbole, and its thesis is all the more pious and honorable in that its intention is to glorify Christ, not to belittle him or favor worldliness in any way. The same remarks apply to monophysitism, which acknowledges in Christ only one nature, the divine, something it certainly does not do out of impiety; one may censure such "heresies" but to curse them is suicide, and history proves it.

Rightly or wrongly—depending on the case—exoterism operates with alternatives: it does not allow for diverse aspects of the real nor for diverse points of view of the spirit, so that in its eyes a "lesser truth" seems a total error; and let us not forget that psychological, moral, or social usefulness often serves as a criterion of truth.

We said earlier that God re-established a certain equilibrium within Monotheism by means of Islam in that Islam places its stress on the intrinsic Nature of God and not on a particular divine Manifestation. Another balancing function of Islam—on a less fundamental level, though one that is still of great human importance—is the rehabilitation of sexuality and of natural things in general, these having been discredited by what we might without hesitation call the ascetical prejudice of Christians;[18] we have spoken of this on other occasions, but we will nonetheless recall once again the principle involved, adding perhaps a further shade of meaning. There are two possible relationships between the divine and cosmic orders, one that is adequate and one that inverts: if we compare the cosmic order to a surface of water upon which a tree is reflected, we can see that the inversion of the tree does not affect the adequacy of the image; thus the material character of a thing does not keep it from having a divine content or participating in the nobility of its principial prototype; though matter as such separates, nobility of content unites, provided of course that it is put to good use by a spiritual discipline and that it contributes to the equilibrium demanded by a spiritual framework, an equilibrium that is consistent with the profound requirements of nature.

In other words man is created to achieve equilibrium between the outward and inward, between the world and God, or between diversity and unity; to the extent he disrupts this equilibrium by passionately attaching himself to the world, he must renounce the world and throw himself passionately in the direction of God; but if he is able to maintain the primordial equilibrium, which constitutes his very reason for being, he need not persuade himself that the only way to God is through a renunciation that is unconditional and contrary to nature. This does not mean that renunciation is not "spiritually natural" to man—which is why Islam commends fasting, vigils, poverty, and

---

[18] In his treatise on the creation of man, Saint Gregory of Nyssa, referring inappropriately to Saint Paul (Galatians 3:28), asserts that the division into "male and female" is foreign to the divine model of man and that God, foreseeing the fall of man and the impossibility for fallen men to reproduce like the angels—and Gregory does not tell us how they do it!—"established for our nature a means better suited to our slide into sin: in place of the nobility of the angels, He gives us the power of transmitting life to one another like brutes and beings without intelligence". And Gregory judges that God, foreseeing our inclination to evil, "for this reason mixed something irrational with His own image", by which he means the sexes, love, and sexual union—things that according to this author normally belong to the animal realm, not the human species. This means that God created the sexes for the sake of sin even while forbidding sin and that He gave the command to "multiply and fill the earth" while foreseeing the sin that would alone make this result possible, which sin He nonetheless forbade. In saying this Gregory does not explain why Christ and the Virgin are in eternal Glory with their sexualized bodies, which according to him bear witness to the fall into sin and animality, hence into degradation and disgrace.

contempt for one's life in the Holy War—but spiritual renunciation is not just any renunciation; even though by definition it amounts to a disequilibrium, it must be integrated into the equilibrium determined by the profound nature of things.[19]

It is often said that Islam is ambiguous or even contradictory in that neither the Koran nor the *Sunnah* commends asceticism whereas the Sufis preach it without fear of extravagance, or that one and the same man may practice and preach an extreme asceticism while enjoying four wives, and other paradoxes of the kind. The reason for this apparent contradiction lies in the fact—noted above—that there are two possible relationships with regard to the phenomena of the world, namely, opposition and analogy; Islam wishes to take into account all the positive aspects of reality whereas Christianity acknowledges only one point of view, that of opposition; the relationship of analogy is then identified with the notion of sin, directly or indirectly.

Because the doctrine of Christ is a message of inwardness, sincerity, and nonformality, it is therefore a message of relativity in connection with outward practices; there is also the fact that contradictory prescriptions occurring in different religions are necessarily relative, and they become all the more so when man is aware of this *de jure* relativity.

We have said that Islam is the perspective of holy equilibrium and Christianity that of holy disequilibrium: on the one hand stabilizing equilibrium for the sake of ascension, which is its reason for being, and on the other hand propulsive disequilibrium for the sake of inwardness. In Islam natural pleasure is either a sin of "association" (*shirk*) or a merit of "union" (*tawhīd*); in the second case it requires contemplativity on the part of the subject as well as moderation and sacralization; in other words pleasure brings one closer to God when it is limited by sobriety and contained within a framework of religious awareness, for this allows it to convey an element of "benediction" (*barakah*)

---

[19] Let us take this opportunity to call attention to the prejudice involved in thinking that only what is difficult or even disagreeable is pleasing to God and brings us closer to Him. We have read in an old manual of piety that "prayer is difficult and therefore satisfying since the difficulty of good works is the principle of satisfaction". But what becomes of the divine content of certain works and what in particular becomes of the sacramental and satisfying power of the Name of God itself? There is not only transcendence; there is also immanence with all its graces.

and spiritual "remembrance" (*dhikr*). Certain rites of purification are necessary not for their own sake but because the average man is little better than a beast; if enjoyment were for him a recollection of the Divine and not an act of idolatry, there would be no need for him to purify himself in order to appease "divine jealousy". Nonetheless, the *Logos*-Man submits to the rules for the sake of those around him; in doing so he does not purify himself from any particular deed but from human or existential impurity; in a certain way he purifies others in himself, for being identified with "Universal Man" (*Insān Kāmil*) he recapitulates all men within his own form.

In rejecting the prescriptions of the Pharisees, Christ teaches—referring moreover to Isaiah—that it is necessary to keep to the essential, and this principle is clearly related to what we might call the *religio perennis*, the primordial, universal, and underlying religion. This is what Koranic language designates by the term *fitrah*: the primordial norm, the profound nature of things.[20]

A very important aspect of Christian morality—not so much its social as its intrinsic morality—is its refusal to exact justice: this attitude presupposes our consciousness of immanent justice on the one hand and of our own quasi-congenital injustice on the other, natural egoism and the danger of pride being traces of the Fall. The renunciation of our rights indicates a presentiment that justice is always there, that it is in God even if we are wronged, and that in claiming our rights we risk adding one injustice to another, given the fact that we are imperfect and our individual claims—being in a sense premature—may therefore compromise our aspiration to perfection and our contemplation of what alone is perfect. As a result one must therefore offer the left cheek; and "all they that take the sword shall perish with the sword".

As with the issue of pleasure, Islam maintains a balanced and noncontrasting attitude with regard to the question of justice: while

---

[20] The fact that Christianity gave up the practice of circumcision and the observance of dietary prohibitions is not unrelated to what we have just said.

integrating the viewpoint of Christ into its perspective, it also considers the rights of nature, taking into account the fact not only that every natural right is in itself harmless to the soul, but that it contains the possibility of virtue and mystical alchemy, which is precisely what makes it natural. This means that the Muslim draws the sword "for God" and "by God" but without forgetting to be generous, wherever generosity can and should be shown; this at least is the *de jure* perspective of Islam, which is to be applied by every Muslim who is scrupulously faithful to the *Sunnah*. From another point of view—and we have made this point on a number of occasions—every possible moral or spiritual attitude is to be found in some form within every religion: it is impossible for Christians not to fight even though war does not enter into their perspective; conversely, it is impossible that a pious Muslim would never find himself in a situation where, leaving aside what is authorized by Islam, he felt obliged to renounce his rights for the sake of "poverty" (*faqr*) and from fear of God; for it is "better to blush in this world than in the next".

In accordance with their respective points of view, Christianity advocates the monastic life whereas Islam acknowledges *a priori*—in keeping with the Muslim pattern—that life in the world is consistent with sanctity, or more particularly with a sanctity that has become "radiation" (*jalwah*) after having first been "solitude" (*khalwah*).[21] "There is no monasticism in Islam": the authenticity of this *hadīth* has been contested, but this matters little since Muslims readily make use of it to stress the sacred structure of Muslim society, which constitutes a priestly and not a "lay" world, precisely.

—— ·:· ——

[21] This same idea gives rise to a curious error of interpretation on the part of Meister Eckhart: he concludes that Martha is superior to Mary because she is capable of achieving sanctity in the midst of material preoccupations, a view that contradicts historical truth and even the opinion of Christ; it is in much the same fashion that an Ibn Arabi comments on the verses of the Koran, reversing their intended meanings in order to support metaphysical or mystical truths, which however have no need of such a stratagem.

We pointed out earlier that the message of Christ is not directly a message of metaphysical doctrine but primarily a message of interiorization; the idea of the Trinity is perhaps less a metaphysical definition of the Absolute than an instrument of mystical interiorization. From another point of view the voluntarism and epistemological sensationalism of Saint Thomas within the Catholic climate did not prevent the enunciation of the most profound metaphysical truths, notably in the case of an Eckhart and in the very shadow of Thomism.

Be that as it may, if we consider theology directly and at the level of its literal meaning—and this is what it requires—it is impossible not to notice that it is sometimes reduced to the art of reconciling notions that are logically irreconcilable, none of which the theologian is willing to sacrifice: under the pressure of a dogmatic formalism or the moralizing prejudice that is its consequence, he is attached to them all; if he does not succeed in reconciling contradictory but irreplaceable notions, he will gladly resort to the idea of "mystery" and be tempted to denigrate "natural intelligence", and this is facilitated by the conventional association of intelligence with "pride". It goes without saying that religious ideas are not sentimental prejudices in themselves, but this is what they become subjectively in the case of those who refuse to admit that there are aspects in God and points of view in man and that what is true in one respect is not necessarily so in another. That God is triune is true in a relative sense—or "relatively absolute" sense if one prefers—unity alone being unconditionally absolute; conversely, that God is one does not prevent Him from having an aspect of trinity on the already relative level of hypostatic differentiation; but when the two theses are both placed on the level of absoluteness—as a result of "piety" and because of a confusion between the absolute and the sublime—they become irreconcilable.[22]

---

[22] The assertion that the unity of God applies to the Essence whereas the trinity applies to the Persons does not abolish the contradiction between unity and trinity since both are applied to God considered as such, hence as the Absolute; the moment we introduce two different relationships into a consideration of the divine Principle we are in the realm of relativity, at least insofar as one of the two terms is concerned, so that a proposition containing both relationships could not be a definition of God. What is metaphysically contradictory is not the assertion that God is one and three in different respects, one of these being relative and therefore beneath the level of divine absoluteness, but rather the assertion that God is both one and three in the absoluteness

We should mention here the danger involved in ill-sounding, even absurd, formulations, which are doubtless inevitable in a world of voluntaristic and sentimental faith. Thought in this climate is above all "pious", hence self-interested; perfect objectivity and a critical sense can in these conditions easily give the impression of doubt and intellectual pride. According to this way of seeing things, to think in a way that is *a priori* disinterested is to cut oneself off from faith, and it is to reason like Lucifer: on one's own and "outside God"; in short it is to fall into rationalism, exposing oneself to the danger of unbelief. Such a prejudice—which side-steps the mystery of intellection—inevitably produces a flowering of pious absurdities, which can be found to a varying degree in all religious climates[23] and which must be accepted, heroically if necessary, as the price of the human effort to transcend oneself.

Basically, zealots connect the function of the Holy Spirit less with truth pure and simple than with the salvific intention of the *upāya*; now this intention cannot be entirely disinterested, intellectually speaking, since its actual usefulness for people, and therefore questions of appropriateness, must be taken into account. All the divergences between religions come down to the distinction between efficacious, opportune, and conditionally saving truth on the one hand and truth as such on the other; truth as such has found many traditional expressions, likewise outwardly divergent for reasons of form, but it resides

---

that essentially defines Him, an affirmation characteristic of a *bhakti*—a devotionally totalitarian *bhakti*—that seeks to maintain its momentum by means of metaphysical propositions. This does not mean theologians are totally averse to the notion of relativity *in divinis*, but they do not attach the idea of lesser reality to this relativity, as we do, or else they would have to admit that only the Essence is absolutely real; if God is the Absolute, only the Essence is absolutely God.

[23] A typical example, gleaned from a Muslim book: to walk on water or rise into the air is a small matter whereas the greatest miracles are faith in God and obedience to His Law—as if faith and obedience were miracles and not virtues and graces and as if miracles were not the result of graces united with virtues and did not find in them their reason for being. When pious intentions overwhelm common sense, the image is perhaps sentimentally striking, but literally it remains absurd, and this means that while it impresses or flatters some people, it discourages or repels others. In this sort of two-edged thought the motive is obviously to serve the interests of faith—or to praise it—and not to provide a wholly exact image; the fact that one is "preaching to the choir" no doubt provides an extenuating circumstance.

above all in the inward and permanent Revelation that is the pure Intellect; this Intellect is accessible, however, only through formal and outward Revelation, hence through an *upāya*, which allows a man to be fully himself and thus to rise above himself.

Since Christianity is a *bhakti* it would in principle have been consistent and sensible to renounce integral metaphysics and hold fast to a fideism inspired solely by the Scriptures: hence to record with due piety what they say of God—of the Father, the Son, the Holy Spirit—without seeking to erect a system and to remain humbly and lovingly content with mystery; theology, which is *de facto* necessary, could have done without certain speculations inspired by Aristotle. But in fact such total faithfulness to itself, or more precisely to the genius of *bhakti*, was scarcely possible for a state religion: it was not possible in the first place because speculation is in the nature of man and the proximity of philosophers was an invitation to imitate them, especially since men are reluctant to acknowledge qualities in others they do not themselves possess—and this, without euphemism, is called jealousy; it was not possible, furthermore, because a number of converts were themselves Greeks or had been Hellenized and were acquainted with philosophy; and it was not possible, finally, because the pagan environment required vigilant apologetics, and there were Christian heresies that had to be neutralized. But here a new difficulty arises: heresy did not always consist in something contrary to the truth but was too often simply something contrary to *bhakti*; theology therefore developed in response to a twofold necessity or twofold temptation: to appropriate the dialectic of real or apparent adversaries, even if it was foreign to the Christian genius, and then with the help of this dialectic to attack its very essence[24]—in a word, to lay claim to all the rights of *gnosis* or pure intellection while resorting to mystery when this claim came up against a limit, which was inevitable since it is a question here of *bhakti* and dogmatism.

This irregularity or inner contradiction does not explain the phenomenon of heresy and its repression—this is found to some degree

---

[24] Now the essence of Hellenism pertains to *jnāna* and not *bhakti*—to intellectuality, which is by definition disinterested, and not to the voluntarism of love; rationalism and scientism are deviations from and caricatures of this intellectuality, and this was the case beginning with the period of so-called classical antiquity.

in all religions—but it does explain the extraordinary magnitude of this twofold phenomenon in Christianity; if so cruel and persistent an ostracism was inevitable, it is because there is a problematical element in doctrinal formulations, one that favors heresies on the one hand and the pedantry of the judges on the other. Nonetheless, if this problematical element has a *de facto* right to its place in the official doctrine of an intrinsically orthodox religion, it is because God tolerates it in just the same way that He tolerates the phenomenon of the *upāya* itself and just as in His patient Mercy He tolerates religious divergences; He tolerates this element, in short, in the same way that He tolerates the fact that man, even while making his way toward Heaven, is always man and nothing more—not man with his sins but man with his limitations. In any case each religious community has its own genius, which is at once divine and human, and therefore its own Law, by which it is judged in accordance with this genius and not in accordance with that of another community; some will be judged according to their love and others according to their faith; God accepts from one man what He would not accept from another, forgiving in one what He would not forgive in another.

It is possible to choose an example of divine tolerance from a much less important and even insignificant level, that of human desires: even while knowing the vanity and impermanence of these desires, God accepts them and permits their sacralization along with their satisfaction; in other words He allows man to be man—a relative subject confronted by relative objects within a space and a time that are equally relative. On the one hand this relativity is pure nothingness in the eyes of God, but on the other hand it is able to convey a message from God to man and to be a way from man to God.

Muslims acknowledge that God is at once the "Knower" (*'Āqil*), the "Known" (*Ma'qūl*), and "Knowledge" (*'Aql*); one could also say in bhaktic terms that He is at once the "Lover", the "Beloved", and "Love". Muslims would never accept this as the definition of God, however, for the simple reason that God is the Absolute and a differentiation always pertains to relativity even while testifying to a potentiality of the Absolute, which means in practice that the metaphysical validity of the above ternary does not preclude the possibility of other formulations or other numerical crystallizations; in the same way a geometrical figure intended to represent space does not preclude the co-existence of a similar figure, and water may take the form of a particular snowflake without excluding thousands of other perfect forms, each of which also bears witness to the substance that is water as well as to the possibilities of space.

Only the definition of the Absolute as such is absolute, and every explanatory description belongs to relativity precisely because of the differentiated nature of its content; this content is certainly not erroneous, but it is limited and therefore replaceable; if one wished to give an absolute definition of the Absolute, one would therefore have to say that God is One. "The testimony of Unity is one" (*al-Tawhīdu wāhid*), say the Sufis, and by this they mean that within the limits of its possibility an expression must be the same as its content and cause.[25]

As we have said, the message of Christ is a message of mystical inwardness and not metaphysical absoluteness, at least not directly; the Virgin Mary embodies its maternal aspect of gentleness, not rigor; she is a welcoming, not sacrificial, inwardness, and in this sense one can attribute to her the quality of being "black but beautiful", as does the Song of Songs; she does not tear us away from the outward

---

[25] No doubt *Ātmā* is polarized into *Sat*, *Chit*, and *Anānda*, but this polarization results from an analytic perspective pertaining to *Māyā*; one cannot say what *Ātmā* is in itself in an exclusive and exhaustive manner except by affirming that it is, that it is not nothingness, and that everything is it without being it, which is tantamount to saying that it is one, hence absolute. What this means is that *Ātmā* may also be polarized into duality or quaternity: in the first case it is the Absolute prolonged by the Infinite, and in the second it is the Absolute refracted into Wisdom, Power, Beatitude, and Mercy or into inviolable Purity, invincible Strength, unalterable Peace (or Beauty), and irresistible Life (or Goodness), which correspond analogically to the four directions of space. The Judeo-Islamic equation "God = Unity" leaves the door open to all possible polarizations: *Allāh* is not only One (*Ahad*); He is also Total or Full (*Samad*), as is stated in the *Sūrah* "Purity" (*Ikhlās*); and "to Him belong the most beautiful Names" (*al-Asmā᾽ al-husnā*).

world but draws us gently toward the inward; she is hope and not fear. For Islam the Virgin and Christ do not personify a metaphysical and law-giving message but rather sanctity as such; Christ is the "seal of sanctity", and the Virgin is "primordial sanctity"; now sanctity is essentially inwardness: *Ecce enim regnum Dei intra vos est.*

We could also say that the Virgin is the nonformal Alpha of sanctity and that Christ is its formal Omega: according to Sufis, Mary is the "milk" that flows forth from the Holy Spirit, and Jesus is the "seal" that closes the cycle of its manifestations. To say that Jesus closes the cycle of sanctity (*wilāya*) and not of prophecy (*nubuwwah*) means that he represents above all a way leading from the outward to the inward, a way that is *a priori* sacrificial but made gentle by the grace of the Virgin; these two aspects, rigor and gentleness, are in the nature of things, for God is at once Majesty (*Jalāl*) and Beauty (*Jamāl*).[26]

Religious life is a complex system that includes the whole of man and thus engages the soul, leaving nothing outside; this system is presented to us as an indispensable condition of salvation, outside of which there is nothing that could save us, even though other systems, just as demanding and exclusive, co-exist beside it.[27] This being so, there must necessarily be a level where these systems as such lose much of their importance and where by way of compensation the essential elements they have in common are affirmed, elements which, whether one likes it or not, give the systems all their value;

---

[26] From a certain point of view it is permissible to compare the respective mystical functions of Jesus and Mary to two Mahayanic schools, best known in the West in their Japanese forms, Zen and *Jōdo*: the first bases itself on personal effort, expressed by the term *jiriki*, "self-power", whereas the second relies upon the merciful and saving grace of Amida, whence the term *tariki*, "other-power"; this is expressed in a certain way in Islam by the two words *salāt* and *salām*, the meanings of which might be rendered respectively as "enlightening grace" and "calming grace". The first of these modes corresponds to what could be called the "Christic" way, the second to the "Marian" way: the first of these ways is "narrow" and difficult, virile and sacrificial, whereas the second is "little" and in a sense "easy"; the two modes also belong to Christ alone, whose "yoke is easy" and whose "burden is light", but the second is nonetheless incarnate in the Virgin the moment we consider the complementarity of these holy beings.

[27] And yet: "For he who is not against us is for us", which is in its way a definition of universality, for it is a question of miracles done "in my name", that is—according to this interpretation—in the name of the one *Logos*.

and we gladly define this level as the domain of Mary, the Virgin Mother, who—according to a symbolism common to Christianity and Islam—has suckled her children, the Prophets and sages, from the beginning and outside of time.[28]

We deliberately close our survey of inter-religious alternations and compensations with some reflections on the Virgin Mary. Mother of all the Prophets and matrix of all the sacred forms, she has her place of honor within Islam even while belonging *a priori* to Christianity;[29] for this reason she constitutes a kind of link between these two religions, whose common purpose is universalizing the monotheism of Israel. The Virgin Mary is not merely the embodiment of a particular mode of sanctity; she embodies sanctity as such. She is not one particular color or one particular perfume; she is colorless light and pure air. In her essence she is identified with merciful Infinitude, which—preceding all forms—overflows upon them all, embraces them all, and reintegrates them all.

[28] During the Night Journey (*mi'rāj*) the Prophet had to choose between water, wine, milk, and honey; he chose milk, which signifies that he chose the primordial nature (*fitrah*), hence the original religion; and in fact Islam presents itself as a restoration of the primordial religion (*din al-fitrah*).

[29] Mary is Virgin, Mother, Spouse: Beauty, Goodness, Love—their sum being Beatitude. Mary is Virgin in relation to Joseph, Man; Mother in relation to Jesus, God-Man; Spouse in relation to the Holy Spirit, God. Joseph embodies humanity; Mary incarnates either the Spirit considered in its feminine aspect or the feminine complement of the Spirit.

Part Three

ISLAM

The Idea of "The Best" in Religions

Every religion by definition wants to be the best, and "must want" to be the best, both as a whole and in its constitutive elements; this is only natural, or rather "supernaturally natural". The fact that Sufism shows solidarity with the religious perspective for which it aims to be the esoterism—whether justifiably or not, according to its modalities—is for us one more reason to clarify this question of maximal religious worth or, more precisely, of the *pro domo* evaluations resulting from a given religious perspective.

Before broaching our subject as such we must return once again to the general question of religious oppositions since the particular question of "the best" depends upon it. Let us remark at the outset that religious oppositions cannot but be, and this is so not only because forms exclude one another—even when the word "exclude" is taken in a principial, hence metaphorical, sense—but because in the case of religions each form conveys an element of absoluteness that constitutes its very reason for being; now the absolute does not tolerate otherness or, with all the more reason, plurality.

To say form is to say exclusion of possibilities, hence the necessity for those excluded to become realized in other forms; and since form by definition excludes, it is condemned to repeat itself. The contradiction between a contingent recipient and a quasi-absolute content cannot be peculiar to religions alone, and in fact it is prefigured in nature: more than once we have had occasion to mention the example of the paradoxical plurality of subjectivity within the order of conscious creatures. Individuals exclude one another because none of them can be the other, and they are opposed to one another because subjectivity by its nature is one—empirically and logically there can be only one "I"—although we are obliged to acknowledge the mysterious evidence of subjectivity endlessly repeating itself outside us.

Religions are like lamps of colored glass; now a lamp illuminates the dark because it is luminous and not because it is red or blue or yellow or green. On the one hand the color transmits the light, but on the other hand it falsifies it; if it is true that without a given colored lamp one would see nothing, it is just as true that visibility cannot be identified with any one color. This is what every esoterism ought to be aware of by definition, at least in principle and to the extent permitted by its knowledge of facts.

As every religion corresponds to a "divine subjectivity"—or "theophanic individuality"—it cannot be expected to be "objective" with regard to another religion, or at least not *a priori* or exoterically; for a religion as such—as a form precisely—the elements of other religions are scarcely more than symbols or points of reference, which can be used—most often in a pejorative or negative sense—within its own imagery and in keeping with its characteristic perspective. There are examples of this in ordinary experience: thus the appearance of things in space can give rise to an immutable symbolism even though the appearance may be different from another spatial point of view and may even reveal that the preceding appearance was an optical illusion. The earth seems flat, and the stars seem to revolve around it; the symbolism based upon appearances has nothing to fear, however, from their illusory character, which cannot invalidate it; the reality symbolized was before the symbol. The immutable truth makes use of the material at hand, so to speak, whose adequacy or legitimacy can be based upon a general subjective experience; the efficacy of the symbol does not depend exclusively upon an exact perception nor for all the more reason upon a perception inaccessible to general human experience. On the one hand truth is independent of its possible symbols, and on the other hand it consecrates them even when they are objectively inadequate: the relative error becomes "canonical", hence serviceable within a given context, in connection with the truth it manifests to one degree or another.

No doubt God show His solidarity with a form that has issued from His Word, but He could not be in solidarity with this form alone; what this means is that God always commits Himself to a given form sufficiently but never exclusively; He keeps His word "within" the formal system without binding Himself "from without" and without having to explain to anyone the modes of His Liberty or the requirements of His Infinitude. God makes Himself human in speaking to man, but in His own Nature He transcends the human, and this is no more difficult to acknowledge than many an enigma in the Scriptures.

Since every exoterism contains exclusive and excessive affirmations intended to buttress its unique value, it is above all necessary to consider the following factor: whatever its level every spirituality is based upon intelligence and will, hence upon discernment and concentration—discernment of the absolutely Real and concentration on the supreme Good. Now a religion requires a "myth" that can provoke this concentration; the will and the soul cannot concentrate with perfection and perseverance except on what is unique, incomparable, irreplaceable. It is not enough for God to be absolute; the means and circumstances of His manifestation must also be absolute, or appear to be so to the greatest extent possible; a realizational will and the sentiment accompanying it tend to transfer the sublimity of God to the contingent elements that testify to it. As a result there is a possible conflict between operative faith, which gives us wings, and speculative discernment—disinterested by definition—which communicates to us the truth pure and simple; one cannot help but notice that there are men who lose their faith to the extent they think and who no longer know how to think to the extent they have faith. This is an altogether illusory conflict in the final analysis, for faith is perfect to the extent it issues from pure truth, and truth is understood to the extent it confers faith.

Because it is exclusive, hence limitative, dogmatism is situated as it were between esoterism and apostasy: esoterism, which brings limitations back to their unlimited archetypes, and apostasy, which rids itself of them in favor of nothingness.

— ·:· —

Christianity as such has no opinion concerning Islam for the simple reason that Islam came six centuries after it; Christian opinion concerning Islam is first implicit and then conventional, but strictly speaking not canonical—or only indirectly so and by way of conclusion. For its part Islam contains canonical opinions concerning Christianity, and necessarily so since it arose alongside of Christians; hence it concerns itself with Christians just as it concerns itself with Jews and pagans, and just as Christianity in its fashion concerned itself with paganism, alongside which it lived, and Judaism, from which it emerged.[1] Everything that is partial in these diverse evaluations is

---

[1] It is useful to recall that for Christ the pagans are those who on the one hand think

excused by the intrinsic truth of the perspectives in question and also, subjectively speaking, by "zeal for the house of the Lord".[2]

Aside from other categories, there are two types of spirituality, which are in fact often opposed, namely, the cult of "Essence" and that of "Form"; this is the antagonism between Vedantism and Krishnaism or between Zen and Amidism. Beginning with this distinction one notes that Islam belongs to the first category and Christianity to the second, and one can easily understand why Muslims are sometimes astonished, more or less implicitly, by the fact that Jesus was not able to prevent the "deviation" they attribute to Christians, a reservation directed fundamentally against the antagonistic perspective rather than the person of Christ.[3] But there is not only an antagonism—formal and not essential—between Christian "personalism" and Muslim "transcendentism"; there is also an opposition—again only formal—between an anthropology based upon original sin and another based upon the unalterable theomorphism of man; here again Islam necessarily sees in Christianity a limitation to be transcended whereas the Islamic position appears to the Christian as a concession to "nature" and a failure to understand "supernature", the first being "flesh" and the second "spirit". Christ incarnates the victory of

---

only of the things of this world and on the other hand profess an outward and quantitative religion—or one that is superficial and prolix—for the sake of the goods here below.

[2] It is only too evident that *de facto* esoterism, which is largely at the mercy of information and experience—at least in its secondary sectors—is not always at the level of esoterism *de jure* or "in principle"; Ibn Arabi was scarcely more informed about Christianity than Saint Bernard was about Islam. Let us note, however, that Gilson somewhere quotes a medieval text that, in the midst of Christian Spain, ranks Muhammad among the great law-givers.

[3] Rigorously centered upon the worship of God alone and hostile to the dispersion of piety, Islam could not permit forms of mysticism such as the contemplation of the sorrows of Mary, propagated above all by the Servites of the thirteenth century, or the cult of the Sacred Heart, which arose in the seventeenth century. Moreover, when the Koran says that Christians "have forgotten a part of what they had been taught" and that "We (*Allāh*) have placed enmity and hatred between them until the Day of Resurrection" (*Sūrah* "The Table Spread" [5]:14), it refers on the one hand to Christianity's *de facto* exclusion of the doctrinal and moral elements accentuated by Islam and on the other hand to the scissions produced in the Christian world by theological specifications concerning points that would have permitted—or even required—a certain margin of indeterminacy.

"spirit" over "flesh"; Muslims acknowledge this, but their point of view does not allow them to give this victory the significance of an absolute value. The Prophet for his part embodies the sanctification of the element "flesh" or "nature", and this is something Christians have difficulty recognizing; one cannot hold this against them too much unless they have a thorough knowledge of Islam, for this sanctification, whatever its benefit may be, hardly ever appears in the phenomenal realm, except of course in a subjective manner and thanks to the spiritual economy of Islam—to the extent this economy is fully taken advantage of; this last reservation means that everything depends upon sincerity (*sidq* or *ikhlās*), without which there is neither "faith" (*īmān*) nor "effectual virtue" (*ihsān*). Moreover, to sanctify the gifts of nature is to be sanctified by them; it is to realize through them a "remembrance of God" and to encounter in them a divine Presence, and this requires the correlative observance of two conditions *sine qua non*, namely, *oratio* and *jejunium*.

If we start with the idea that Islam presents itself under three aspects—namely, faith in the One, obedience to the Law, and the sincerity of these two attitudes[4]—we can understand without difficulty that the Islamic perspective recognizes in Christ only what is in keeping with this pattern and therefore excludes the sacrificial and sacramental aspect of Christianity, and this is expressed especially by the Koranic negation of the Cross. And if Sufism sometimes appears— quite paradoxically from the Christian point of view—as the "religion of love", this is in reference to the element "sincerity", which opens to both love and *gnosis* and thus interiorizes all the religious formalism, though without wishing or being able to abolish it in fact.

Christianity is the perspective of redeeming divine Manifestation, a Manifestation that is presented as the only possible link between God and man; it offers the Sacrament, which regenerates, and demands the Sacrifice, which interiorizes. Islam comes into collision above all with the axiom that this Manifestation is the only possible link, hence the only path of salvation, and it postulates on the contrary that the fundamental, and therefore invariable, link between God and

---

[4] This is the ternary *īmān-islām-ihsān*, the third element giving rise to esoterism. On this subject see the chapter "The Religion of the Heart" in our book *L'ésotérisme comme principe et comme voie*.

man is divine Truth and thus human Faith; this Faith entails abstention from what draws one away from God and accomplishment of what brings one closer to Him; this means that everything lies in the Unity of God and the sincerity of man. For Islam Christ could only re-actualize this fundamental and primordial religion, whatever may have been his particular means; according to the logic proper to its perspective, Islam could criticize Christianity for having subordinated the essential and invariable religion to these means, but in fact it does not limit itself to this reproach, for its particular religious character precludes its recognizing these means as such; nonetheless its specific attitude metaphysically and esoterically includes the mitigated meaning mentioned above.

Whatever the metaphysical cogency of the Muslim point of view, one can and must stress in this context—and this is obvious—that the specifically Christian theophanism is a fundamental possibility in the salvific economy of God, and therefore it had a perfect right to appear in the human atmosphere at the cyclical moment reserved for it. In any case the apparent dissonances between the religions are resolved in their underlying harmony, just as the accidents are resolved in the substance.

When reading passages in Muslim books that tend to exalt the merits of Muhammad or, for the same reason, to diminish those of other Messengers, it is necessary to consider the following principle of Muslim piety: it is morally beautiful to seize every opportunity for praising the Prophet, provided one does not say he is the son of God. The pious intention—the desire to fulfill a quasi-religious duty—seems to take precedence over every other consideration, though this is true only on the plane of speculation, not on that of historical information, where on the contrary the scrupulous noting of facts and evidence concerning the Prophet and the Companions is required and where pious embellishments are therefore excluded; information is one thing, interpretation another. The first encompasses only the history of Islam; the rest is a matter of symbolism.

Muslim theologians enumerate three great "Messengers" (*Rasūl, Mursal*), namely, Abraham (*Ibrāhīm*), Jesus (*ʿĪsā*), and Muhammad—

to whom they sometimes add Noah (*Nūh*), though without being able to categorize him, or so it seems; in bluntly formalistic fashion the criterion of "greater" or "lesser" is apparent conformity with the Muslim dogma of Unity.

In theology just as in philosophy—though to varying degrees—one encounters a deliberate way of reasoning in a given manner and in a given direction that is meant to support a certain axiom and to exclude from the intelligence all possibilities that do not serve this end; subjectivists will say that the same holds true for all demonstrations, but this is not true, for in the case of a certainty independent of all sentimental postulates the arguments result objectively from the certainty to be demonstrated and not subjectively from our desire to prove it.

But let us return to the Muslim enumeration of the great Messengers: here one finds oneself in the thick of schematic and indirect symbolism; it is not a question of defining the Messengers but simply of making use of their names in order to support the scale of values proper to Islam. In the same order of ideas we may mention the following example: during his "Night Journey" (*Mi'rāj* = Ascension) the Prophet traversed the seven Heavens and met successively Adam, Jesus with John (the Baptist), Joseph (the Patriarch), Enoch, Aaron, Moses, and Abraham; other enumerations differ slightly from this one, and this fact reinforces the impression that the apparent hierarchy is founded only upon associations of ideas that are altogether extrinsic, fragmentary, and allusive and not upon the intrinsic eminence of the personages.[5] The inspirationist impulsiveness of the Arab-Oriental temperament, a temperament that lacks a critical sense regarding formal coherence but that is all the more sensitive to moral and mystical intentions and their subtleties, favors or even conditions this way of proceeding. Doctrinally, as we have said, this associative play of ideas is explained by the fact that Islam reduces every "Message", and therefore every "Messenger", to a single, strictly monotheistic pattern, so much so that differences for it are more or less secondary;

---

[5] For example, a given author thinks that in order to imitate Jesus, who had no fixed abode, it is necessary to be continually on a journey, and other details of the kind; the true personality of Christ is here reduced simply to his preaching of monotheism, with the addition of a few particularities mentioned by the Koran.

the unitary idea, which is the principle, measure, and criterion of the distinctions, is in another respect the very element that indirectly blurs or even abolishes them.[6] The Koran itself forestalls all artificial hierarchizing when it declares that "we (the believers) have no preference (*nufarriqu* = we make no distinction) for any one of them" (*Sūrah* "The Cow" [2]:136 and *Sūrah* "The Family of Imran" [3]:84); in a complementary fashion, when the Koran declares that "We (*Allāh*) have given to certain Messengers a distinction (*faddalnā*) over certain others" (*Sūrah* "The Cow" [2]:253), it is concerned with particular qualities and characteristics and not their value as a whole; in other words it is speaking of qualities or graces that are a matter of indifference from the unitary point of view since they are "horizontal" and not "vertical". Be that as it may, what most offends Christian logic and sensibility is the "horizontalization" of Christ—which contains certain compensating nuances, however—in the wake of the "verticalization" of Muhammad alone, an enhancement of the Prophet's worth that is not Koranic but results from the *Sunnah*. What remains to be seen is the meaning of this exoteric partiality from the point of view of pure and simple Truth.[7]

— .:. —

The dogmatic assertion, which is self-evident in Islam, that the Prophet is "the best of men" or "of creation" (*khayr al-khalq*) or "the best of those whom God hath chosen" (*khayru mani 'khtāra 'Llāh*) is in itself independent—and quite paradoxically so—of the conclusion that other founders of religion would be inferior to him. In the first place this designation as "the best" refers to the *Logos*, which is the prototype of the cosmos in the Principle or of the world in God; and in this case the epithet does not refer to any man.[8] In the second place

---

[6] At times one has the impression that there are two divergent but intertwining hierarchies, one centered on monistic purity and on Abraham and the other on sanctity and on Jesus and Mary, the second perspective being emphasized only in Sufism.

[7] A partiality of which every exoterism by definition offers us a counterpart—in keeping with the psychological requirements of the voluntarist perspective.

[8] If the *Logos* is nonetheless termed "Muhammadan Light" or "Muhammadan Truth"

"the best" is Muhammad inasmuch as he manifests or personifies the *Logos*; but in this respect every other "Messenger" (*Rasūl*) is equally "the best". In the third place "the best" is Muhammad inasmuch as he alone manifests the *Logos* in its entirety, other Messengers manifesting it only in part, in accordance with the framework of this perspective; this amounts to saying that Muhammad is "the best" inasmuch as he personifies the Islamic perspective or because he personifies it; within this perspective the man who reveals it is necessarily "the best", but obviously the same can be said of every other Messenger within the framework of his own Message. In the fourth and final place Muhammad is "the best" inasmuch as he represents a quality of Islam by which it surpasses other religions; but every integral religion necessarily possesses such an incomparable quality, for otherwise it would not exist.

A point we must raise here, one that will doubtless make certain eulogistic expressions seem less abrupt, is the following: in Arabic the comparative can have the meaning of the superlative—*Allāhu akbar* means both "God is greater" and "God is greatest"—and as a result the superlative easily conveys something of the comparative. Thus it can signify an indefinite extolling and not an absolute surpassing, as is shown precisely by the numerous sayings beginning with the expression "the best" (*khayr al-*); the same is true, though in an opposite sense, for those sayings beginning with "the worst" (*sharr al-*), which would often be excessive were it not for the grammatical nuances we have just pointed out.

What this means is that for the Arabs, and perhaps for all Semites, the superlative can signify not only what is unequaled but also what is unsurpassable without being incomparable.

But let us return to the pre-eminence that redounds upon the Prophet from the quality by which Islam surpasses the religions pre-

---

(*Nūr Muhammadiyyah* or *Haqīqah Muhammadiyyah*), it is because Muhammad proceeds from it and because he is supposed to synthesize all the other Prophets. Let us specify that the idea of the *Logos* is polyvalent: if God is "Beyond-Being"—which He never is in ordinary theology—the *Logos* will be creating or conceiving Being; if God is Being, the *Logos* will be His creating or efficient Word; if this Word is God, the *Logos* will be the reflection of God in the cosmos, that is, the universal Intellect, the Koranic *Rūh*, whose fundamental functions are manifested by the Archangels; Beyond-Being, Being, Existence.

ceding it: it is obvious that Muslim theology focuses solely upon this quality for the sake of its Messenger as well as for its own sake, for the Message is the measure of the Messenger; what is true for the first is true for the second, the *Rasūl* being defined according to the *Risālah*. For Islam the essential Truth, the one that takes precedence over all others, is the nature of God together with the consequences of this nature: namely, that God is absolute and infinite in His Essence, that He is perfect by His Qualities, and that He presents Himself as both transcendent and immanent; and just as He radiates because He is the Sovereign Good, He creates the world and reveals Himself to it.⁹ Now Muhammad personifies the sincere, hence effectual, awareness of this essential Truth, and this is shown by the fact—Islamically speaking—that he is the final "Messenger"; this "finality" is supposed to manifest a principial primacy through inverse analogy; it is for Islam what the Sinaitic Revelation is for Judaism and what the Virgin Birth is for Christianity, and history shows in fact that no world religion has seen the light of day since Islam.¹⁰ Nonetheless, if this finality were to imply the absolute value attributed to it by the *'ulamā*—according to whom the merits of Muhammad are weightier than those of all the other Messengers taken together—it would amount to the *Parousia*, for so superior a manifestation of the *Logos* would *ipso facto* imply a dimension of finality and not of simple succession. Of course this

---

⁹ "Say: He, God, is one; God is limitless and immutable" (*Sūrah* "Sincerity" [112]:1-2). The first adjective, *ahad*, signifies the absolutely One, hence the Absolute as such; the other two adjectives are expressed in Arabic by a single word, *samad*, which in reality here means the Infinite, though considered in relation to the totality of its possibilities, which can be neither increased nor decreased by anything and which—like space-ether—contains neither emptiness nor change, whence the idea of total plenitude proper to this word. Another term that *de facto* expresses the idea of Infinitude is *Rahmān*: it contains the notions of Goodness, Love, Compassion; according to the Koran it is almost the equivalent of the name *Allāh*, which means that it refers to the "radiant" dimension proper to the Absolute, a dimension that becomes *Rahīm*, the "Merciful", at the level of the "qualities" (*sifāt*), hence at the level of creating Being.

¹⁰ It could be added that Islam seems like an anticipatory protest and providential resistance against the worldly and as it were anti-Biblical civilizationism of the declining West, "civilization" being the suicide of Christianity, all things considered—a suicide inaugurated by the Popes of the Renaissance despite the warnings of a Dante and Savonarola and despite the very Christian and very innocent Mount Athos, which moreover and quite paradoxically was protected by the Turks.

objection holds true for all expressions of favoritist zeal, whatever the religion.[11]

According to certain authors, what constitutes the superiority— possibly "absolute"—of one prophet or saint over another are his qualities; now in order to prove these qualities the person's merits are stressed, for example the fact that Abu Bakr was the first to convert to Islam, as if this fact—in any case disputed[12]—were necessarily linked with a quality or as if a quality necessarily depended upon such a fact.[13] Furthermore, when one asserts that Abu Bakr—because of his "merits" promoted to "qualities" and because of his "qualities" supported by his "merits"—was "absolutely" superior to the other three "rightly guided" (*rāshidūn*) caliphs[14] and that each of them was superior to his immediate successor, what this implies is that each was inferior in "qualities-merits" to his predecessor; thus it means quite paradoxically that the last of these caliphs, Ali, the son-in-law of the Prophet,[15] had fewer merits and thereby fewer qualities than the other three; faced with this hierarchization, perfunctory to say the least, the Shiite cult of Ali appears as an inevitable reaction or as the disproportionate explosion of a misunderstood reality. Of course we do not deny that the primacy of Abu Bakr can be explained by his particular gifts or that in the case of Ali there could have been

[11] The state of the Muslim world in our time of cyclical end clearly shows the relative import of the argument from finality; the human fall is general not with regard to every individual but with regard to collectivities or the average man.

[12] It is not known whether the first convert to Islam—after Khadijah—was Abu Bakr or Ali.

[13] If this logic were applied to Saint Paul, his attitude before his conversion—which was providential and in no way self-willed—would constitute an argument against his quality as an apostle and his degree of sanctity; the same holds true for the apostle Peter with his denials of Christ and also *mutatis mutandis* for Mary Magdalene.

[14] *Hadīth* in favor of Umar: "If God had willed that another Prophet appear after me, it would have been Umar." Another *hadīth* favorable to Uthman: "Uthman is my flesh and my blood, and the husband of my eyes (my two daughters)."

[15] Of whom the Prophet said: "I am the city of Knowledge, and Ali is its gate"; also: "O Abu Bakr! whosoever wishes to see the man of my family who has the highest rank and the most perfect merit . . . let him look upon Ali! His hand shall be in mine on the Day of Resurrection; he shall enter withersoever I shall enter; his hand shall not leave mine until he enters Paradise with me."

extrinsic factors making his triple eviction opportune; what we deny is that these advantages and disadvantages—if one can express it this way—coincide with so many merits and demerits, so many qualities and deficiencies.[16]

And in the same way, if we are assured that the Prophet is superior to other Messengers—including Christ, of course—and that he is so in an absolute fashion; that the love offered God by the others and therefore also by Jesus was less perfect than that of Muhammad; and that the other Messengers—including Christ as always—were not raised to the degree of "friend" of God as the Prophet was, Abraham being so only to a lesser degree: then we must object that at the level of the founders of religions such evaluations are devoid of meaning and only serve to prove the ignorance and fanaticism of those who conceive them. Although in itself the symbolism of the superiority of a given Messenger within his own religion is "subjectively" legitimate—since each religion sees in its founder the total *Logos*—the arguments used are nonetheless inadmissible from any point of view; already unfortunate when they come from the pen of a theologian, they are all the more so coming from that of an esoterist.

From another standpoint it must be admitted that the offensive nature of certain formulations is sometimes due to misunderstandings: for example, when a Bedouin told the Prophet that Jesus had walked on water, the Prophet replied that he, Muhammad, had raised himself up to the throne of God; this is an answer that seems offensive if one is unaware of the interplay of intentions. In reality the Bedouin did not wish to recount a piece of history but to express doubt as to the

---

[16] In certain *ahādīth* the Prophet states that Abu Bakr is an extremely virtuous and spiritual man and that his merits gained in the cause of Islam are immense; from this the Sunnites rightly conclude that what the Prophet meant is that the slight faults Abu Bakr might commit in the future were pardoned in advance. For the Shiites the praises of the Prophet do not refer to Abu Bakr as he is in himself but merely to his past merits at the time the Prophet spoke, and for them saying that the future faults of Abu Bakr would be pardoned in advance means that he was henceforth free, from the Sunnite point of view, to commit every crime, given his past merits precisely. This logic is characteristic of religious fanaticism, as if the Prophet would have taken the trouble to praise Abu Bakr had there been in his nature the possibility of committing crimes—on the contrary praise here expresses the fundamental impeccability of the personage—and as if the Sunnites would absolve anyone of crimes because of previous merits!

legitimacy of the Prophet, and the Prophet did not mean to diminish Christ's miracle but simply wished to refute the Bedouin's doubt by asserting that ascending to Heaven is more than walking on water and that not walking on water is not a blemish in someone who like himself has ascended to Heaven; he responded to a provocation and not to mere information. In a similar manner, when Muslim texts seem to belittle persons or phenomena pertaining to Christianity, it is not with an intrinsically pejorative intention but merely in order to stress the littleness of the creature before its Creator in contrast to what seems the Christian tendency to divinize the creature; rightly or wrongly, it is in order to re-establish an equilibrium. No doubt the means are not always apt, but their intention is *ad majorem Dei gloriam;* their imperfections or dissonances should be imputed to religious sentimentality, whose misdeeds are not an exclusively Muslim phenomenon, as will be readily acknowledged. Immoderation is here the religious price that must be paid for the underlying metaphysical perspective, which cannot prevent a certain "tilting at windmills" from occurring on the surface, human nature being what it is.

Islam is the Message of Unity and therefore of the Absolute and the Essence, and in principle this implies that along with the simplifications and impasses of theology—whose authority in Islam is after all somewhat fluctuating—it offers all the mysteries comprised in Unity by its very nature; it therefore postulates not only transcendence, which is separative by definition, but also immanence, which is unitive, linking man existentially and intellectually to his divine Origin. As a result the Testimony of Faith has a separative sense and a unitive sense, depending on whether it is considered in relation to transcendence only or in relation to immanence: the first mystery is symbolized by the "negation" (the *nafy,* that is, the words *lā ilāha,* "there is no divinity") and the second mystery by the "affirmation" (the *ithbāt,* that is, the words *illa 'Llāh,* "if not the sole Divinity").

These two levels or dimensions make it necessary to give the fundamental concepts of Islam two different meanings—different but not contradictory since the Message is homogeneous and could not be otherwise; thus the crucial concept of "servitude" (*'ubūdiyah*)[17]—the quality of "servant" (*'abd*) and the attitude resulting from it—means either the duty of submission and obedience or the vocation of liberating conformity: conformity to That which is and conformity because we are.

— ∴ —

In our book on the unity of the religions, we wrote that for Christianity esoterism is to be found in sanctity whereas for Islam sanctity is to be found in esoterism; the second assertion scarcely poses a problem since Muslim sanctity coincides with Sufism, but the first no doubt requires further precision. To understand it properly one must realize that Christianity as such is an esoterism in comparison with the "Old Law", but a relative and not an absolute esoterism—partial and not total, intermediate and not integral—and this is because it represents by its general Message a perspective of love, *bhakti*, not of knowledge, *jnāna*; and this *bhakti* is what is fulfilled in a sanctity based upon the general and specific means of the Christian religion; it is in this sense that Christian esoterism is realized in sanctity. As for Christic *gnosis*, it goes without saying that it implies an appropriate doctrine, one based on the equation "*Logos*-Intellect"—"Christ within us"—and on the complementarity between "Incarnation" and "Deification"; with this reservation it can be said here as well that esoterism is fulfilled in sanctity since *gnosis* does not require any particular institutional framework in the Christian climate.

---

[17] The divine complement of this element being "lordship" (*rubūbiyah*, from *Rabb*, "Lord", "Master"). These concepts can be interpreted in different ways, not with regard to their metaphysical essence—for the Absolute is the Absolute and the relative is the relative—but with regard to their human application, which depends in turn on whether the concepts and their respective moral concomitances are addressed to a mind that is "opaque" or "transparent"; all this is without losing sight of the fact that an idea can be addressed to every man "to the extent" he is either one or the other: either a "hylic" or a "pneumatic", a fact that constitutes a bridge between diverse degrees of receptivity. This point of view is characteristic of the Semitic monotheisms in general and Islam in particular; leveling exoterism abuses it, precisely.

Let us now return to considerations relating more directly to our subject. We have pointed out more than once that Christianity puts the emphasis fundamentally upon "divine Manifestation" since its essential thesis is "God become man" and that this theophanic perspective determines the very idea of God; in an altogether general sense it could be said that every Revelation is a divine Manifestation and that the only difference between religions is the mode in which God wishes to manifest Himself.

Now it is characteristic of Islam that God, while remaining irreducibly One and transcendent, nonetheless occasionally enters into human affairs without disdaining their possible insignificance; this can already be seen in the God of the Bible, but it is still more striking in the lives of the Prophet and the saints of Islam. The idea of an absolute "best" becomes inoperative here, for styles cannot be mixed, and this is a difficulty that providentially reinforces the barriers between religious systems.[18]

Since the legislating "divine Person" must affirm Himself within human relativity, He could not have a unique and absolute "form" or "subjectivity", for this quality of absoluteness can pertain only to the Divinity in itself.

"God became man that man might become God": this audacious and elliptical formula of Saint Irenaeus, which we have cited more than once, defines Christianity and yet at the same time transcends it; in reality "God became man" in every religion as soon as He expressed Himself in human language; every sacred Scripture, beginning with the *Vedas*, is "God become man".[19] Divine anthropomorphism responds to human theomorphism: if God can manifest Himself in human

---

[18] In Buddhism "God" makes Himself *Nirvāna*, *Buddha*, and *Bodhisattva*, in multiple polarization as well as in unity; we mention this example because Buddhism is too often described as "atheistic", such that our considerations concerning theophanic modes would not seem to apply to it.

[19] As a result the formula "true God and true man" also applies to the revealed Books in an appropriate manner.

modalities, it is because man is "made in the image of God", and this is the very reason for man's existence and for the cosmic miracle that he is. The timid deism of the naturalistic philosophers, which does not want to allow God to be more than a "power", stems from a fundamental blindness with regard to the human phenomenon: one is so used to "everyday man", to man as "Peter or Paul", to the ordinary and insignificant man, that one is no longer capable of seeing this earthly God nor therefore the proof of God that man as such truly is. Deism—without even mentioning atheism—is one of the measures of the intellectual smallness of a man who is forgetful of his own nature.

A remark concerning the form of the Islamic Revelation is called for here. The style of the Koran—which is in large part uneven, dry, discontinuous, and tautological, causing admiration in some and leaving others perplexed—incontestably poses a certain problem, but this is altogether secondary when one considers the celestial origin of the Book. If the Koran were the work of a man, it would reflect the character of its author: it would be given to either anger or clemency, punishment or pardon. Now the Koran expresses both dispositions; just when it appears to be pitiless, it proclaims that God is ready to forgive every sin, provided one does not lose faith in His Mercy; at the same time it stresses that God does what He wills, that He is therefore outside all psychologically definable human characteristics—all of which a mere man, mindful of human logic or human interests, would never have had the idea of writing. And let us add that the dialectic of the Koran proceeds by antinomic formulations, like that of all sacred Scriptures.

Here we may once again make use of the Buddhist idea of *upāya*, the spiritual "means" or salvific "stratagem" that makes it possible to capture the greatest possible number of souls. The "sacred monstrousness" of the exoterisms results from the fact that, in order to be able to say that a circle alone describes space, one must deny that a cross, a square, and a spiral do so as well—and in some respects even more explicitly than a circle does; of course the circle contains the other fundamental figures potentially and in its own way, just as they in turn contain the circle, their center and origin being the point. But the essential thing is to be aware of this fact, and this awareness could never be the mission of the exoterisms, which by definition are formal and thus formalistic.

When the divine Light descends upon the human plane—"incarnating" itself to some extent—it undergoes an initial limitation, and this results from human language and the requirements of a given collective mentality or cycle of humanity; then it undergoes a second limitation inasmuch as this mentality pushes the specific limitation of the *upāya* as far as possible by needlessly dotting "i's" and thus provoking divergences and heresies.

The true content of Muhammadan "finality" is the message of equilibrium: to say that Islam is a synthesis—or the synthesis—is to say that it wishes to realize, and in its fashion does realize, an equilibrium between the outward and inward, the earthly and heavenly, in keeping with the nature and vocation of man. For man is *pontifex*: through him God wishes to be sought and known starting from the world, from contingency, from outwardness; man must therefore combine and harmonize both dimensions: on the one hand a world restored to its value and transfigured and on the other hand a contemplation, at once human and divine, of the Real.

Concretely, and in the person of the Prophet, the equilibrium is this: first, implacable and fearless adherence to the Truth, hence perfect sincerity; second, a combination of strength, courage, justice, generosity; third, simplicity of behavior joined to a Bedouin poverty, which together with fasts and vigils constitutes asceticism; fourth, love of beauty and—not to be disdained—love of cleanliness; and finally, the hallowing of woman and sexual life, with an emphasis on contemplativity and generosity.

The question of miracles poses a certain problem here in that the prodigies of Christ are in a way the self-evident consequence of the superhuman grandeur of the Word made flesh, whereas in the case of the Prophet they appear at first glance as a superadded element; they do not emerge from a typological and historical foundation that would render them necessary or even plausible. The reason for this is the following: whereas with Christ miracles are brought about by the God-Man himself, with the Prophet they are brought about by God through the man; the miracles of Muhammad are in reality the miracles of God alone, who lends them to whomever He wills and who quite obviously lends them to His Messenger in the interest of the Message. It goes without saying that Muslims do not conceive of miracles in any other way, and thus it comes as no surprise when the Koran, in relating the miracles of Jesus, adds the words of God: "with My permission" (*bi 'idhnī*); from the Christian standpoint this is virtually meaningless, but it makes sense within the rigorously theocentric perspective of Islam.

Be that as it may, there is an aspect of Islam—rather disconcerting from the Christian point of view—that we might account for in the following terms: "Small causes, great effects" (*Kleine Ursachen, grosse Wirkungen*), says a German proverb, and in fact a twofold principle of disproportionality can be discerned between an underlying reality and its expression: in its very form the expression may be less than the reality—and this is independent of the limitation contained in the expression as such—or on the contrary the reality may be less than its expression, as is the case in profane literature and especially in the deceitful skill of many writers. In the first case a precious meaning is clothed in a relatively plain expression, and this is found particularly in Islam but sporadically in the most diverse traditions; if Muslims see in the Koran not only a sacred Scripture but also a sublime literary work, it is partly—all semantic subtleties aside—in order to do justice to the immensity of its meaning, which is rather veiled by the form, with its dryness, discontinuities, and tautologies, despite its poetic beauty.

The disparity between form and substance also appears in the person of the Prophet and therefore in the *Sunnah*; it is precisely the formal modesty of his person that seems to provoke compensatory, hagiographic hyperbolisms, which the real nature of the hero does not need and which in the eyes of the non-Muslim serve instead to diminish the intelligibility of the portrait.[20] The grandeur of Muhammad appears above all in the immensity of his success in a work that is ascendent and constructive—not descendent and destructive—and in the moral and mystical efficacy of his personality over the course of centuries, a personality made of spiritual idealism, adamantine vigilance, irresistible strength, generosity, and simplicity.

---

[20] See the chapter "Insights into the Muhammadan Phenomenon" in our book *Forme et substance dans les religions* and the chapter "Oriental Dialectic and its Roots in Faith" in *Logique et transcendance*.

Muslims argue—or could argue—that God spoke to Moses, but for Israel only; that Jesus separated men from the natural in order to lead them to the supernatural, but that he offered them nothing from the realm of nature, which after all has its rights since the supernatural itself grants them to it; that Muhammad restored the rights of nature while cutting man off from whatever could harm him in it—not as much in itself as through his own fault. To summarize, what constitutes the norm and summit for Islam is not just an emphasis on the intrinsic and extrinsic Unity of God, but also an equilibrium, which results from this emphasis, between two apparently opposite attitudes or disciplines: consecration of natural values on the one hand and detachment from this seductive and evanescent world on the other; this double perfection or equilibrium coincides with the primordial perfection (*fitrah*) of the man-pontiff,[21] and in the eyes of Muslims it constitutes a value of totality or integrality, which they tend to deny pre-Muhammadan Messengers.

We may define this sentiment by saying that from the Muslim point of view Christ was the personification of sanctity—whence the title "seal of sanctity" or "seal of the saints" = *khatam al-wilāyah/al-awliyā*—but not of the quality we might call "practical sense" or perhaps "foresight" on the strictly human or natural level; moreover this seems to be indicated by the declaration that "my kingdom is not of this world".[22] Most curiously, the same reservation can be

---

[21] Man is *pontifex* by definition since he must combine and balance his life in the world with his life in God. It is a fact that in Christianity there is something like a principle of instability: having abandoned Jewish Law, Christianity oscillated between Roman Law and various common Laws, and this is not to mention the slow elaboration of the liturgy and the notion of "theological progress". The fact that the slow Christianization of the West amounted to a form of progress favored *a priori* the progressivist illusion of the moderns, whereas Islam—being rigidly retrospective—is stable as a matter of principle and excludes *a priori* all progressivism.

[22] It goes without saying that this does not signify any intrinsic lack. Christ was what he should have been and willed to be, and nothing more, his spiritual type excluding precisely the horizontal or, if one will, "Mosaic" dimension. What amounts to a lack from one point of view contributes to a form of glory from an-

applied to the son-in-law of the Prophet: Ali is regarded in Islam as the personification of sanctity and mystical science, but no one can maintain—without being partisan—that he was a statesman, which in fact amounts to saying that he lacked practical sense and foresight; equally unrealistic, moreover, was the intention of his supporters to institutionalize and politicize sanctity and esoteric science.

Aside from the different interpretations we have set forth above, the quality of "best of creation" pertained quite naturally to the Prophet in the minds of the Arabs of that time and of subsequent generations, and it did so with the dazzling self-evidence of a prodigy one has witnessed oneself, directly or even indirectly; but this has no connection with the false comparisons that may be introduced *a posteriori*—and in the abstract—as if to conserve or shore up a sacred memory. And this leads us to the following consideration: if the Prophet had wished—supposing Islam were the product of his mind—he could also have declared himself the son of God, he could have declared the Arabs a chosen people, and he could have founded a dispersed and dispersing cult, which would have placed himself, the Archangels, some pagan divinities, and possibly one or more of his wives alongside God; and he would certainly have done so if he had had the character still all too readily attributed to him in the West. That he did not do so proves in any case two things, namely, a character of absolute integrity and an authentic Message from God; both of them—the human qualification and the divine intervention—are necessarily combined, for the Messenger must be in conformity with the Message and must in some manner anticipate it by his character and gifts.

We have spoken above about the quality of "finality" in connection with the idea of "the best"; now the Islamic claim to this qualitative finality is for Christians a key motive for their categorical rejection of Islam. Indeed the terminality of Christ and the Church is logically

other point of view, and this follows from the fact that we are in the formal order and within its compensatory play of exclusions and inclusions.

absolute, possessing a self-evident character and a plenitude that permit no reservation or *a fortiori* any subsequent finality; now it goes without saying, given the claims of Islam for its own finality, that it must deny Christic finality in order to take its place, which from the Christian point of view merely aggravates those claims—if indeed they can be further aggravated in this perspective. Unquestionably, to say finality is to say unique, hence irreplaceable, phenomenon; finality can be defined according to different perspectives, however, and in this sense we shall say that if Christianity is the last word of God in the monotheistic cycle, it is so only in a certain respect, whereas Islam is so in another. Christianity is this last word as "summit", as theophanic phenomenon, whereas Islam is so as synthesis, equilibrium, and "quintessence"; it is a kind of "unexpected" outcome, resulting from a dimension Christian logic leaves outside its doctrinal "iconostasis" and sphere of action.

But considered from the standpoint of the doctrine of the human cycles, according to which the movement of humanity is descendent and not ascendent—the "Golden Age" renewing itself nonetheless with each religion within the framework of a given cyclical period—finality includes a privative aspect along with its triumphant aspect, which the Gospel characterizes by saying that "the light shineth in darkness; and the darkness comprehended it not". The "Muslim miracle" was not only the lightning-like expansion followed by the adamantine stability of the new religion, but also the transformation of a people as passional and undisciplined as the ancient Arabs into the vehicle of the final religion and of one of the great civilizations of mankind; and yet from another point of view it cannot be denied that the Arab character imposed certain limitative traits on Islam, for which the Revelation is not responsible but which are nonetheless "providential" in the economy of the divine plan. In a similar way, if on the one hand the Europeans constitute the predestined ethnic vehicle for Christianity, on the other hand they have superimposed upon it certain imperfections, extrinsic of course and inevitable by virtue of the universal principle that *tenebrae eam non comprehenderunt.*

— ·❖· —

Faith, Obedience, Inwardness, Equilibrium: such is the entire Semitic monotheistic cycle. Abrahamism is Faith; Mosaism is Obedience, and the Law requiring this Obedience is already a mode of cyclical finality; Christianity is Inwardness, which is able to transcend the Mosaic culmination because it is situated in another dimension. Finally, Islam is Equilibrium between the preceding positions but with multiple accentuations in the sense that it gives primary emphasis to the elements Faith and Equilibrium, the alpha and omega; then, as a result of these two elements, comes the factor Obedience, hence Law, but with the stress on Sincerity, which as it were paraphrases Christian Inwardness.[23]

Still in connection with a finality that intends at the same time to be a primordiality, we shall once again summarize what is essential in the Islamic Revelation. Unquestionably, Islam is a Message—or the Message—of metaphysical Unity, for this is its fundamental and ubiquitous affirmation; next comes the Remembrance of God since for Sufis the purpose of all ritual institutions is this Remembrance, which contains everything else. Another fundamental aspect of this Message is submission to the Will of God, hence holy resignation, which the very term *islām* expresses from the outset and which is a characteristic trait of Muslim piety. Two no less important characteristics of Islam are its concern for moral and social equilibrium, this being founded on the primordial and universal nature (*fitrah*) of man and on the hallowing of natural things—notably sexuality—in keeping with their essential and positive symbolism and thus their intrinsic nobility. Then comes holy battle for the cause of God, hence for the Truth: a battle that is first of all outward but then inward and coincident with the aims of esoterism; this is the distinction between a holy war (*jihād*) that is "little" and another that is "great". This entire Message is found in the Koran and constitutes its principal value, without forgetting the richness, depth of symbolism, and theurgic power of the holy Book.

---

[23] The Alid movement and then Shiism afterwards can doubtless be explained by a desire to stress the element Inwardness even more; in fact this movement plunged into a "personalism" close to the Christian position, and this seems to be required by the element Inwardness in one form or another and by a kind of compensating necessity, whence also the hypostasizing cult of the Prophet in Sufi Sunnism.

Leaving aside the content of the Message, the two most striking "signs" of Islam—if one may put it this way—are what we have called its lightning-like expansion and its adamantine stability, that is, the merit it has of having overwhelmed a fragmented and hesitating world and of having perpetuated the Biblical world. Within the framework of this double merit or double miracle, the absolutely honest, simple, disinterested, and generous personality of the Prophet—we speak as a historian and not a "believer"[24]—reveals proportions that transcend the commonly human.

Other "signs" of Islam are the strength of Muslim faith—of a piety composed of certainty and serenity—and the characteristic virtues of authentic Muslims, which must have a cause; and one must also mention, on a much more outward but in the final analysis no less important plane, the traditional art of Islam, which cannot come from nothingness and whose expressivity proves its spiritual content.

Like every religion Islam includes both a Message and a Language. We have given an account of the Message; as for the Language, being Semitic it is distinctively voluntaristic, moralistic, and inspirationist, and to the extent that exoterism is the equilibrium and salvation of the greatest number, this Language is specifically addressed to the "average man"; from the perspective of an esoteric climate and pure esoterism this poses a certain problem—contingent and not insuperable—although it has no connection with the Message as such, which opens directly to *gnosis*. For everything is in the Testimony of Unity and Remembrance of the One.

— ·⫶· —

True finality—the glory of being the omega—is not realized by any one religion as opposed to another but by esoterism in relation to all religion; it is in this sense that Sufis reinterpret the dogmatic finality of Islam; such a reinterpretation goes hand in hand with a mixture that is

---

[24] Muhammad was disinterested with regard to his own person, not with regard to religion; and he was generous to the extent that generosity is possible and legitimate within the framework of justice and political necessity. Christians should be well aware of this, they who profess to "love their enemies".

strictly speaking improper but that can be found, quite obviously and *mutatis mutandis*, within every religious system.[25] If access to *gnosis* is made possible in Islam by the metaphysical truth of the Testimony of Unity, which is well suited for conveying the distinction between the Absolute and contingency, this access has its root in Christianity in the union of the two natures of the God-Man, whence *theosis* or *deificatio*; in other words, if Islam opens esoterically to *gnosis* because its essential Message is the metaphysical Truth, Christianity does so because its Message is the divine Man—*Māyā* united to *Ātmā* and in this respect identical to *Ātmā*; hence Union, metaphysics realized, the mystery of the *jīvan-mukta*.

"God alone is good," said Christ. Strictly speaking, "the best" is neither this nor that but "That which is", or else what conveys the plenitude of Being within the order of phenomena.

---

[25] In Hinduism the glory of finality is replaced by that of primordiality, which in this case amounts to the same thing.

Images of Islam

Islam burst forth in the form of an epic: now a heroic history is written with the sword, and in a religious context this sword assumes a sacred function; combat becomes an ordeal. The genesis of a religion amounts to the creation of a relatively new moral and spiritual type; in Islam this type consists of an equilibrium—which is paradoxical from the Christian point of view—between contemplativeness and combativeness on the one hand and between holy poverty and hallowed sexuality on the other. The Arab—and the man Arabized by Islam—has four poles, as it were: namely, desert, sword, woman, religion. For the contemplative the four poles are interiorized: desert, sword, and woman become so many states or functions of the soul.

On the most general and *a priori* outward level, the sword represents death—the death one deals and the death one risks; its perfume is always present. Woman represents a similar reciprocity; she is the love one receives and the love one gives, and thus she incarnates all the generous virtues; she compensates for the perfume of death with that of life. The deepest meaning of the sword is that there is no nobility without a renunciation of life, and this is why the initiatic vow of the Sufis—to the extent it relates historically to the "pact of the divine Acceptance" (*Bay'at al-Ridwān*)—includes a promise to fight to the point of death, bodily in the case of the warriors (= "martyrs", *shahīd*, *shuhadā*) and spiritually in the case of the dervishes (= the "poor", *faqīr*, *fuqarā*). The symbiosis between love and death within the framework of poverty and in the face of the Absolute constitutes all that is essential in Arab nobility; indeed we do not hesitate to say that here lies the very substance of the Muslim soul of the heroic epoch, a substance Sufism tends to perpetuate by sublimizing it.

To say that Islam was born in the form of an epic means that it possesses essentially a political dimension that was foreign to early Christianity and that Christianity possessed only as a profane appendage even when it became a state religion. Now politics is divisive by its very nature because of the diversity of possible solutions and individual qualifications: the Companions of the Prophet were politically divided by force of circumstances, and what was at stake was nothing less than the final and lasting victory of Islam; they lived alongside one another like closed systems, not unlike different religious perspectives, which also exist side by side without understanding each other; each identified himself in his very being with his own particular intuitions of what was right and efficacious. The remarkable stability of Islamic institutions through all the vicissitudes of history proves that worldly ambitions were very far from the minds of the Companions and, on the contrary, that at the very heart of their dissensions was a concern for immutability and incorruptibility. In a word, each kept himself enclosed in his point of view with a holy obstinacy, if one may put it this way, the rigidity of their attitudes being the result of their sincerity.[1]

Unlike the Apostles, the Companions did not live in the shelter of a *Pax Romana*; they were founders and defenders of an empire, every question of religious perspective aside. The situation of nascent Islam was complex because of the inevitable rivalry on the one hand between the Qurayshite masters of Islam and the Bedouins, who had become heroes of the conquests, and on the other hand—among the Qurayshites themselves—between the Hashimites and Umayyads; the first of these, which was the clan of the Prophet, represented a strictly religious point of view (*dīnī*) and the second, which was the clan of his early adversary, Abu Sufyan, tended either to a more specifically political point of view or even to one that was plainly worldly (*dunyāwī*). Moreover the core element, which was opposed by the rising tide of the victorious and newly enriched Bedouins—who were represented above all by the cities of Basra and Kufa—was not simply the tribe of the Quraysh, from which the Prophet issued, but also the group of Medinese Companions (*ansār*) of the Prophet; together they constituted precisely the spiritual aristocracy that is designated by the term "Companions" (*sahābah*); but in addition, and at the antipodes of this quite general rivalry, there was the opposition between the Alids and all other pretenders to the Caliphate. All these oppositions were in the logic of things—let us remember the bloody birth of Latin Christianity at the time of Clovis and Charlemagne—and there is no need to attri-

---

[1] It would have been contrary to the nature of things, however—given the contingent character of its motives—for such holy rigidity to have been unconditional: before the famous "Battle of the Camel" the Companions were on the point of being reconciled, but the battle was joined through the fault of subordinates who had an interest in division.

bute such clashes to questions of personal interest when they occurred on a plane where only the sword could decide; history itself proves the contrary and shows that parallel to the play of historical contingencies there was an unfolding of the highest moral values, not to mention the immutability of the sacred mold that is religion.

A point of view that may be worth mentioning here is the following: the range of the Arab soul extends from the most violent impulsiveness to the most generous serenity;[2] but it is not alone in possessing these characteristics and gifts—upon which, however, it confers an original quality precisely because of its impulsiveness—and it has bequeathed these same traits to a greater or lesser extent to foreign peoples, above all to nomads and semi-nomads, through the process of Islamicization. The historical facts that illustrate this Arab-Muslim magnanimity are numerous, and we shall here recall two examples: after the capture of Jerusalem, the Caliph Umar refused to pray in the basilica the Patriarch had placed at his disposal in order to avoid its being claimed later by Muslims; and the Saracens abandoned the siege of Toledo because the queen of the city appeared on the ramparts to tell the assailants that her husband the king was absent.[3] In summary, the particular disinterestedness that is generosity necessarily confers upon strength its stamp of nobility; strength owes it to itself to be generous to the extent it is legitimate.[4]

—— ·:· ——

[2] The mixture of aggressiveness and generosity that characterizes the pure Arabs reminds us of an incident we witnessed among the Bedouins: two women in dispute were pulling each other's hair and hurling invectives like furies, but suddenly they had had enough and released each other, each going her way with dignity as if nothing had occurred; we have never been able to forget the expression of detachment that suddenly adorned their faces.

[3] In this case chivalric honor also enters into play; one does not wish to go against a frail woman even if she is surrounded by warriors.

[4] The greatness of the soul of Saladin—a Kurd—is well known. In the midst of battle he presented a richly caparisoned horse to his enemy, Richard the Lion-Heart, whose horse had just been killed; and this was one of the least of his acts of generosity.

In every religion there are three spheres or levels: the Apostolic, the theological, and the political; the first has a certain quality of absoluteness, the other two being more or less contingent, although clearly to very different degrees. In Christianity the theological element is directly connected to the Apostolic, the political era beginning only with Constantine. In Islam, however, the political element is found in conjunction with the Apostolic, strictly theological elaboration coming only later. Now the Apostolic environment—the intimate circle of a prophet—inevitably involves oppositions when the political element comes into play, offering as it does different solutions to the problem of efficacy; but it cannot contain elements of hypocrisy or other forms of baseness in its very substance: differences of perspective, yes, but not petty and sordid conflicts of interest. The Apostolic sphere is pure, or else it is nothing;[5] and it is in this sense that Sunnism accounts for the Apostolic epoch of Islam. But the appropriateness of the traditional Sunni version of events involves taking into account the quasi-avataric nature of Fatimah's posterity, which it does through its doctrine of the *sharīfs*:[6] the *sharīfs* cannot suffer damnation, any sins they may commit being forgiven them in advance, and they are entitled to respect and love, easily becoming saints—in short, being "pneumatics", gnostically speaking, even if most of the time they are so only in virtuality. None of this should be taken to mean that a "psychic" can never become a saint or that there are no "pneumatics" outside the Fatimid line; this is self-evident.[7]

From a certain point of view the significance of the battles between the Umayyads and Alids is in practice the conflict between

---

[5] The Epistles of Saint Paul contain an echo of grave disorders in the early Church, but the people or groups concerned were converted pagans, not Apostles; they were therefore outside the Apostolic sphere just as were those Arabs who entered Islam after the taking of Mecca and who can be counted neither among the "emigrants" (*muhājirūn*) from Mecca nor the "allies" (*ansār*) of Medina.

[6] The descendants of the Prophet through Fatimah; the Arabic word *sharīf* (plural *shurafā*) means "noble".

[7] The "psychic" is saved through "conversion" whereas the "pneumatic" is saved by "nature". The second of these accepts the truth—as did Ali and Abu Bakr—without the least hesitation and from the heart by virtue of an almost existential "recollection". One must bear in mind that in Pauline language the "psychic" is the earthly and fleshly man, hence practically the "hylic" man of Gnosticism.

political efficacy and sanctity, two things few men are capable of combining. Abu Bakr and Umar succeeded in doing so, apart from certain blunders that need not concern us in this context; as far as the Caliphate of Uthman is concerned—and still more that of Ali—it is important not to underestimate the terrible difficulty of holding in balance a mass of men as passionate, ambitious, and turbulent as the ancient Arabs, who were always divided among themselves and therefore unaccustomed to unity and discipline.

The early Caliphs were fully aware of how dangerous it would be for the austere Bedouins, who had become conquerors, to adopt the decadent customs of the Sassanids and Byzantines; this is what the later Caliphs did all too readily, to the point of betraying the dignity and virtues of their race, and this is what the Shiites wished to prevent by claiming the Caliphate for the Alids alone. Moses broke the Tablets of the Law upon seeing the Golden Calf and then, so it is said, received others of a less rigorous character; this image expresses a principle of fluctuation or adaptation, the effects of which may be observed in diverse traditional climates and also, precisely, in early Islam, where the political regime that was ultimately viable did not correspond to the original ideal. Sunnis resign themselves to this fatality whereas Shiites enclose themselves in the bitter memory of a lost purity combined with that of the drama of Karbala and, on the level of the mystical life, with the noble sadness that an awareness of our earthly exile can arouse—an exile then seen in a particular aspect: that of injustice, oppression, frustration with regard to early virtue, divine right, and everything that represents them.

Be that as it may, the fundamental explanation of Shiism and its reason for being cannot be situated on the political plane alone; what must be said is that in Islam, and above all in the person of the Prophet, there are two tendencies or mysteries—this latter word indicating something rooted in the celestial order—namely, "Fear" and "Love", or "Cold" and "Heat", or "Dryness" and "Humidity", or "Water" and "Wine"; now there are grounds for saying that Ali, Fatimah, Hasan, and Husayn represented the second of these dimensions, whereas Aisha, Abu Bakr, Umar, and Uthman personified the first, at least from the point of view of a more or less outward accentuation. Ali and his family—politically ineffectual as they were—collided with the world of "Fear", "Dryness", efficacy; and what is remarkable is that Fatimah came up against this world not only in the person of the first Caliph but even in relation to her father, the Prophet, who as we have said combined both tendencies. It goes without saying that the element Love could not have been lacking in the Abu Bakr group—the love for the Prophet among all the Companions proves this[8]—and conversely it is unthinkable that the element Fear would have been missing in Ali and his people, for in their case too it could only have been a question of accentuation, not of privation;[9] in short, what was more or less implicit in the case of the Sunnis became no doubt more explicit in that of the Shiites. One could enlarge indefinitely upon this entanglement of religious attitudes, and we would have preferred not to mention it, especially since it is a difficult and thankless task to do justice in just a few words not so much to the parties involved as to all the points of view. One related observation is essential, however: upon contact with the Sunni world—where the general atmosphere is one of resignation in God and serenity through faith—one does not *a priori* have the impression of dealing with a perspective of Love while one does have this impression in the climate of Shiism, whatever the reasons may be. It is true that resignation and serenity characterize Islam as a whole; it is equally true that in Shiism an emotional element is added, to the point of being superimposed upon these qualities, an element that has an approximate equivalent among Sunnis only in the Sufi brotherhoods.

Be that as it may, a most important point must still be clarified: when we speak of the element "Love" in the case of the Prophet, there can clearly be no question of anything other than the love of

---

[8] This love is still to be seen in our time from one end of the Muslim world to the other in forms that are surprising in their intensity and touching in their spontaneity. Let us draw attention here to the fact that Sunnis criticize Shiites for not loving the Prophet sufficiently in that they love Ali, Fatimah, and their descendants too much; and let us cite this by no means irrelevant *hadīth*: "Not one of you is a believer unless I am dearer to him than his sons and his father and all men together".

[9] The question of there being an alternative between Fear and Love could not arise in the case of an Ali or Abu Bakr; but within *gnosis* itself it is possible for either the "humid" or the "dry" aspect to predominate.

God; when we attribute this element to the Companions, it becomes somewhat fluid with regard to its object, which may be either God or the Prophet or both, or again Ali and his family, whereas the object of "Fear" is always God. What has to be understood above all is that in Islam the love of God is not the point of departure; it is a grace God may bestow upon whoever fears Him; the point of departure is obedience to the Law and the fear—perfectly logical—of punishment. "What matters is not that you should love God, but that God should love you," a canonical collection on the Prophet declares,[10] and it continues to this effect: if you wish God to love you, you must love His Messenger by following his *Sunnah*. Love of God thus passes through love of the Messenger; among Shiites love of the Messenger passes *de facto* through love of Ali and his family, and this introduces into this mysticism—for historically plausible reasons—an element of resentment and mourning on a level where such motivations may be reconciled with a movement toward God.

The question of the spiritual style of Islam as a whole is also clarified by the following example: "If I turn in repentance toward God," says a man to Rabiah Adawiyyah, "will God turn in Mercy toward me?" "No," replied the saint, "but if He turns toward you, you will turn toward Him." It will no doubt be objected that this way of thinking—typically Muslim—implies a kind of inoperative tautology, which may even have a paralyzing effect; now it is necessary to know that the intention here is to arouse in man the consciousness of his impotence before God and to prevent him from attributing his virtuous actions to himself, hence to make him profoundly aware of the fact that the positive cause of his good actions is the divine Agent; without this concrete certitude—in the Islamic perspective—effort is compromised at its very root. This is doubtless a question of point of view, but points of view have their efficacy.

---

[10] *Al-Anwār al-Muhammadiyyah* by the *faqīr* Yusuf ibn Ismail al-Nabahani. The saying quoted appears to contradict the Law of Love proclaimed by the *Torah* and Christ, but this is not so, for the difference can be reduced to a question of terminology: whereas in the Bible the love of God has a significance that is primarily volitive and operative, this same expression refers in Islam to a contemplative grace, a grace that is doubtless active and yet conditioned by a divine inspiration. "Love God and therefore obey Him," Christ seems to be saying. "Obey God until you love Him," says Islam in turn; and there is obviously a point where the two perspectives meet and intermingle.

— ∴ —

But let us now return to the question of denominational divergences: for Shiites, and according to a perspective that is at once symbolic and schematic, hence simplifying and abstract, protagonists of the "dry" dimension—that of earthly efficacy—become personifications of the "world"; only the family of Ali represents the "spirit". No doubt this makes no difference from the point of view of pure mysticism, but on a more outward level it does render more plausible the polemics against the great figures of Sunnism, especially since Sunni doctrine renders homage not only to Ali and Fatimah but to the great "imams", to whom precisely the Shiites refer;[11] in short, it is at the very least paradoxical and tragic that a denominational branch that aims to identify itself with esoterism would at the same time include a particularly virulent and problematical exoteric ostracism. Shiism on the whole is a mysticism of the providential and provisional defeat—ultimately changed into triumph—of the *Logos* in its earthly exile, and in this way it rejoins the mystical geometry expressed by Saint John: "And the light shineth in darkness; and the darkness comprehended it not"; thus we are far from the idea of an immediate victory, one necessitated by the divine origin of the message. The criteria are now inverted in that the minority status of Shiism is a sign of superiority from their point of view: for Sunnism, which is the perspective of the necessarily victorious divine message—a perspective that must therefore be held by the majority—to be in the minority is a sign of heresy, but for Shiites it amounts to a criterion of orthodoxy since *lux in tenebris lucet et tenebrae eam non comprehenderunt*. This criteriology applies unquestionably to esoterism, and in this respect the two denominational points of view of Islam coincide; Sunni Sufism is necessarily a minority in the context of the common religion, and Shiism claims the same quality of "inwardness" that Sufism aims to represent. Nonetheless what Shiites

---

[11] To the imams of the Shiites correspond the Sunni Shaykhs, who rule to the extent that they influence monarchs. Shiites like to support the legitimacy—or transcendence—of the imams on the basis of such and such a numerical or cosmological symbolism, but Sunnis can do as much, *mutatis mutandis*: there are four Caliphs who are *rashidūn* and four founders of ritual schools (*madhhab*) just as there are four rivers of Paradise, four Archangels, four words in the *Basmalah*, four sides to the Kaaba.

seem to want to say is basically this: "Islam is esoterism"; and Sunnis seem to reply: "First allow it to exist on earth." Or again, to the Shiite assertion that esoterism is Shiism, the Sunni reply is basically that esoterism cannot be a religion and furthermore that esoterism is found where exoterism is found. The fact that Shiism in its fashion recognizes the distinction between the "outward" (*zāhir*) and the "inward" (*bātin*) does not modify its basically esoteric claim, as is proved by its theory of the imamate.[12]

But let us return to the symbolism *lux in tenebris*: if the political failure of Ali and his successors on the plane of Islam as a whole proves that the Prophet's son-in-law could not alone be the personification in every respect of spiritual and temporal authority for Islam as such, the very existence of Shiism nonetheless proves an element of victory in Ali himself and by extension in his family. Sunnis do not deny this eminence, praying indeed for blessings upon the Prophet, "his family (*āl*), and his Companions (*sahb*)", and honoring the "*sharīfs*".[13]

Let us note parenthetically that the elements "light" and "martyrdom", which are attached to Ali and his family, allow us to interpret the affair of the Fadak Oasis in a particular sense: after the death of the Prophet the caliph Abu Bakr refused Fatimah the right of inheritance; now the Prophet had owned the oasis of Fadak, and his daughter greatly wished to keep it.[14] Clearly there could have been no malice toward anyone on Abu Bakr's part and *a fortiori* not toward Fatimah—he was ready to allow the inheritance as long as he was presented with a direct witness to the *hadīth* authorizing it—but he was providentially obliged to play a negative role, though in an altogether outward sense, in relation to Fatimah insofar as she was the personification of an otherworldly light; it was necessary for him to assume

---

[12] A fact worthy of mention is that the majority of the descendants of Ali and Fatimah are Sunnis and that there were Alid dynasties that were nevertheless not Shiite.

[13] Many *ahādīth* accepted in Sunni collections take account of this. This proves moreover that one cannot accuse Sunni authorities of having in bad faith suppressed texts favorable to Ali and corroborative of the Shiite thesis, especially since the Caliph Umar II, who had the first written collection of *ahādīth* made, was not hostile to the Alids.

[14] Which, it must be admitted, poses a certain problem for non-Muslims in the absence of documents that would explain this attitude in relation to its hagiographic context.

this incidental role on the material plane by virtue of his thoroughly extrinsic function as guardian of legal principles, or let us say of legal abstraction. The affair of the inheritance refused to Fatimah is an example of the dilemma or conflict between a principial abstraction and a particular concrete case lying outside its purview.

The intertwining of characters and destinies that concerns us here includes the strange case of Fatimah. Embodying the purest sanctity, according to unanimous tradition,[15] she was put aside, deprived of her rights, forgotten; on occasion she was treated with harshness—even, it seems, by the Prophet, her father. In this is contained the whole drama of a celestial soul predestined to be a martyr of terrestrial life; her abasement is like a shadow cast by her spiritual elevation, human individuals appearing in her destiny as the cosmic instruments of her painful alchemy. There is something similar in the case of the Virgin Mary, treated not without a certain coldness by the Gospels and passed over to a large extent in silence by the rest of the New Testament, to reappear afterward in all the greater splendor; a comparable example in a totally different world is that of Sita, wife of Rama, who was never happy on earth but was deified in Heaven, or again that of Maya, mother of the Buddha, who was nearly forgotten and yet later glorified in the form of Tara, "Mother of all the Buddhas"; we mention these things here to show that the destinies of saints of the highest order show forth symbolisms that it would be vain to analyze solely from the point of view of individual responsibilities. As for Fatimah, this saint's attachment to her father clashed after his death with the inflexibility of the first caliph, who in refusing her certain elementary favors took into consideration only the rigidity of the principles of Islam, which in reality could have allowed for a wider interpretation in this particular case; but it was the destiny of Fatimah to be deprived of the consolations of this lower world. This example is typical of the oppositions between the Companions: the clash is not between pas-

---

[15] The written documents contain nothing, however, that would oblige us to acknowledge this sanctity; if we do acknowledge it, this is because there is no effect without a cause: the cult of Fatimah throughout Islam and throughout the centuries cannot be explained without the sanctity of the person, and the world of Fatimah is too near our own to be legendary in its essential features.

sions but between good intentions, inspired by a totalitarian mentality ever prone to irreducible alternatives.

All things considered the drama of the Companions is that of human subjectivity: there would be no problem if there were only the good and the bad, but the great paradox is the existence of the good who differ with each other to the point of not being able to understand each other—differing not so much by nature as with regard to situation and vocation. The great epic poems, such as the Iliad or the Song of the Nibelungs, show in all their tragic grandeur this intertwining of temperaments, positions, responsibilities, duties, and destinies: combat outwardly in the current of forms, but unity inwardly in an unchanging quest for the Light that liberates.

The moral courage of Muhammad was immense; the physical courage of Ali, unsurpassable hero on the battlefield, was no less so. Muhammad liked to speak of the general religion and to give practical counsel; Ali was the metaphysician of the community, and he would even broach the most transcendent subjects during moments of respite in combat.[16] Now men are diverse; in many cases the law of affinity as well as that of complementarity could have worked in Ali's favor, and this must have given the impression—not altogether mistakenly—that some people were less attached to the Prophet than to his son-in-law. But even if this were not the case, one can admit that the forerunners or ancestors of the Shiites, if they were not those among the Companions who most loved the Prophet, certainly were the ones who put the love of his Family in the foreground—to the detriment, say the Sunnis, of the more impersonal elements of the divine Message or a more objective evaluation of things. We could perhaps say that the "pre-Shiites" were those Companions who could

---

[16] According to the testimony of Hasan al-Basri, Ali was "the theologian of the Community". "I am the city of Knowledge, and Ali is its gate," said the Prophet, according to a *hadīth* that was reported to us in a Sunni country; it means that Ali was concerned with explaining and commenting upon what the Prophet expressed in an elliptical manner.

not live without the presence of the Muhammadan Family and who had no other choice but to attach themselves to what remained of it in its descendants, whereas the Sunnis were those who could not accept any substitute whatever for this presence and who therefore had no choice but to live by the memory of it and in its *Sunnah*.

One must assume there was something fascinating about Ali, something particular to him that determined a cult nearly independent of that of Muhammad; Ali appears above all as the "solar hero" and the "lion" (*asad* or *haydar*) of God; one loves him as the *gopīs* loved Krishna,[17] and his tragic death adorns him with a halo of martyrdom and cries out for a quasi-mystical and cosmic vengeance. Nonetheless—and this is an altogether different matter—the hero was not a statesman or even a strategist; he wielded the sword superlatively but not so diplomacy; he disdained diplomacy out of purity and uprightness, we are assured by his partisans, who forget that the Prophet—without being any less pure or upright than his son-in-law—was an accomplished statesman, perfectly capable of cunning when dealing with the enemy and of making concessions that seem surprising at first but are extremely efficacious, even decisive, in the final analysis. Ali lacked foresight because of a spirit of integrity and was indecisive because of detachment from earthly things; this explains why he did not gain full endorsement at the time of his election.[18] In the person-

---

[17] "Love for Ali consumes all sins, as fire consumes dry wood," proclaims a Shiite *hadīth*. For the extremists Ali is even greater than the Prophet.

[18] Even among some of his partisans his prestige dropped during the war against his rival Muawiyah. The majority of Ali's army having pressed him into accepting an arbitration that in fact turned out to be disastrous, a part of the army—the Kharijites—revolted against him and separated from him; it was one of these Kharijites who later killed him at Kufa in order to avenge the defeat Ali inflicted upon them at Nahrawan. Let it be noted that a Hasan al-Basri and an Ibn Sirin, young contemporaries of Ali and great stars in the firmament of nascent Sufism, were totally Sunni: they criticized certain aspects of Ali's behavior and accepted without hesitation the Caliphate of Abu Bakr and Umar and, with serious criticisms but with resignation, the Caliphate of the Umayyads, while at the same time excusing Uthman, an attitude that would be inconceivable on the part of saints of that epoch if truth and right had been the monopoly of the Imamists. This is all the more significant in that the initiatic genealogy of the Sufis connects Hasan al-Basri with Ali himself, which indicates, if not a direct initiatic link—although we do not see why this link has been brought into doubt—at least a particular and typical spiritual relationship.

ality of Muhammad, by contrast, it is not the physical hero who stands out, but the leader of men, the strategist, the farsighted and invincible statesman: he who does not merely win a day's battles by the strength of his sword but who brings about a millennial world empire thanks to his genius, humanly speaking. Now Abu Bakr, Umar, and others were more responsive to this kind of power than to the heroic radiance of an Ali; for men like the first three caliphs there could be no question either of a cult or of hostility in relation to the Messenger's son-in-law.

The quasi-exclusion in Shiism of what we have termed the element "dryness" may fundamentally explain—though not justify—the Shiites' misinterpretation of the first three caliphs and of the Prophet's favorite wife, and this is the price paid for the exoteric coagulation of Shiism; it is indeed the way of all exoterism to become hypnotized by a single aspect of reality and interpret everything in terms of this exclusivity.[19] Let us recall in this connection the general condemnation of all forms of "paganism" by each of the three monotheistic religions or in particular the Christian underestimation of the *Torah* and the inward dimension of Judaism, or again in Islam the reduction of Christ's role to that of a forerunner. For Shiite spirituality the question of knowing who an Abu Bakr or an Aisha really was does not arise: only principles count—whether positive or negative and whatever the images in which they find expression. Be that as it may, the extent of the dissemination of the theses that are the most hostile to Sunnism and—it must be said—most passionate and most unconvincing appears to have been somewhat variable; they are to be found above all in theological works of the Safavid epoch, works that do not possess any absolute authority, however, since the application of the canonical principle of "personal judgment" (*ijtihād*) is freer among Shiites than Sunnis and thus opens the door to far more pronounced divergences, whence by way of compensation the less obligatory character of the opinions expressed.

---

[19] This sort of ostracism—and the negative symbolization of proper names—is found almost everywhere, even in the Hindu world and even outside exoterism: for the partisans of Madhva, Shankara is the incarnation of a demon; his name, which means "Savior", becomes for them *Sankara*, "bastard". The partisans of Shankara do as much in return, declaring that Madhva was the bastard of ignoble parents, who set himself the mission of falsifying the *Vedānta*.

Regarding the origins of Shiism, the emphasis we have placed on these factors must not however cause one to lose sight of the role of political contingencies after the death of Uthman and above all after the death of Ali, when the city of Kufa aimed to remain the capital of the Empire and did not dream of effacing itself in favor of Damascus, the capital of Muawiyah. While it is true that ideas create vested interests, it is no less undeniable that vested interests can in turn create ideas or ideologies, for such interests encourage accentuations—and corresponding doctrinal elaborations—with all the prejudices and exclusions these can bring in their train; these two factors, idea and interest, are sometimes difficult to disentangle in a climate of passion that is at once mystical and political. From an entirely different point of view, it is possible that Shiism, which was *a priori* a purely Arab movement, was subjected *a posteriori* to the influence of concepts having a Babylonian and Mazdean origin: we are thinking here particularly of the metaphysics of Light and the related idea of an esoteric and quasi-superhuman Priesthood.[20]

There are those who have wished to see the esoteric aspect of Islam in Shiism, which is false if one concludes from this that Shiism is a pure esoterism and that Sunnism may be reduced to the corresponding exoterism; but it nonetheless contains an element of truth to the extent that Shiism can be explained by an intention of "inwardness", which however it readily translates into the terms of "outward" theology;[21] thus Shiite exoterism is instilled with the flavor of a quasi-esoterism of an emotional type, whereas in Sunnism the two dimensions, the outward and the inward, remain in principle separated and in equilibrium.[22] In a certain approximate manner Shiism

---

[20] We have very little inclination to acknowledge borrowings of this kind, but in the case of Shiism—above all, or at the very least, in its extreme and relatively late forms—such influences seem to us probable if not certain; they may be explained in this case by a convergence of motivations.

[21] Mention must be made of a particular sector, namely Shiite Sufism, which is very close to Sunni Sufism. One comment on the subject of the etymology of the word *sūfī*: the fact that in Persian this Arabic term has often been translated as *pashmīnah-pūsh*, "wearer of the woolen cloak", indicates that the Arabic word is derived from *sūf*, "wool", and not from *safā*, "purity", nor for that matter from the Greek *sophos*, "sage", as has been claimed.

[22] Both popular Sufism and Sufi Asharism appear to some extent to contradict this, but

is the "Christianity of Islam":[23] its fundamental theme is the "divine humanity" of its great saints,[24] then the martyrdom of the uncomprehended light, and finally the sacramental presence of this light in the form of the imamate.[25]

The quintessence of Shiism is imamism: instead of being humanized in the Prophet alone, the *Logos* is also manifested in the twelve imams by being as it were refracted in them, and this begins with Ali. The pure Intellect, which is immanent in the heart of every man but actualized only in the sages and saints[26]—in varying degree and different modes—is in itself infallible, and it is a ray of the divine *Logos*; now since this *Logos* has been humanized not only in the Prophet but also in the imams, it is from them that the human Intellect stems in practice according to the Shiite point of view. There is no wisdom and no sanctity without the grace of the imam, even if "hidden"; to know God is to know Him through the imam since all spiritual knowledge comes from the Intellect. This is the thesis of Shiism, and it will be noted that it pushes to its limits the humanization, indeed politicization, of principial realities.[27]

---

these are inevitable phenomena, for it is impossible that the two dimensions would remain anywhere totally independent from each other.

[23] Shiism is to Islam what Arianism is to Christianity, but in an opposite sense since it accentuates the human Manifestation of God whereas Arianism accentuates Transcendence.

[24] Though not in the sense of Christian incarnationism (*hulūl*). The avataric quality of the Muhammadan Family, which is in any case relative, implies an innate and *a priori* radiant sanctity—which may not manifest itself in distant descendants, to say the least—but the absence of this quality in no way implies that the highest spirituality is impossible.

[25] To pretend that all Muslim esoterism is derived from the *shī'ah* is to play with words. The Sufi notion of the "pole" (*qutb*) results from the nature of things, and it is not the fault of Sunnis if for the Shiites the "pole" is the Alid imam and no other; it is clear that the immediate descendants of Husayn, the son of Ali, were "poles" since they combined the Sharifian nature with personal sanctity. As for the opposition of certain imams to Sufism, this concerns only some particular manifestations of Sufism; one need not be a Shiite in order to notice a "two-edged" innovation in the foundation of the brotherhoods, but this has no bearing on *Tasawwuf* as such.

[26] According to the accepted view, the first of these terms accentuates intellective perfection and the second volitive perfection.

[27] Imamism justifies its narrowly systematic conception of the "cycle of sanctity"

The particular greatness of the imams, Fatimah eminently included, resides in the conjunction of what might be called their celestial substance with their personal sanctity, this sanctity having been effectively realized down to the twelfth imam, who withdrew from the sight of men and is supposed to reappear as the *Mahdi* at the end of the world. But this conjunction—of which one sees another example in the ancient Brahman caste, which issued from the *Rishis*, and yet another in the case of the first emperors of Japan, who descended from Jimmu Tenno—does not mean that sanctity cannot appear outside an avataric line of descent; the imams are to be identified with the *Logos*, but the *Logos* is not to be identified with the imams;[28] the Sunni *qutb*—the "pole"—embodies the *Logos* as does the Shiite imam, but without having to be a *sharīf*. And we shall add this: if the very existence of Shiism proves the particular greatness of the "House of the Prophet", the Sunni perspective, or the existence or actual importance of this perspective, points on the contrary to the relativity and the limits of imamism.

From the fact that Shiites have in their own way emphasized certain ideas or realities of early Islam or of Islam as such, it does not follow that these ideas or realities belong to Shiism alone nor that all who acknowledge them are indebted to Shiism or are openly or even secretly Shiites. From a more general but related point of view we would say that saints certainly have a right to think and speak as their vocation permits and within the framework of their denominational milieu, but their teachings should not make us lose sight of the fact that all Islamic sapience flows from quintessential and primordial for-

---

(*wilāyah*) by a corresponding retrospective interpretation of the "cycle of prophecy" (*nubuwwah*), but in reality the liberty or discontinuity of the latter cycle is an argument in favor of the Sunni conception of the "pole" precisely because this has nothing dynastic about it. And in any case how can one attribute perfections or talents as diverse as personal sanctity, metaphysical intellectuality, and political capacity to a whole dynasty—that of the Alid imams? On this subject let us note that there are divergent opinions about the person of the imam, which is all the more surprising, to say the least, given the fact that knowledge of the imam of the period is supposed to be a condition of salvation.

[28] Just as one may accept that Jesus is God but not that God is Jesus. Let it be noted that for the Nusairis, the Ali-Ilahis, the Bektashis, and others, Ali is God veiled by a human appearance; one might ask what the motivations are for such extravagances.

mulations, namely, the *Shahādah* and certain *ayāt* and *ahādīth*[29] that make its essential intentions more explicit or specific in relation to union as well as doctrine.[30]

No believer doubts that God may sacrifice certain possibilities of Mercy to the imperative demands of Truth, for otherwise no Justice would be possible; but it must also be acknowledged—though there is no symmetry between the two—that God may sacrifice truths that are in practice secondary to the imperatives of saving Mercy, for otherwise there would be no religious or denominational divergences. This means that in practice a secondary truth is no longer truth when it is discarded in favor of an essential truth, just as a lamp is no longer light in the presence of the sun and is even a cause of obscurity since it then casts a shadow; this also means that error as such could not come from God but is on the contrary prefigured—if it figures extrinsically in a traditional symbolism—in the very structure of the human receptacle. God never gives less than He promises and never takes away anything positive without compensating for it or giving it back on a higher level; therefore the errors—always extrinsic—of religions or

---

[29] Koranic verses and sayings of the Prophet.

[30] When one possesses a rigorous notion of esoterism or *gnosis*, it is impossible not to feel uneasy in observing that the sayings of the imams, which are supposed to be the only sources of esoterism, have given rise to voluminous compilations and require in turn whole volumes of commentary. One of the crucial differences between Sunnis and Shiites is that for Sunnis the apostolic quality belongs only to sayings of the Prophet—there are some thousands—whereas for the Shiites it extends right down to the last of the imams, toward the end of the ninth century, hence more than three centuries after Muhammad; it is as though one were to add all the Fathers of the Church to the New Testament. These remarks will be better understood if one considers the subjective, empirical, emotional, inspirationist, prophetising, and even political character of a certain type of esoterism, one founded above all on hermeneutics (*ta'wil*) and an eschatology that is audacious, to say the least.

denominations that are orthodox[31] in themselves necessarily coincide with spiritual truths, at least with those that are negative.[32]

When the Scriptures say that the sun rises, moves, and sets, they are not lying, even though from the point of view of facts the sun is motionless in relation to its planetary system; they are simply using the language of terrestrial appearances. The same is true of the human facts contained in the sacred perspectives; every formal element is subject to the relativity of "aspects" and "points of view", only the divine Intention—made of intrinsic Truth and liberating Attraction—being immutable. "Elias is come," said Christ, thinking of Saint John the Baptist, even though John had denied he was Elias; it is true that Christ was referring only to the function and not the person whereas the Forerunner was speaking of his own person and not the function; but Jesus' indirect and elliptical expression nonetheless illustrates the liberty that prophetic language may take with the facts when a principial truth is at stake.

Whatever the divergences between the Muslim denominations, the metaphysics of Unity and Union dominates the entire horizon of thought, just as much Shiite as Sunni; and in the final analysis a Muslim is orthodox to the extent that he identifies himself with the fundamental thesis of Islam and assumes all its consequences. On this basis we can say that quintessential orthodoxy is sanctity, which combines or transcends all partial truths in the purity of its experience.

---

[31] A denomination or religion is intrinsically orthodox when it includes a metaphysical doctrine that is at least adequate and offers both the notion and the phenomenon of sanctity.

[32] Not positive, for it is a question here of things rejected. Shiites are right in condemning Pharisaism; their associating it with the names of Companions is quite another matter. Hindu meditation on an image is one thing, and the Semitic reproach of idolatry is another.

Dilemmas of Muslim Scholasticism

Theology, founded as it is upon the inevitably antinomic and elliptical—but by no means contradictory or irreconcilable—facts of the sacred Scriptures, is a mental activity that interprets these facts by means of the reason and in relation to a piety that is often more fervent than enlightened; this occasionally results in theories that are doubtless opportune and effective in a given psychological or moral context but restrictive or even aberrant from the point of view of pure and simple truth and in any case unacceptable on the plane of metaphysics. Muslim theology affords us a primary example of this in the antagonism between "comparison" (*tashbīh*) and "abstraction" (*tanzīh*): some protagonists of "abstraction" have gone so far as to maintain that God is unknowable in an almost absolute sense and that, though the Koran attributes certain beneficent Names to Him, this tells us nothing about the divine Nature, for this Nature is "absolutely other" and God has merely "given Himself" these names in Revelation without our being able to grasp His motive for doing so.[1] Obviously, there is both resemblance and incomparability between God and the world; this may be expressed by saying that God does not resemble the world but that the positive qualities of the world resemble God and are intelligible through Him alone. God is in no sense a terrestrial light, but it would be absurd to maintain that physical light tells us nothing about the divine Nature, for otherwise there would be no point in revealing to us that God is Light.

Asharite theology in particular offers more than one example of a form of reasoning inspired more by zeal than discernment. God cannot be unjust—Ashari reasons[2]—because injustice consists in invading the

---

[1] The Shaykh al-Alawi remarked on the contrary that "the men most removed from their Lord are those who most exaggerate His unknowability", that is, His *tanzīh* ("incomparability"), because of which nothing is like him. "What is important," the Shaykh also said, "is not to exaggerate 'incomparability' (*tanzīh*) but to know God by means of 'analogy' (*tashbīh*)"; and again: "Comparison linked to the certitude of Unity is worth more than abstraction joined to the veiling of Unity."

[2] Ali al-Ashari, Arab theologian of the tenth century, founder of Muslim scholasticism (*kalām*). Let us specify at once that in Islam theology is in principle open to question and therefore has a more or less optional character; but it is always difficult to establish

domain of someone else, and there is no domain that does not belong to God; therefore, even if God were to act like the most unjust of men, He would not for that reason be unjust; anything coming from Him is necessarily justice precisely because everything belongs to Him. There is a strange forgetfulness of intrinsic values here: because of fear and despite the Koran, one seems to lose sight of God's infinite Goodness (*Rahmah*, whence the names *Rahmān* and *Rahīm*); a sort of "moral vacuum" is presented, whose only characteristic is an unintelligible and unpredictable willfulness. If this were the truth, no name signifying a quality could be applied to God; human intelligence would be pointless since there would be nothing to understand; it would not exist any more than would the virtues, which by definition reflect something of God. All that could be asked of man would be a sort of obedient animality, perfectly proportioned to a blind Law.

When Ashari depicts the unlimitedness of Omnipotence, he strangely loses sight of what a quality is in itself as well as of what the divine Nature is; he seems to discern only extrinsic qualities or situations—such as the fact that a monarch has to take orders from no one—and seems to see God only in situations of this kind. Nonetheless the love of God is incumbent on every man, and this presupposes—and proves—that God is supremely lovable and furthermore that this love is thereby in the profound nature of man, so much so that loving God means being entirely true to oneself; now the "Good Pleasure" God of Ashari or Ibn Hanbal is not lovable since the only motive for His actions is "what He wills" and "because He wills". Certainly, the Koran teaches that God "doeth what He will", but it does not say that this constitutes the very definition of God or the sufficient reason for worshipping and loving Him. There are two flagrant pieces of nonsense in totalitarian obedientialism: one concerning God, whom one wishes to make sublime by means of a blind hyperbolism in connection with freedom, and the other concerning man, who is reduced to nothingness by means of a no less blind abdication of common sense. All things considered the error consists in subordinating Being to Power, *Ātmā*-God to *Māyā*-God, or Essence (*Dhāt*) to Qualities (*Sifāt*); now Power is a reality that is already relative—although still in

---

lines of demarcation in such matters, all the more so as Sufism feels quite free with regard to theology.

a divine way—since it presupposes a level that is not God over which He is able to exercise control. Since power is relative to this level, it has no effect on the divine Nature, which is absolute; power can neither limit nor extend itself because its substance is derived from the divine Nature and not from the will of a given *Hypostasis*; God cannot make His Omnipotence less than it is or cause it to modify the divine Nature and thus trespass on the Essence, which is the Absolute.

If it is impossible for God to lie, this is because lying is an imperfection; this being so, Omnipotence does not imply that God might decide—as Ashari maintains—that lying is a perfection; if lying is not intrinsically an imperfection, there is no reason to suppose—as Ashari does—that God cannot lie. And if it is impossible for God to pray—to cite something Ashari wrongly takes as a proof of his opinion on lying—this is because prayer, as an act of subordination, implies the imperfection of separation and duality, but it also implies the perfection of love and union, and in this connection its prototype is in God. Moreover, when Ashari asserts that God cannot lie, one wonders why; he even specifies that God, while creating lying "for others", cannot Himself lie, just as God, in ordering prayer for others, cannot pray Himself since there is no one above Him; this reasoning is fallacious, for prayer necessarily has its origin in God in its positive and essential content, as we have just mentioned. Moreover the same applies to lying: the purely negative side of lying is certainly foreign and opposed to the divine Nature, and yet God can hide truths, as is proven on the one hand by the diversity of Revelations and on the other hand by the existence of esoterisms; this is not lying, but lying nonetheless is derived—by perversion and privation—from the capacity of God to veil Himself; if God veiled nothing, the whole world would be instantly consumed by His blinding Truth.

Monotheistic theologies claim that creation has a beginning but not an end, which is metaphysically absurd; since it is more pressing for the average man to save his soul than to be a metaphysician, however, and since it is better to make spiritual progress without metaphysics than to stay behind with a metaphysics that is poorly assimilated, God accepts the limitations of men and expresses Himself accordingly. It is in their interest for Him to veil particular truths, given the requirements of a specific and average mentality, while it is the duty of the sages to interpret symbols and recover the total truth, as Ibn Arabi pertinently observed. Paradoxically, it is moral or passional limitations rather than intellectual limitations that make it inopportune to reveal certain truths, which means that the risk of incomprehension lies more readily in the will than in the intelligence; the capacities of intelligence become inoperative when the will and affectivity are surrendered to the passions. It is obviously better to approach God while not being sharp-minded than to pull away from Him by being sharp-minded, which amounts to saying that it is better to go naively to Heaven than lucidly to hell; intelligence has no value without truth.

But let us return to the impasses presented by a certain type of theology, for we live in a world where it is better not to leave them unmentioned; we do so in the interest of truth as such and without prejudice for the religious perspectives: in claiming that lying is an evil because God has declared it so and for no other reason, one completely forgets to ask why God declared that lying is evil; and one forgets even more to tell oneself that this "why" or motive is in God Himself. An evil is what is opposed to the divine Nature, not what God—because He is "omnipotent"—has decreed to be evil; the very content of the divine declaration confirms the self-evident fact that lying is an evil; it is not the fact of the declaration that creates its evil character. In teaching—or reminding—us what we must do or not do, the Ten Commandments teach us at the same time what God is and is not.

— ·∴· —

For Ibn Hanbal and Ashari it would seem that God owes nothing to man and can owe nothing to him; the truth is that God, having created man "in His image" and having consequently given him intelligence, owes His intelligent and theomorphic creature an intelligent and consequential attitude because He owes it to Himself;[3] it is because God is homogeneous and because His homogeneity penetrates creation— or because the divine Nature is essentially good and true—that man

---

[3] It is in this sense that the Koran declares that "God prescribed Mercy for Himself", which means that Mercy is part of the divine Nature, which by definition is intangible; according to a *hadīth qudsī*, God said: "In truth My Mercy precedeth My Wrath", which indicates the essentiality of the first and the quasi-accidentality of the second.

cannot be excluded from the logic of the divine Nature, if one may put it this way.[4] The reciprocity between Creator and creature comes from the nature of the Creator, and God cannot change His nature; "can" and "will" are here synonymous.

If we know that God rewards the good and punishes the wicked, this is because He has told us so—or so Ashari thinks—and not because He is obliged to act this way. With his passionate desire to instill in turbulent souls a pious abnegation before God, the theologian loses sight of the fact that God has likewise told us that He is the Good, the Merciful, the Just, the Generous; if we must believe this— assuming we had no means of knowing it other than simple information—then by the same token we must necessarily conclude that God acts in accordance with goodness, mercy, justice, generosity. It is true that in certain cases we may not know how these divine Qualities ought to—or will to—manifest themselves, but in precisely the case mentioned by Ashari we do indeed know, and it is the express will of God that we should.

Dazzled as he is by his awareness of our nothingness, Ashari thinks God does not owe us any explanations; but he forgets that God "wishes to owe" explanations, and that if God creates an apple tree it is to produce apples and not figs; God "wishes to owe" human intelligence all the clarifications for which it was made just as He "wishes to owe" a given womb the species of creature for which it was made, not some other species. And if God thus keeps His word, ontologically and humanly, it is certainly not from lack of freedom but because He is Truth and Goodness and because ontologically His Freedom wills the good.

—— ·:· ——

We may recapitulate all these considerations in the following way: theological voluntarism begins by asserting that both good and evil are in the world and that both are created by God; if these things exist

---

[4] It goes without saying that we are using the word "logic" in a transposed and not a rational sense. As a positive discipline logic necessarily reflects a quality of the divine Intelligence.

in space or happen in time, it is because God "wills" them; to reduce God in this way to voluntarism there is but a single step, and Ashari takes this step by declaring that it would not be bad for God to punish believers and reward unbelievers and that our only reason for saying He will not do so is that He has informed us to the contrary! And all this—still according to Ashari—is because no one can command anything from God since He is the supreme Monarch, so much so that He is free to do whatever He will, and nothing He does can be evil.

We have alluded above to the strange opinion that lying is bad "because God has declared it bad" and that "it would be good if God had declared it good"; if God Himself does not lie, this is "not because lying is bad but because it is impossible for God to lie"! The error of this reasoning comes entirely from the equation "God-Will" and from the fact that All-Possibility is regarded—as the result of exoteric anthropomorphism—as a freedom to will anything whatsoever; the error here—we want to stress this—lies in subordinating even the true and the good to the arbitrariness of an unrestricted Will and in forgetting that man is made in the image of God, with the result that his intellections depend not on divine "declarations" but on the nature of things as derived from God's perfection and as revealed to the primordial, and in principle normal, understanding of man. Doubtless nothing exists or happens without being divinely willed, or let us say without an ontological causation; but this Koranic doctrine would be unintelligible without the essential affirmation, placed at the head of each *sūrah*, that God is "the Infinitely Good, the Ever Merciful"; it follows from this that evil "created" or "willed" by God can only be a provisional element in a greater good and that this evil is therefore integrated and dissolved in the final and decisive good; and it is this—and not the notion of a gratuitous "Omnipotence"—that explains why nothing can be evil on the part of the Sovereign Good.

It has been said, in Islam and Christianity alike, that evil comes from substances that do not accept omnipresent Goodness; it remains to be seen why they do not. The reason is that these substances, although they are ontologically derived from the divine Good, are called upon to manifest remoteness from the Principle and thus a sort of nothingness—this in accordance with cosmic equilibrium and the rhythms it implies; though they are bad in their privative particularity, these substances are nonetheless good by virtue of their cosmic function, a function that is necessary for the sake of the good known as universal Manifestation.

"If someone were to ask me," remarks Ghazzali, "why God does not wish all men to be believers, I would reply that we have no right to ask questions about what God wishes or does. He is perfectly free to wish and do whatever He pleases." Now this is a weak response and beside the point; but what is curious—and significant with regard to the "twofold thinking" of many esoterists—is that Ghazzali himself gives the correct answer later on: "In creating unbelievers and wishing them to remain in this state, or in creating snakes, scorpions, and pigs—in short, in willing everything that is evil—God has wise motives in view that it is not necessary for us to understand." He should have said this from the start! For this answer completely contradicts the one he proposed earlier; what should have been said at once is that divine production can have motives that may well escape man's understanding, whether in principle or in fact, or in any case the understanding of a given man; to ask questions is normal for a human being and to admit that his understanding has fundamental or accidental limits is likewise normal. To take intelligence to task in the name of a divine "good pleasure" is convenient, but it has no relation to the inalienable rights of our nature, nor—needless to say—does it have anything to do with the problems of Universal Manifestation and All-Possibility.

If we look at a scorpion—to keep to Ghazzali's example—and if we consider it in relation to pure existence, we see a good and not an evil, namely, existence precisely, the divine word "Be!", which is like a victory over nothingness; the same is true if we consider the scorpion in relation to its existential, vital, and sensorial qualities, for a faculty is everywhere and always a faculty; the same applies if we consider it in relation to its function in the economy of nature; and if we looked at everything this way—if we were interested in making the effort or if it were possible for us to do so always—we could say with Ibn Arabi and with certain Indian *bhakta*s that there is only good in the world, provided we had clearly discerned the relationships that authorize us to say this and that we never denied that an evil is an evil in the particularity that characterizes it. It is all very well to object that this particularity is only privative, that it is "pure inexistence", as Ibn Arabi would say; but this does not prevent the particularity from being what it is in our experience, which means that the concrete reality of imperfect or maleficent things will not be abolished, for this privation or "inexistence" does indeed exist, or else it would be impossible to speak of an evil; if pain were but a nothingness, it would not be felt. And yet this reality, let it be said once more, is necessary, and it becomes a good by virtue of its function in the universal economy—quite apart from the good that is existentially immanent in all things—without which no creation would be possible.

To manifest divine Perfection is to make it different from God or "other than He"; without this difference or alterity, there would be no manifestation; now to be different from pure Perfection involves imperfection, hence also—on certain existential levels—what we call evil. And the manifestation of divine Perfection results from the infinity of this Perfection itself; this dimension, which is both expansive and restrictive, is none other than *Māyā* or *al-Hijāb*, the Veil that at once manifests and separates.

It is curious that a man like Ghazzali, who was certainly aware of the dangers of *kalām* since he thought this science was liable to trouble faith, would have inadvertently bowed before the *fait accompli* of theological opinions that had come to be established as dogmas; like Ashari he piously believes that God is able to punish or cause suffering without the creature's having deserved it and without there being any subsequent compensation, whereas it would have been neither difficult nor indeed superfluous to specify that a destiny always results from the nature of the being who undergoes it—this is independent of the question of individual sin—and furthermore that the creature is always free to turn his destiny into an occasional cause of spiritual victory, for otherwise the Koran would not speak of merits or demerits. Ghazzali thinks that it is blameworthy (*makrūh*) to devote ourselves to a science which exceeds our strength and that only Prophets and saints—not theologians and philosophers—have the capacity and the right to scrutinize the mysteries of God; whether Ghazzali was a saint or not—and we are of the opinion he was—we admit that we sometimes prefer the opinions of the philosophers he attacks to his own.[5]

---

[5] Let us note in passing that the epithet "philosopher"—taking the word in a limitative or pejorative sense—may not be applied without reservation to such minds as Farabi and Avicenna, for they were primarily Neoplatonists in spite of some Aristotelian influence. And let us also note in this connection that the role of the sage is not to

The real, hence adequate, intuition of a perspicacious intelligence is worth more than the hurried and faulty speculation of a contemplative mind, even an outstanding one, and the fact that a given error may have—subjectively speaking—only a provisional and accidental character obviously adds no value to it whatsoever.

The opportunity presents itself now to call attention to the following point: wisdom consists not only in knowing truths and being able to communicate them but also in the sage's capacity to recognize the most subtle limitations or hazards of human nature. Since for various reasons this condition is not always fulfilled—and extenuating circumstances are by no means lacking—we encounter certain types of errors even on the part of traditional authorities; this deserves mention despite those who see such authorities in far too superhuman a light. It is a fact that the doctors of the Law and the Spirit contradict one another quite apart from any question of heresy, and they do so on grounds that are not always reducible to a point of view, unless one uses the phrase "point of view" to label a lack of intellectual intuition or a false piece of reasoning; moreover the orthodox doctors do not criticize one another for "ways of seeing things"; they criticize one another for errors. All the same, there is an essential distinction to be noted here: there are errors situated within the framework of comprehensive truth, and there are errors that shatter this framework, and here lies the whole difference between sacred and profane thought. It is sometimes said that no doctrine is completely wrong and that everything contains an element of truth, but this is completely false, for fundamental—and thus decisive—truths can neutralize the minor errors in a doctrine whereas minor truths are valueless within the framework of a major error; this is why one must never glorify an error for having taught us a given truth nor look for truth in errors on the pretext that

explain things from zero or to construct a system—as in the radically mistaken view of the moderns—but first to "see" and second to "cause to see", which means to provide a key; it is therefore absurd to accuse Platonists of "constructing" a theory of knowledge on the basis of an image of the world already presupposing such a theory.

truth is everywhere the same, for there are critical nuances here; and above all one must not reject a fundamental and comprehensive truth because of a minor error that may happen to accompany it.

Be that as it may, the human soul is capable—paradoxically and up to a certain point—of combining spiritual knowledge with a singular incapacity for expressing it in the way the total context requires and according to the logic of things; there is basically no common measure between the inward man seized by the radiations of the Infinite and the outward man living on preconceived notions and habits and moving his thought, by the way, on a level that is proportionately far below his intelligence; it is of course desirable for a man to match his thought to his real knowledge without letting any purely formal doubts persist, but this is a particular grace, which may not be realized and which, in the case of certain Sufis influenced by Asharism, is only partially realized.

In the logic of the omnipotentialists, our possible ignorance of divine motives comes to imply a possible absence of motives in divine activity; this is a characteristically subjective judgment, one that must be kept in clear view if we wish to extract a plausible meaning from certain verbal utterances that have become more or less traditional but are not obligatory. In the same realm of ideas the following example is perhaps worth mentioning: the opinion—repeated by Ghazzali—that God can ask man to do something that he is unable to accomplish is completely in keeping with the anti-metaphysical and finally immoral omnipotentialist-obedientialist outlook of the Asharites; the Koranic prayer "Do not impose upon us what we have not the strength to bear" (*Sūrah* "The Cow" [2]:286) in no way authorizes this opinion, especially since the same verse tells us that "God imposes on the soul only what it can bear". The meaning of the prayer just mentioned is that God—in this case *karma*, as Hindus and Buddhists would say—may punish a sin and that the punishment may be greater than the actual strength of the sinner; but in this case the human weakness is an aspect of the sin and reveals its importance, which amounts to saying that through our own fault we may be accidentally incapable of bearing what we normally—and with sufficient faith—could bear.

In short what the prayer means is this: remove from us a *karma* that in fact might crush us; in other words loosen this knot or reduce its effects since we put our trust in Thy Mercy. But it could never mean that God can ask us to perform things that cannot be objectively realized.

We have already mentioned in passing the strange idea that God could chastise the good and reward the bad "if He so wished": to wish to draw this blindly totalitarian conclusion from the Koran is to forget that the Koran itself excludes it. When God says that He will punish sinners "according to their deserts"—while specifying that He will reward the good far more than they deserve—He expresses a causal relationship and not an arbitrary and unintelligible decision; we see absolutely no reason for God to be less logical and less just than virtuous men just because He is omnipotent, not to mention the fact that according to the Koran the essence of God is Generosity and Mercy. This last point has been amply developed by the Sufis, notably Ibn Arabi, who refers everything to the divine *Rahmah*.[6]

The idea of the unlimited rights of God, which in itself constitutes a curious juridical incursion into the realm of All-Possibility, gave rise to the following paradox within the climate of Sufism: when on God's command a man asks God for a certain gift, God rewards him for having obeyed this command even if the request is not granted; but when a man makes a request on his own initiative, even though it may be granted, it may also happen that the man concerned will be deprived of a grace in Paradise in proportion to the gift received on earth—as if God could command a petition without granting it and as

---

[6] Broadly speaking, Ashari, Ghazzali, and Ibn Arabi are the three landmarks of Sunni Islam, setting aside the founders of the four orthodox ritual schools: Abu Hanifah, Malik, Shafii, and Ibn Hanbal. Ashari, previously a Mutazilite, presented orthodoxy in a philosophical and scholastic form; Ghazzali rendered this scholasticism more supple and profound and assured Sufism an unquestioned and henceforth unquestionable place within general orthodoxy; Ibn Arabi dedicated himself to making explicit the doctrine, which is essentially inherent in Koranic monism, of the nonduality of the integral Real and the essence of the merciful Love (*Rahmah*) of this Real—this essence also being proclaimed by the Koran—and in this way he demonstrated the absoluteness and universality of the Muhammadan message. And it is precisely this quasi-definition of Unity as *Rahmah* that the protagonists of omnipotentialism are so ready to forget, hypnotized as they are by a piety where fear and scruple predominate and where an emphasis on Mercy appears like a temptation to do things the easy way.

if He could grant a request and cause it to be paid for in the hereafter, He who never promises more than He gives and never gives less than He promises and who not merely permits but commands that one make requests of Him![7] The Koranic sentence "God doeth what He will" means that we may be unaware of His motives and ways but not that He can be intrinsically inconsistent, as certain arguments do not hesitate to insinuate, propping themselves up as they do with the contradictory and tautological idea that nothing can be inconsistent on the part of God; this is contradictory because divine perfection excludes all intrinsic inconsistency—and if it is not intrinsic then it is pointless to speak of inconsistency—and it is tautological because God, being perfect, could never be considered inconsistent. Be that as it may, God is ever ready to grant humble, charitable, reasonable, and fervent prayers, but sometimes He grants them later, and sometimes He grants them in a form different from what the supplicant had in mind; indeed a refusal on the part of God sometimes amounts to a kind of granting in that it foretells a better gift, to the extent the prayer had the qualities required.

The correctness of an argument—its adequation, not just its formal validity—depends essentially on the truth of the elements it uses as well as on the presence of sufficient information; this is what philosophers and theologians too often forget, whence reasoning of the following type, metaphorically speaking: "A bird is an animal, and it has wings; a cat does not have wings; therefore, it is not an animal."[8] A fallacious argument of this sort, taken from the catechism of Fudali, is the following: "Let us suppose that a temporal thing resembles God—that

---

[7] One may assume, however, that reasonings like the one we have just commented on have more a didactic than literal import—unless they are simply poorly formulated, but this would only be a very relative excuse since correct formulation is part of charity.

[8] This type of argument is used in particular to deny the validity of other religions: one attributes an absolute significance to one's own axioms without realizing that, while they are intrinsically true, they belong only to a "point of view" or "aspect".

God is such that one could attribute to Him qualities that one also observes in temporal creatures; in this case He too would have to have a temporal origin and consequently would need to have a Creator." This conclusion is false because the temporal character of things has no connection with their qualities but simply pertains to their level of manifestation. It is as if one said: there is no resemblance between the moon and its reflection in water because if there were a resemblance the moon would have to be liquid! And let no one say that this kind of reasoning is the prerogative of theologians; modern science reasons no differently when it ventures into realms that are by definition beyond its scope, given its initial prejudice against everything transcending the senses; it was this kind of logic that created evolutionism, psychology, textual criticism, history, and the science of religions.

The great problem for Ashari was to replace Mutazilite rationalism with something that would channel the very need that gives birth to rationalism but without being rationalism; at the same time it was a question of making contentious men feel that God owes them no explanations and that it does not behoove the creature to dispute with his Creator. Moreover the long opposition in Islam to any rationalization of the faith is well known; this is the opposition between the partisans of *naql*, the Koranic and Muhammadan tradition, and those of *'aql*, or rational interpretation. There is wisdom in the restraint of the partisans of tradition alone; their principle, "Without asking how and without comparison (*bilā kayfa wa lā tashbīh*)", while being a two-edged sword inasmuch as it violates a right resulting from human nature, nonetheless acts as a protection against the cerebral exaggerations of a singularly totalitarian piety, and yet without sacrificing any of the possibilities of inward enlightenment.[9]

Moreover the early partisans of tradition had a positive and overriding reason for mistrusting rational speculations: namely, that the Testimony of Faith, the *Shahādah*, constitutes a sufficient metaphysical key and that many pitfalls would subsequently have been avoided if people had always known how to apply this fundamental formula to

---

[9] The early Muslims did not hesitate to declare theological speculation "illicit" (*harām*). "If men knew to what extent theology includes evil passions, they would flee it as they would a lion," declared Shafii, and this was also the sentiment of the three other founders of ritual schools (*madhhab*).

theological problems. For instance, instead of being only half grasped it would have been understood that every human quality is prefigured in the divine Nature and is possible only as a result of it and that no manner of acting is therefore possible for God that would be base for men, the blind argument of the unlimited rights of All-Possibility notwithstanding; and it is precisely the fact that a given manner of acting would be base for men that proves by analogy that it cannot be part of divine Freedom, the Infinite Source of all earthly qualities. As we have said, we must not allow our ignorance of God's motives to lead us into concluding that there could be imperfect attitudes in God, hence attitudes incompatible with the divine Nature: if an act of God is apparently unjust, this is not because God has the right to be unjust or because injustice on His part would not be unjust, but because we do not perceive a divine act in its entirety and are instead like a child who receives a bitter medicine and who may not be aware that one is doing him no harm. To say that God "does not have the right" to be unjust means that He "does not want" to have this right, and to say that an injustice would remain unjust even on His part means precisely that it is incompatible with His nature; if it were not so, God would not possess the quality of justice nor therefore the name "the Just" (*al-ʿAdl*), and the divine Names would tell us nothing, *quod absit*.

Intellectually speaking, the weakness of the Asharite mindset consists in humanizing the Absolute, in speaking about Omnipotence when it is a question of All-Possibility, and in attributing an individual and almost juristic character to Omnipotence to the point of forgetting the fundamental Goodness of Being. What amounts to an overflowing of Infinity in God becomes an unfathomable tyranny for the Asharites and their like, at least in certain sectors of their thought: God keeps His word, they say, because He cannot lie; but they do not tell us, first, why God cannot lie and, second, why He would be acting from authority and not simply from truth when He tells us that lying is wicked. This detour by way of an authority that merely decrees could of course mean that God is the source of every quality and measure, but in that case the matter is very badly expressed, as always happens when one forces metaphysical truths into the mold of a perspective that is narrowly human, hence voluntaristic and sentimental.

Incidentally, this Asharite doctrine of causality throws light on an aspect of exoterism as such, for we find similar theories—similar, that is, with respect to their formal inadequacy—in the most diverse religious climates. The function of this doctrine—this atomism or occasionalism—is in essence to keep us always reminded that God is present and active in all things and to suggest to us that the world would be nothing but a discontinuous chaos were it not for the divine Presence; regarded this way Asharite atomism is a reminder of this Presence or an introduction of the transcendent—of the marvelous, one might say—into everyday life. Man must feel that faith is something other than rationality and that it sees things in relation to God, not the world; because of this the believer himself is not entirely of this world, and his faith is not a "natural" thought but a "supernatural" assent; what is divinely true seems absurd to unbelievers, who follow only a worldly process of thought. According to this perspective the unbeliever thinks in a horizontal sense, the believer in a vertical and ascending sense, according to the "straight path"; and the divine transparency of earthly things—since the divine Cause is everywhere and is alone really present—confers upon faith a sort of concrete and sacramental mystery, a miraculous element, which turns the believer into a being marked by the supernatural. From the metaphysical point of view all of this is an unnecessary luxury since the Intellect has resources other than pious absurdity, but from the theological point of view it is without doubt a victory. All things considered, if unbelief in the form of atheistic scientism admits only physical causes and denies the transcendent causality operating in them, Asharism has replied in advance, and has done so radically, by denying physical causes; it is like a surgical operation or a preventive war. Certainly neither the scientism of the Ancients nor the Renaissance could have taken form in an Asharite climate.

In just the same way, omnipotentialism—which in practice denies that the human mind has any capacity at all for understanding divine motives and refers our intelligence to Revelation alone—has the function of suggesting that it is "God alone who knows", but it does this arbitrarily *ab extra* and forgets that, if it is indeed God who is always the thinker, He is also the thinker in us and in pure intellection or inspiration; for one cannot utter a truth about God "except by the

Holy Spirit". But Asharism thinks of one thing alone: to make the immensity of God concretely present in the world, and it is perfectly realistic in its presentiment that the acceptance of higher truths passes through the will and not the Intellect in the case of the average man and that it is therefore the will that must receive the shock; this shock, at once crushing and sacramental, is provided precisely by a quasi-blind omnipotentialism. Just as the negation of secondary causes transforms the world into a discontinuous chaos of spatial and temporal monads, which can be held together only by the miracle of a divine Will that is renewed at each instant,[10] so also the negation of intellectual and moral logic with regard to what concerns God transforms our intelligence into a vacuum only Revelation can fill; plausible or not, it is an application of the principle according to which one must die in order to be reborn. As Ashari sees it, in order to be concrete and efficacious, theology must be "folly in the eyes of the world"; and Sunnism, sensitive to this moral and sentimental value of Asharite theology, has accepted it—*de facto* rather than *de jure*—as the best possible solution to the ever-threatening antagonism between reason and faith.

Muslim theology, like Christian theology, believes it must stress the gratuitousness of creation: God creates things in order to manifest His Power or Will—always voluntarism!—and without needing to create them, hence without any necessity; He has the right to do whatever He wishes in His creation, and this could never be an evil on His part, and so on. Here we have the almost classic confusion between necessity and constraint on the one hand and between liberty and arbitrariness on the other: one forgets that necessity can be a perfection and is by no means opposed to liberty and at the same time that arbitrariness—or "gratuitousness"—is an imperfection and thus cannot be an

---

[10] In basing themselves on the Koranic idea that God never ceases from creating and that He has no associates, Hanbalites and Asharites believe that the world returns each instant into the void to re-emerge the next instant and that the continuity of phenomena from one *creatio ex nihilo* to the next depends solely on an unpredictable divine decision and not on the nature of the phenomena.

attribute of the divine Nature. It seems one also loses sight of the fact that if God can "owe" man certain things—something totalitarian voluntarism will not permit—this is not because He can be subjected to constraint but because His truthfulness, faithfulness, and goodness involve consequences whose roots are not in human "rights" but in divine Perfection itself: in fulfilling what He promised God submits to His own Will, and this submission is no more contrary to divine Freedom than the honest or noble action of an honorable man is contrary to human liberty. Theological voluntarism appears to forget that it is contrary to the divine Nature to will the absurd; it will no doubt be said that the absurd willed by God is no longer absurd since God wills it, but this precisely is the height of absurdity and of the sentimentalist perversion of intelligence. If God "owes" us the truth, this is because He is perfect, noble, good, and truthful, and He cannot but wish to be what He is and to act in a consequential way; He does not have the "power" not to be perfect, hence not to be God. It is important to understand that from the moment God created the lion He "owed" it zebras that look like zebras and nothing else; the apparent divine "debt" is nothing other than the immanent logic of the cosmos; in other words this "debt" does not result from a lack of freedom or power but simply from the necessary homogeneity of the world.[11]

In order to express the idea that man is mere nothingness in relation to the Absolute, one could say he is only a dog, which would be false, for a dog is not nothingness, nor conversely; but this is what certain theologians seem to say, metaphorically speaking. Viewed from the stratosphere, man in fact disappears, as he likewise disappears in the abyss of time; thus there are points of view that reveal the nothingness of man, but there is no point of view that can reduce him purely and simply to an animal, nor is there any point of view that allows one to think the human mind is unworthy of logic on the part of its Creator; otherwise religious teachings would be in vain.

By reducing the nature of the Universe to the exclusive relationship "Creator-creature", thus confining it to an inescapable alternative, one is prevented from being able to recognize that creation is necessary, or rather that it has an aspect of necessity. Intellectually,

---

[11] For "all things are *Ātmā*"; it is this homogeneity that is expressed by the Hindu myth of the "sacrifice of *Purusha*".

however, this restrictive opinion is not inevitable: indeed we fail to see why it would be an imperfection for God to manifest Himself by necessity when everyone admits that it is neither restrictive nor humiliating for Him to have qualities He necessarily possesses; we have said this already and do not hesitate to stress it again. Universal Manifestation—creation—is nothing other than the pouring forth of a divine Quality, and if its necessity is by no means imperfect but on the contrary signifies a perfection, this is precisely because Manifestation, inasmuch as it is a divine Quality, goes beyond the alternative "Creator-creature"; from this point of view the world is "none other" than an aspect of *Ātmā*. *Māyā* is a divine aspect mysteriously projected toward a nothingness that is by definition nonexistent and therefore never attained but always intimated; *Māyā* is this intimation itself, extending from Being down to the most infinitesimal privations and the spatial void. The duality "Creator-creature" is situated in *Māyā*; *Ātmā* alone transcends it.

In reply to the argument that creation must be "gratuitous" on pain of imputing "constraint" to God—as if gratuitousness did not have an aspect of infirmity and as if necessity did not have an aspect of perfection derived from absoluteness—we might express ourselves thus: God is unlimited, and He will therefore manifest His Unlimitedness; He is good, and He will therefore manifest His Goodness; He is powerful, and He will therefore manifest His Power; and this is why He creates the world.[12] Manifestation is not a constraint from outside—from a nonexistent outside—but a dimension of the divine Nature, if one may put it this way, and indeed it has as much right to be so described as any other quality of God; and if we assert that God is One, we do not inquire whether He is obliged to be so. Divine Necessity is free, and divine Freedom is necessary; God is not limited by His Nature, and His Freedom cannot not be.

Like all Semitic theologians Ashari has in mind only the opposition between the created and the Creator and not the participation—none-

---

[12] According to Saint Thomas Aquinas, "Every power manifests itself by its effect, for otherwise it would be vain." He also says, "Whatever implies contradiction is not contained in the divine Omnipotence, because this is outside the notion of the possible" (*Summa Theologica*, Part 1, Quest. 25, Art. 2 and 3); this answers erroneous speculations concerning the limitlessness of divine Possibility, speculations that tend to attribute inconsistencies to God for the sake of gratuitous glorification.

theless necessary—of the former in the latter, whence the negation of secondary causes and natural laws that is characteristic of Asharism. It is as if one could see only the warp and not the woof in a piece of fabric; this is a curiously fragmentary image of the cosmos, one that pays no attention to a whole dimension of existence—that of cosmic or natural causality—but replaces it arbitrarily by God. We say "arbitrarily" because one could put God in the place of any other cosmic reality, denying for instance the role of the Prophet on the pretext that God alone speaks, not an intermediary. We could equally well maintain that only fruits are real and trees nonexistent because God alone provides the fruits.

In replying to the criticism of Averroes, Ghazzali thinks it is possible to defend the Asharite negation of secondary causes by replacing them with angels, by means of whom—or in whom—God causes physical burning; but this is wasted effort, for if God can or must use angelic powers or subtle substances to bring about burning, He can also use—or must use—physical substances or powers. "Must" does not in this case mean "being forced" *ab extra* but remaining within the logic of His own nature; for if we say that God cannot not be God, this does not at all mean He is "forced to be God", hence determined *ab extra, quod absit.*

If on the one hand there is opposition between Creator and creature, there is also on the other hand unity of Essence; this is what the exoteric point of view cannot grasp, incapable as it is of allowing for more than one relationship and of understanding the simultaneity of antinomic relationships. It therefore admits only one, which is the most apparent and opportune relationship from the human point of view, and since this relationship alone is not enough to satisfy all the presentiments of our mind, the gaps are filled with emotional sublimations, in which the very excessiveness of the image takes the place of profundity and mystery.

One of the characteristic features of the Semitic mind—all the glory of which is to be found in its prophetism and nowhere else—is the tendency to reduce things to simplistic and all too readily moralizing alternatives; this tendency has its symbolic value and efficacy, but it gives rise to many abuses. Theologians know—metaphorically speaking—that a given object is not white and therefore conclude that it is black, as if this were the only choice; and if perfection is roundness and they conceive of this exclusively in the form of a circle, they will declare that a sphere is not round because it is not a plane figure, and so on. We have here what is undoubtedly a general characteristic of the human mind insofar as it is easily duped by "points of view" and "aspects"—this is even necessary to one degree or another at the level of doctrinal formulation—but there is an essential difference between a limited starting-point that opens up horizons and a limiting concept that closes them in advance; this has no bearing on mystical intuitions, which retain all their freedom as well as all their secret.

Alternativism—that is, the prejudice of seeing in every relative and therefore reconcilable opposition a fundamental and irreconcilable one that would force us spiritually and morally into a violent choice—induced the early rationalists of Islam, the Mutazilites, to see an incompatibility between the Qualities of God and His Unity; from this resulted a tendency either to deny the diversity of these Qualities or even to deny them altogether. One finds the same alternative for the Mutazilites between Justice and Predestination and the same incapacity for seeing that these are two faces of a single reality or two different relationships. The inability to reconcile the pure spirituality of God—or His "nonmateriality"—with the possibility of a beatific vision stems from the same intellectual limitation.

Asharism reacted against the rationalism of the Mutazilites but was unable to overcome the alternativist tendency or, in general terms, a certain lack of sense for the relativity of things, and this meant that it could not get beyond the passional logic or the anthropomorphist and simplistic voluntarism that are typical of exoterism. One sees this in the inability of the Asharites—and before them the Hanbalites, of whom they are in some respects heirs[13]—to reconcile relative or cosmic causality with absolute or divine causality and in their violent and stubborn choice of the second at the expense of the first; this is a choice clearly observed in their claim that it is "hypocrisy" (*nifāq*) to

---

[13] Though quite paradoxically, for Hanbalism is the open foe of all interpretative speculation (*ta'wīl*); but Ashari took care not to oppose any of its orthodox theses, including those of Ibn Hanbal.

admit ordinary causality—the laws of nature, for example—because this would be to "associate" (*ashraka*) an "aid" (*walī*) with God, of whom He has no need and whose existence is impossible since God is One; but this is to suppose that earthly causality, which merely reflects divine causality, could prevent it from being what it is and from acting simultaneously with the appearance of physical causation! Such simplistic alternatives are the price one must pay for a doctrine that is intended to teach us about God but that contains no more than can be grasped by the most rudimentary and uninspired reason, whence the paradox of a wisdom that must force metaphysical truths into the mold of a mentality unable to encompass them.

When one sees the effect of a fire there is unquestionably a certain spiritual beauty in admitting that God alone performs the miracle of burning or, when one grasps an object, in admitting that this power of movement can come only from God, who alone is powerful—hence in remembering thus and on every occasion that "there is no god but God"; but one would prefer these to be spontaneous acts of awareness, limited to the particular relationship they perceive, and not the applications of a scholasticism that violates the natural evidence of things and thus common sense.

An inability to understand the notion of *Māyā*—which is basically that of relativity and of the infinitely varied play of relationships between the relative and the Absolute—may be either fundamental or accidental; if accidental, it may result either from a man's surroundings or else from a spiritual vocation that preceded doctrinal reflection and that determines it in the direction of an emotional mysticism. But it may also be the result of a simple difficulty of expression or a concern for religious psychology, and in these two cases it is merely apparent; it enters nonetheless into the destiny of those concerned—not as an "incapacity", certainly, but as an "absence" of complete or fully conscious understanding. Certain ideas can be found in the works of theologians that prove them capable of understanding a particular truth they deny or that prove they understand it indirectly or virtually, or that they could accept it if they had the opportunity to approach it in a completely different way; in short, the rejection of a notion may be the result of surroundings, vocation, or destiny; in such cases the accent is not on intellectual intuition but on realizational fervor. For some individuals a given truth may have the effect of neutralizing this fervor, while for others it can stimulate it; there are spiritual outpourings that need a certain narrowness and instinctively refuse openings that are too large. Thus it is not exclusively a question of truth, whether more or less ample or profound, but also of spiritual economy and equilibrium of energies.

What we have just said allows us to specify further that there is a link between religious exoterism and the systematic way of love, a bhaktism that is at once limitative and explosive: salvific certainties that engage the whole man act on the sensibility and provoke enthusiasm; this enthusiasm is in turn concentrated upon a single point, neglecting or rejecting all the rest, and it is for this reason that the elephant—to borrow an Eastern metaphor—is identified by some blind men with the trunk, by others with the tusks; such simplifying concentration is all the stronger inasmuch as man is will—from the point of view in question—and truth is what is capable of determining the will in a spiritual direction. Certainly every truth determines the will in one fashion or another, but it is the emphasis that counts here; a will integrated into the contemplation of truth is one thing, and a notion of the truth narrowed to suit the needs of a volitive nature is another. Some souls present a curious mixture of contemplativity and impulsiveness: profound intuitions unleash violent exteriorizations—exteriorizations that are one-sided precisely because of their very violence; such souls find compensation in a quasi-rationalism, which tends to codify both contemplation and impulse.

Only the idea of *Māyā* permits the combination of two causalities—the physical, which is "horizontal", and the metaphysical, which is "vertical"; in the absence of this idea one "takes short cuts", that is, one must sacrifice the bothersome dimension. This is the meaning of the Buddhist *upāya*, the "saving means", which is itself illusory: a spiritually effective error is a mercy, and it is its very efficacy that here takes the place of truth; in fact a notion that leads to truth, whatever the reason, is virtually true, which amounts to saying—to reverse the order—that truths that are too elevated may actually become errors in the consciousness of a man who is too earthly or passionate. Let us take this occasion to note that the idea of *upāya* essentially implies the ideas of "aspect" and "standpoint", which means that every formulation is derived objectively from "aspect" and subjectively from "standpoint"; this is also set forth in the introductory sentence of the *Tao Te Ching*: "The name that can be named is not the true Name."

In order to situate the Asharite mentality correctly, we must therefore take into account the fact—paradoxical in some respects—that it coincides largely with the viewpoint of love, not in the sense of *bhakti* itself but of its doctrinal systematization. The protagonists of Vishnuism, whose sanctity is obviously no more in dispute than that of the great spokesmen of *kalām*, see fit to assert against the *Māyā* of Shankara that souls, like the physical world, are real, which is something Shankara never denied, for the notion of *Māyā* does not contradict relative reality but simply annuls it at the level of absolute Reality; now it is precisely the alternativist mindset, the inability to reconcile apparent antinomies on a higher plane, and the failure to understand both relativity and absoluteness that are common to Semitic exoterism and Hindu bhaktism. The great Vaishnavas—especially Madhva, with his abrupt dualism (*dvaitavāda*)—conceive only of creative Being and not the unqualified Essence, for their ontological "positivism" cannot reconcile two levels of reality, one of which annuls or in a way absorbs the other, though without preventing the other from remaining fully real at its own level; being above all operative and emotional, this "positivism" cannot accept a reality that is woven of relativities and that is in a way transparent and fluid, for according to its way of looking at things it needs solid bases, hence simple and definitive distinctions—a simplicity, given the complexity of Reality, that becomes crude wherever it does not really apply.

Every religious exoterism is voluntaristic, hence moralistic, and in its fashion belittles intelligence; bhaktism does the same: for Ramanuja, *gnosis*—*jñāna*—can be nothing more than a merely mental meditation on the divine perfections, and this is something that obviously has no direct relationship to Deliverance. It is moreover significant that bhaktism feels itself obliged to reduce the divinities—the personified "divine aspects" of the Hindu pantheon—to mere creatures; its alternativist mindset prevents it from reconciling these aspects with the One and Personal God it needs.

If we look for a prime mover in Asharism, it is the wish to relate everything, absolutely everything, to the divine Cause alone: it is the negation of all cosmic or "horizontal" relationships in favor of "vertical" or ontological relationships, as if the first were incompatible with the second and as if the "horizontal" relationships were not on the contrary the necessary images of the "vertical" and invested with the same right to existence as the things to which they refer.

The Near-Easterner of earlier times was unquestionably a man of impulse: on the spur of some apparently obvious fact, whether real or illusory, he would leap at it and pin it down, all the while embellishing it with superlatives; these three responses come easily to the combative temperament, for the warrior must charge: without exaggerating he would not conquer, and without pinning things down he would allow himself to become distracted. When we encounter an apparently absurd idea—one that is in fact absurd at the level of its expression—we must strive to disentangle these three factors: leaping, pinning down, and exaggeration, so as to reach the cause of the phenomenon, namely, an intellectual or mystical bedazzlement in response to some aspect of the Real. A classic example of how extravagance can be the price of profundity or sincerity is the following argument: a man who loves God must not wish to go to Paradise since God would perhaps prefer to put him in hell—as if God did not wish Paradise for those who love Him and as if for this very reason He did not want man to wish the same! Certainly a man may abstain from every eschatological desire as a result of contemplating the Immutable, but then he remains humanly neutral; he does not confuse his individual sentiments with the affairs of the Absolute, nor does he express his metaphysical neutrality by human absurdities; no man ever dreamed of committing suicide simply because he is nothing in the eyes of the Absolute.

A well-known Sufi saying belongs to much the same category: "Paradise is the prison of the sage (*'ārif*)"; the meaning is not hard to make out: the created could never constitute the bliss of those who have taken hold of the Uncreated or been taken hold of by it; but in reality Paradise is so constituted that it is a prison for no one; the over-simplification of such a formulation has absolutely no connection with the complex and multidimensional nature of the celestial states. While we are on this subject we might note that the sentimentalist cult of suffering in Catholicism gives rise to entirely similar excesses:[14] a mystic has said that the angels envy earthly men for being able to suffer for the love of God, which would justify our inquiring whether Christian saints regret being in heaven and unable to suffer any longer and, if so, what the bliss promised to the elect consists of. As in similar Islamic formulations, there are two aspects to consider: first, the objective aspect of absurdity, which pure and simple truth does not allow us to overlook; and second, the subjective aspect of "zeal for the house of the Lord", which the love of God obliges us to discern unhesitatingly and even to approve.

Arab thought, at least in certain sectors, is above all an act; it seems that the more spiritual it is, and therefore the more prone to inspiration, the more volatile it is and the more it segregates things; for this reason it easily takes on an appearance of impulsiveness and discontinuity, and to understand it we have to interpret its expressions in depth, not necessarily according to a long-winded logical sequence but more often than not according to underlying intentions that are more or less isolated from one another. In any case what this segregating exaggeration aims to insure—an exaggeration that violates the logic of a context that has in fact been forgotten—is the distinctness of the image on the one hand and the effectiveness of the discourse on the other; the European is rather insensitive to this dialectic, and the result is an immense gap between the two mentalities, which is both regrettable and providential.[15]

At the heart of Muslim obedientialism there is the profound truth—already indicated by the term *islām* ("surrender")—that man is fundamentally happy only in obedience, and this is because he is

---

[14] We do not criticize this cult, which is the subjective means of a certain type of mysticism, but we reject any doctrine that presents it as the sole truth and the sole means of reaching God.

[15] To these difficulties may be added another, namely, that the Arabs—given their linguistic narcissism, if one may so express it—are sometimes more preoccupied with semantics than logic in the sense that even an indirect or conjectural verbal connotation can take the place of argument, sometimes counter to what is otherwise obvious.

a fragment, or rather a "fragmentary totality", and therefore does not have his final end within him. But in order to produce its full effect—that is, in order that obedience may be compounded of certainty and peace—it is necessary for its motive to be intelligible, for whoever says "faith" says "trust", and man cannot submit in truth and with happiness to the unintelligible and absurd; it is precisely this that is forgotten by theologians, who tend to reduce metaphysics to a sort of morality, thus running the risk of robbing their moral concern of its entire basis. But it is necessary to reserve for human nature a certain right to error within the framework of truth, and it is for this reason—because a man rarely has the gift of being complete in every dimension of the spirit—that "divergence among the doctors of the Law is a blessing", according to the Prophet.

The logical "segregationism" or "fragmentarianism" we referred to above has the grave disadvantage of not bringing out an entire thought when it ought to be brought out: one-sided assertions are proffered, whose limitations are nonetheless known, and the proof they are known is that diametrically opposite assertions are presented elsewhere. For example, when Ghazzali opines that "listening to the voice of a bird and looking at the greenness of a landscape mean a greater privation in the next life", it is impossible to assume that he was ignorant of the root of the question, which is that everything depends on whether our attitude is one of passionate attachment or contemplative nonattachment, and indeed he suggests this crucial truth in his reflections on *gnosis*, which consists in seeing God everywhere or everything in God, and on equilibrium, which consists in avoiding extremes;[16] or again, if in one passage the same author expresses himself like the most limited Asharite by declaring outright that God is the cause of both good and evil, he explains in another passage—quite judiciously

---

[16] It is curious, to say the least, that a man who acknowledges metaphysical transparency in the case of sexuality forgets this transparency in the case of other phenomena that are no less symbolic; but it is possible Ghazzali simply neglected to indicate a particular relationship—in keeping with the habit of Muslim writers—and that he was referring to the fact of "shutting oneself" inside a sensation rather than "moving through" it. In other words sensual pleasure is either an "association" (of something else with God, *shirk*) or an indirect experience of "unification" (between the soul and God, *tawhīd*); without this second possibility there would be no sacred art, not even Koranic calligraphy.

this time—that God "wills the good to the extent it is good, but He wills what is evil, not to the extent it is evil, but for the sake of the good it contains, evil being accidental and good essential." In spite of his all too ostentatious solidarity with Asharite *kalām*, Ghazzali does not forget to point out that "God does not disappoint the hopes of the one who loves Him"; this should have been said alongside the troubling paradoxes of conventional omnipotentialism. Finally, Ghazzali has the merit of emphasizing—against the opinion of the most dryly obedientialist theologians—that man cannot "love by obedience since this is instead the consequence and the fruit of love, love itself being the key"; this is what one would like to have heard *a priori* in keeping with the Koranic verse on the pre-eminence of Mercy.

Someone could perhaps find fault with us for the same fragmentarianism by pointing out passages in the works of the authors we have criticized that we have not taken into account, but this has no connection with our purpose; for it is one thing to criticize authors while being unacquainted with certain passages in their works—and they deserve such criticism precisely because of the defect of fragmentarianism—and it is another to present weighty truths in a fragmentary manner, which inevitably leads to confusion. Ashari defended himself by claiming that it was necessary to have read him completely in order to judge him, but one cannot logically demand the acceptance of an absurd idea because of what one will write the next day, *Deo volente*, or because of what one has written in another book. A partial proposition must always include the tenor of the whole message, at least negatively by avoiding absurdities.

—— ·:· ——

The great weakness of the protagonists of *kalām* is to apply anthropomorphism to what most completely eludes being made anthropomorphic in God, namely, Beyond-Being or the supra-ontological Essence, and to confuse Beyond-Being with its ontological self-determination: creative, revealing, and saving Being.[17] This is to confuse—in the

---

[17] Let us note here that Meister Eckhart clearly defined this *distinguo* by calling Beyond-Being *die Gottheit*, "the Divinity", while reserving the word *Gott*, "God", for

absence of the notion of *Māyā*[18]—two totally different divine subjectivities, the first corresponding to *Paramātmā*, in Vedantic terms, and the second to *Īshvara* or even *Buddhi*,[19] according to the degrees considered; and it is this confusion that constitutes the characteristic infirmity of Asharism in particular and *kalām* in general, and even of all doctrinal exoterism to one degree or other.

According to Ibn Arabi, the meaning of sin is that God orders a legal or virtuous act but may not wish for it to be realized, or he wishes a forbidden act to happen but *a priori* forbids his servant from accomplishing it;[20] this is a typically Asharite formulation, for the divine Subject here is double, the "God" who orders an act being in no way the same Subject as the "God" who does not "wish" the realization of this act. There is something monstrous about an anthropomorphic *Paramātmā*, and all the speculations based upon it lead to a deficient metaphysic—those for example that seek to show that Iblis, the devil, obeyed the "divine Will" even in violating the commandment of God; it can be seen here how this anthropomorphic concept of the "divine Will", which encompasses realities that are in some respects antinomic, confuses the ontological and the moral, the Absolute and the human. Moreover, the error in question cannot simply be reduced to the anthropomorphist confusion of Beyond-Being and Being; by the same token it also implies a confusion of Pure Being with determinative and existence-generating Qualities, and this again amounts to a mixture of two universal but in fact different Subjectivities, always without prejudice to the unity of essence.[21] This whole

---

Being, which is the divine self-personification.

[18] Or rather in the absence of its application, for *Māyā* in Islam is *Hijāb*, "Veil".

[19] The macrocosmic Intellect, the manifested "Spirit" of God.

[20] Ibn Arabi distinguishes between an "existential commandment" (*amr takwīnī*) and a "circumstantial commandment" (*amr taklīfī*); to the extent the respective objects of the two commandments are ontologically different, hence unlikely to come together in the same domain, this necessitates taking into consideration a distinction internal to the Divinity.

[21] This principle of the pluralization of the divine Subject, or of a given *hypostasis* of this Subject, finds an application in the plurality of the law-giving *Logos*, hence of religions: when Heaven speaks to man, it personifies itself in relation to a human receptacle or a particular possibility of formal expression, whence the apparent contradictions not only between one religion and another but sometimes also within the fold

problem—like the corresponding problems in Christianity that result from the dogma of the Trinity—shows that it is impossible to practice integral metaphysics on the basis of axioms treated apart from the key notion of *Māyā*.

By the very nature of things the early Muslims necessarily had at their disposal an intrinsically sufficient doctrine, although in fact it was insufficient for dealing with heresies that were to arise later on; witness this saying of Hasan ibn Ali: "One does not obey God by compulsion, and one does not disobey Him under the sway of an irresistible force; He has not left His servant completely without initiative in His Kingdom"; witness also this perfect formulation of Kalabadhi: "By free will we mean that God has created in us a free will, and this is why there is no question of compulsion in our conforming (*tafwīd*) to God." The theologians would not deny this, but they annul it all the same—in fact if not in intention—by a simplistic and heavy determinism.

The "Supreme Subject", Beyond-Being—*Ātmā* or *Paramātmā*—cannot "will" cosmic manifestation; being able to will only itself, its lack of creative will must manifest itself in some fashion even within creation, which is willed by the creative *Hypostasis* of *Ātmā*, and this is a distant, paradoxical, and mysterious cause of what we call evil; the creative and conservative "will" of Being conveys the negative "indifference" of Beyond-Being in a subtle and mysterious manner.[22] The other causes of evil are those we have indicated on more than one occasion: on the one hand the remoteness of the world in relation to

of a single religion, depending on its historical span. On the one hand Beyond-Being could never speak; on the other hand Being does speak, but since it adapts itself to the interlocutor, whether singular or collective, the language may vary from one interlocutor to another and give the impression of different subjectivities.

[22] Jili opposed Ibn Arabi on the subject of Omnipotence: whereas for Ibn Arabi God did not create things by taking them out of inexistence but by transferring them from Being-Intellect to Being-Existence, Jili maintains with good reason that there is no antinomy here and that the transfer from one mode of Being to another takes place together with *creatio ex nihilo*; in fact, if existentiation is the projection—into the realm of contingency—of the archetypes contained in creative Being or Prescience-Being, Being in turn is *Māyā* in relation to the supra-ontological Essence; therefore, Prescience also arises *ex nihilo* since only the Pure Absolute—Beyond-Being—is Reality as such and pure Omnipotence. Being—the ontological Principle—is a "divine self-revelation" (*tajallī*) arising *ex nihilo* in relation to the supra-ontological Essence (*Dhāt*).

Being—and this remotion also results from Beyond-Being—and on the other hand the equilibrating function of evil, or let us say simply its "unreal" and limitative reality, whatever its mode or degree.

Voluntaristic theologians and philosophers make two fundamental mistakes: first, they attribute cosmic effects that are in reality derived from different universal Sources to a single divine—though in fact humanized—Subject, forgetting that divine Functions are not Substance or Being and that Being is not Beyond-Being; second, they use the word "will" to refer to all causes even though only some of these are entitled to this anthropomorphic analogy. It is true that the Koran uses symbols that seem to justify all the simplifications in question here, but theology is supposed to be a commentary precisely, and a commentary is for explaining and clarifying things, not complicating them or making them intellectually unintelligible and morally unacceptable.

Even the most narrowly unitarian Muslim is obliged to admit that the divine Quality called "the Merciful" is not the same as the one called "the Avenger"; he must also admit that the Qualities are not the same thing as the Essence. God "wills" the virtuous act since He commands it, while at the same time "willing" sin since sins are committed and nothing happens without the "Will" of God; but the metaphysical cause of sin is something other than the divine Command. On the one hand there is for every man a divine Will that commands the good; on the other hand there is for the world a divine Will connected with a certain cosmologically inevitable or necessary quantity of evil; and every man has the freedom to appropriate this or that universal Will by choosing either good or evil;[23] finally, there is divine Foreknowledge of the choice man will make thanks to the freedom God has bestowed upon him, a freedom that takes the form of a relative participation—real on its own level—in absolute Freedom. And it is only through and in this that man makes himself completely free: the choice of the good is the choice of Freedom.

---

[23] This is what Ashari had the merit of teaching; he opposed the massive determinism of the Jabriyyah with the doctrine of the "appropriation" (*kasb* or *iktisāb*) of divine causes by man.

As for our reservations concerning Asharism and similar theses of an earlier or later date, the root of the problem is basically the whole issue of the evil "willed" by God; let us summarize once more and for the sake of clarity what the problem is. From the point of view of divine Subjectivity, the Will that wills evil is not the same as the Will that wills good; from the point of view of the cosmic object, God does not will evil to the extent it is evil but as a constituent element of a good, hence to the extent it is good. On the other hand evil is never evil in its existential substance, which by definition is willed by God; it is evil only through the cosmic accident of a privation of good, which is willed by God as an indirect element of a greater good. If we are criticized for introducing a duality into God, we acknowledge this without hesitation—though not as a criticism—just as we accept all the differentiations in Divinity, whether hypostatic degrees or qualities or energies; the very existence of polytheism proves our point, notwithstanding a possible deviation and paganization.[24] It is important in any case to distinguish between the divine Will with regard to existence and the divine Will with regard to man, who is intelligence and will: in the first relationship everything that exists or happens is willed by God; in the second only truth and the good are divinely willed.

There is a truth that philosophers are prone to ignore either through unawareness or else by prejudice and on principle: a formulation does not exist to exhaust the reality it expresses but in order to provide a key to the realization of that reality; the spiritual passage from the formulation to the reality is always discontinuous—it is like a leap into the void—just as there is no common measure between the most perfect geometrical figure and the reality of total space, which cannot be depicted.

[24] In its origin polytheism considers the Divinity both as *Ātmā* and in relation to *Māyā*; it becomes pagan only when it forgets *Ātmā* and grants absoluteness to diversity, hence to relativity.

It is doubtless no exaggeration to say that theology occupies a less important position in Islam than it does in Christianity; the best proof of this is the absence of Councils in Islam. In Christianity theology has majestic prototypes in the Gospel of Saint John and in the Epistles, followed by venerable models in the writings of the Fathers of the Church, including Dionysius the Areopagite, and on this foundation it gave rise to the great Scholastics and to the Palamite doctrine in the East. But theology in Islam has no sacred prototype; neither the Koran nor the *Sunnah* contain any such thing, and the first attempts at theology, as we have seen, met with a categorical rejection on the part of the traditionalists, so that in fact the legitimacy of *kalām* remains an open question or one at least not entirely settled; it would therefore be unjust to compare the two theologies—Christian and Muslim—when their respective roles are by no means equivalent except in a completely extrinsic respect. What corresponds best to Christian theology in Islam are the four orthodox ritual schools; but while one cannot be a Catholic without being a Thomist,[25] at least under normal conditions, one can easily be a Malikite or other kind of Muslim without having to accept all the Asharite theses, except of course those clearly coinciding with the unanimously recognized meaning of the tradition.

In other words—to speak very approximately—theology in Islam is rather like what Aristotelianism is in Christianity; Islam, however, is more theological than Christianity is Aristotelian. Theology is a vital element in Christianity whereas in Islam—though it cannot do without it—theology even has an appearance of "innovation" (*bid'ah*), hence of something either blameworthy (*makrūh*) or illicit (*harām*). This last position is that of Hanbalism; and yet it is from Hanbalism that Asharite *kalām* inherited its most questionable theses.

We must mention here certain merits that greatly contributed to the success of Ashari in the Sunni world. First, he safeguarded the rights of interpretative intelligence against the extremists of literal tradition (*naql*) but without minimizing the rights of Revelation, whereas before him the religion seemed to know only extremes—though this does not imply any shortcomings on the part of anti-rationalist traditionalism insofar as it might coincide with Sufism. Furthermore, Ashari

---

[25] Apart from the few Thomistic theses the Church has not retained.

successfully established the right definition of the Koran: according to him it is a Message at once created and uncreated; and he did the same for human liberty, which he defined in a way that was acceptable from the theological point of view by preserving both divine determination and human responsibility. All this—taken together with that hymn of exaltation, his omnipotentialist doctrine—will suffice to explain why Ashari's thought became the bulwark of Sunni exoterism, though not of Islam itself; it is important to stress this reservation, for Islam as such is to be found only in Revelation and the divine Institutions on the one hand and in the *gnosis* of Sufis on the other.

A point we wish to emphasize further in this context is the following: in questions of religion or spirituality, the reasoning of Semites appears to be determined by the wish to communicate an illuminating shock or a moral emotion—not exclusively so but much more readily than in the case of Greeks and Hindus: the premises of an argument may be based on a dogmatic, intellectual, or mystical certitude, but the function of the logical operation is simply to communicate and reinforce what is evident; compared with a dialectic that is concerned with doing justice to the nature of things, it is not impartial and has ceased to be anything more than an extrinsic factor, and this is what explains the weakness of certain arguments of Sufis themselves. The nature of things is perceived in the fundamental givens, whether these are explicit or implicit, but it is not necessarily followed up in the points of reference that reason believes it should supply; in saying this we are aware of entering an extremely subtle sphere where definitions are always hazardous, but the nature of the problem leaves us no choice; there are things one can express only imperfectly but that nonetheless cannot be passed over in silence without leaving a pressing need for explanation unsatisfied.

It is doubtless fitting to distinguish between a static thought, nearer to the Aryan genius, and a dynamic thought, nearer to the Semitic genius; and in order to grasp the most paradoxical of Semitic expressions it is necessary to understand clearly the nature of this dynamism. In using the word "Semitic" we are also referring by extension to Aryans Semiticized by their respective religions, such as Europeans and Irano-Indians, although in these groups the Aryan mentality is able to co-exist with the Semitic mentality, this being most unquestionably so in the case of Christianized Westerners, in whom there is sometimes a veritable schism, pagan antiquity never having been completely eliminated by Christianity. Humanity being one, these two modes of thought—the static and the dynamic—may be found everywhere; they are nonetheless characteristic of the two great groups of white humanity, though only relatively so since the Semites themselves were partially Hellenized.

Aryan thought is—or seeks to be—a recording of what is; Semitic thought presents itself instead as an act, a process of transmission and persuasion; it seeks to be effective and salvific, and it is right to do so in the sense that the truth is properly transmitted only when it takes hold of a man. In the beginning—in the "Golden Age"—the truth pure and simple was salvific by itself, and to a certain extent this is the point of view of Platonism;[26] later it was necessary to reveal the aspect most conducive to its saving effect, and hence it was necessary to clothe it in an argument efficacious for certain mentalities, and this is what the Semitic religions have done. All the same the fundamental enunciations of the religions remain outside these categories: the Christic assertion that "God descended that man might rise" or the Islamic assertion that "there is no god but God", while being Semitic by virtue of their monotheism and dynamism, have at the same time a universal character that is open to every possibility of the spirit.

An example of what we mean by the Semitic spirit is provided at the level of Revelation by the characteristic notions of a heaven and a hell that are both eternal: no doubt this is objective information in the sense that the elect are once and for all within divine Grace—the *apocatastasis* abolishing nothing positive—and the damned will never return to the human state, a definitive exclusion that may be expressed, like the definitive inclusion, by means of the notion of

---

[26] Christian polemics against Platonism are typical in this respect; it is a dialogue between two different languages, one Semitic and the other Aryan. While Platonism itself is obviously not a "wisdom according to the flesh", it can in fact become so in purely philosophic minds for whom the truth commits one to nothing, and it may so appear to religious mentalities of the Semitic kind, for whom truth must be clothed in forms having a volitive finality—forms intended not only to inform but to capture and transform.

eternity.[27] But what is important above all is the moral and spiritual effect of the dogma: man is confronted with definitive realities, and it is precisely the definitive character that reveals the cosmic and divine reality awaiting him, whatever its modalities in the shorter or longer term. It is this innate point of view—this pre-eminence of effective eschatology over what is objectively exact at the moment—that explains, and excuses if necessary, the excesses of a theology more concerned with salvific efficacy than intellectual adequation.[28] In dogmatic formulations, whether at the level of Revelation or theology, it is always necessary to sacrifice the interest of those whose spiritual dissatisfaction offers the least inconvenience: thus the idea of divine Mercy attracts the naturally contemplative man toward God, but it runs the risk of leaving the passional man in his sin if it is presented in too unilateral a way; doctrine will choose to avoid this risk rather than meet the contemplative on his own terms, who in any event is detached from the world by his very nature; in other words the spirit of the contemplative penetrates phenomena, and he is such that the world is withdrawn from him.

In the face of such an ambiguous intellectual phenomenon as Asharite theology, one cannot continue indefinitely weighing the *pro* and *con*; it is necessary to resign oneself to a conclusion that is at least approximate. We return here to an argument we used earlier, namely, that every opinion intended to proclaim the absoluteness of the One or to serve in any way the cause of God while at the same time fitting within a context of traditional orthodoxy compensates by this very

---

[27] What this means is that the damned are excluded from the Grace that concerns human creatures but not from universal Grace, which may appear in innumerable ways outside the cosmic sector of mankind; this is quite apart from the final and apocatastatic reintegration, which also embraces negative existences by fundamentally transmuting them.

[28] In this realm of ideas one could mention the Mahayanic wish to "save all sentient beings down to the last blade of grass", hence the idea that everything must "become Buddha"; absurd as it is in human terms, this formulation nonetheless conceals a truth—as do all exoteric formulations—namely, the truth of the *apocatastasis*, the final reintegration Origen spoke about. We might also mention the ellipses of Trinitarian theology, in which the one divine Essence and the diversity of Persons give rise to a contradictory but symbolically revealing plurality, the intention clearly being to safeguard both Unity and Trinity, which are presented as real on the same level of reality, which is that of the Absolute.

fact for its possible imperfections, provided it does not have a contrary effect in a given environment; but even in this case such an opinion is at least morally excusable. The same is true for men: we must excuse their limitations and weaknesses, not according to our love for them but according to their love for God.

Paradise as Theophany

According to a *hadīth*, "the majority of the dwellers in Paradise are simpleminded" (*bulh*), which does not mean that they are men of little intelligence but that they are men of holy naiveté. This perfectly plausible meaning has not prevented certain commentators from asserting that the saying refers to simpletons, who "are satisfied with the Garden instead of thinking only of the Gardener"—who stop short, in other words, with the created and lose sight of the Creator.[1] The forced character of this interpretation is apparent in the very form of the symbolism: in fact the image of a garden and a gardener is poorly chosen, for a gardener is there for the garden and not the other way round; a gardener is without interest outside of his professional work, whereas God on the contrary is the reason for the existence of Paradise. Different imagery should have been used: for example, that it is absurd to honor the palace more than the king or to love the wedding gown while forgetting the bride.

But such expressions, though they are adequate in relation to the aspect of separateness, which is the exclusive interest of some men, are nonetheless inadequate in relation to the total nature of celestial reality. Paradise is above all a dimension that unites us to God; rather than being the bride's gown, it is her very body, and it is therefore what manifests outwardly the mystery of the Personality that is loved. In this respect Paradise is a reflection of God and not a veil concealing Him; it is the "Outward" (*al-Zāhir*), which prolongs or refracts the "Inward" (*al-Bātin*), somewhat as a rainbow prolongs or refracts pure and uncolored light. If the created did not have the mysterious function of manifesting the Uncreated, it would be impossible to explain this saying of a Companion of the Prophet: "I never saw anything without seeing God."

It is precisely man's mission to combine the vision of "the Inward" with that of "the Outward", to be at once witness to God as Principle and to God as Manifestation or Theophany, for "everything is *Ātmā*".

---

[1] The Arabic root *blh* gives rise to a double meaning, that of "ingenuousness" and that of "foolishness", but the form used in the *hadīth* has the first meaning and not the second.

Therefore, man has an express right to both these perspectives; they constitute the sufficient reason for his existence and consequently define him; in other words man is essentially *pontifex*, the link between Earth and Heaven and between the Outward and the Immanent.[2]

The very notion of the Beatific Vision implies that the joys of Paradise or modes of Beatitude cannot be situated outside the divine Presence; the idea of preferring a pleasure to God therefore has no meaning here; it is merely an illegitimate transposition of an earthly possibility into the heavenly world. The existence of the paradisiacal degrees, with their increasingly direct and intimate participation in divine Reality, could at most serve as an extenuating circumstance for this idea; it could then be said that from the point of view of the "Paradise of the Essence", which is none other than supreme Union, the other Paradises imply so many modes of separativity or cosmic illusion; but this truth is in fact not expressible in voluntaristic or moral terms.

The problematical image of the "fools who people Paradise"—and who through their foolishness are satisfied with the "Garden" while overlooking the "Gardener"—calls for the following objection above all: to forget God is to sin, and it is even the essence of sin; now in Paradise one cannot sin, and one enjoys moreover the Beatific Vision; thus one could not have an attitude or state that merits the adjective "foolish". The inconsistency of the image of the "foolish elect"—and similar images—shows how little the spiritual and didactic intention found in certain Oriental circles is concerned with the coherence of the imagery; let logic perish, provided the moral or mystical suggestion is saved. Hasty and simplistic disparagements of Paradise obviously serve to stress the supereminence of the Creator, but the immediate objection to this is that God requires praise, which is in our interest, but not flattery, which serves no one and is an insult to Him; in fact the purpose of praise is not to please a tyrant but on the contrary to actualize our awareness of the divine Source of all goods and therefore

---

[2] Christian theology specifies that the blessed in Paradise love the other blessed "in God" and rejoice in their beatitude and that they know creatures "with God"—but not all possible creatures—and everything that relates to their own state. It is taught in Islam as well that being conscious of the glory of the blessed is part of beatitude but that the essence of beatitude is contemplation of God.

to show forth our human function, which consists in connecting the cosmic qualities to God so as to see them in God and God in them.

To say that Paradise is of little value is either a truism or "hypocritical angelism": it is a truism if one means that only the Absolute is absolutely real, and it is "angelism" if one means that the human individual ought to disdain the graces that are proportionate to his nature. Opinions of this kind are morally disproportionate, hence humanly absurd—as would be the assertion that the Prophet merits no consideration since he is not *Allāh*; it is to forget that Paradise—like the Prophet—is a theophany and in this respect cannot be treated as the created ought to be treated when considered in its nondivinity or separativity.

In pointing this out we are not overlooking the fact that the intention of the formulations at issue could be to correct the misinterpretations that the literal meaning of the Scriptures gives rise to in imperfect souls, though without of course correcting this meaning itself, and to do this for the sake of the spiritual disciples to whom these formulations are addressed and whose vocation is precisely to rise above the ordinary human level. All things considered, there are many assumptions and extenuating circumstances that may serve to excuse an idealism that is strangely insensitive to images and words, though even so it is not possible to fully justify a procedure that consists in correcting one imperfection with another.[3]

In this context we would also like to mention the following *hadīth*: "The here-below is forbidden (*harām*) to the people of the hereafter (*ahl al-ākhirah*); the hereafter is forbidden to the people of the here-below (*ahl al-dunyā*); and the here-below and the hereafter are forbidden to the people of God (*ahl Allāh*)." This teaching means that

---

[3] It is necessary to take into account the quality of Arab-Muslim thought, which is inspirationist, impulsive, expeditious, segregating, and contrasting—"henotheist" in a certain sense in its blunt and hyperbolic accentuation of a given aspect of the real but at the same time capable of a perfectly static and disinterested rigor, which after all is just what thought should be when it conveys the truth.

men who desire Paradise must not put their faith in the things of this world, that men who put their faith in the things of this world will not have access to Paradise, and that men who put their faith in God need not worry about either the here-below or the hereafter. Moreover, a distinction is made here between ordinary devout souls, who limit themselves to obeying the divine Law in hope of the promised reward, and initiates or saints, who aspire to God through intelligence and love, hence by virtue of their nature; but this distinction does not authorize our denying a real participation in the Beatific Vision to the simplest of the saved, a Vision that permeates so to speak the entire paradisiacal Substance. In speaking of the "people of the hereafter", the *hadīth* we have quoted says that the here-below is forbidden them, but it does not say God is forbidden them, *quod absit*; in Heaven there are doubtless different degrees of Beatific Vision or Union—"in my Father's house are many mansions"—but there is not one category of blessed souls who alone contemplate God and another of those who do not.

As for the "people of God",[4] it is important not to overlook the fact that the idea of Paradise is part of their perspective with regard to transcendence; Buddhism offers particularly clear examples of this, given its initial concept of *Nirvāna*: the idea of the celestial homeland—the "Pure Land"—comes to refer to a certain mode of nirvanic or divine Radiation, not to a "creation" conceived of as "other than God"; the paradisiacal region appears as the emanation of the "uncreated" Center and as the human aura of the mystery of the Beatific Vision or supreme Union.

The intention of the *hadīth* we quoted is first of all to take into account certain essential differences that are in the nature of things but not to define or delimit these differences exhaustively; next to raise the level of faith by admonishing men to emphasize God alone;[5] then to bring faith—for those so called—to its quintessence and total "sincerity" (*ikhlās, sidq*); and finally to provide a reminder that everything

---

[4] Men whose primary spiritual motivation is the reality of God and not hope for reward or fear of punishment.

[5] The common religion obviously is addressed to fallen man and takes into account his weaknesses. Our *hadīth* makes a distinction first between the worldly and the spiritual and then, among the spiritual, between exoterists and esoterists.

good, whether earthly or heavenly, is such only "through God" and "in God".[6] *Nemo bonus nisi solus Deus.*

The prototype *in divinis* of Paradise—or of the heavenly mansions—is the plane of the divine Qualities, some of which pertain to the Essence itself. The "Garden" is a *hypostasis* before being a theophany.[7]

To speak of man is to speak of divine vision and human ambience. There is an inward vision and an outward vision of the Real: inwardly—"the Kingdom of Heaven is within you"—the intelligence has in principle a presentiment or perception of the divine Self, which is the one and indivisible Essence even though it presents different aspects and degrees to man; outwardly, the intelligence perceives the Real according to cosmic Relativity or according to Possibility unfolded and diversified: in relativizing or exteriorizing itself, the Real unfolds like a fan or the plumage of a peacock. From the point of view of individualistic and sentimental voluntarism, this manifestation—seductive for passional man—will be piously disparaged; from the point of view of intellectual discernment and contemplation, the world appears on the contrary as a theophany, and it is pre-eminently so in its celestial or paradisiacal center, which no longer contains any privative or subversive modality.

In Mahayanic language it is said that the *Pratyeka Buddha* turns his back on *samsāra* and looks toward *Nirvāna* whereas the *Bodhisattva* perceives *Nirvāna* also in *samsāra*—which cannot be of another substance—and thus abolishes the opposition between the outward and the inward. *Mutatis mutandis* this was also the perspective of the Prophet, who—according to Ibn Arabi[8]—perceived God in woman, who "was made lovable unto me" (*hubiba ilayya*) by *Allāh* by virtue

---

[6] But the *hadīth* does not in any case wish to corroborate extravagances such as this: it is better to think of God in hell than to forget Him in Paradise. This may well be a kind of *yin-yang* containing a plausible symbolism, but it is perfectly nonsensical and, practically speaking, a two-edged sword.

[7] The "Graciousness of *Allāh*" (*Ridwān*) is situated as it were between God and Paradise, which means that it is a kind of link uniting them. In fact the Koran teaches us that in Paradise there are streams, pure spouses, and the "Graciousness of God" (*Sūrah* "The Family of Imran" [3]:15) and that this Graciousness is the "greatest" gift (*Sūrah* "Repentence" [9]:72).

[8] *Fusūs al-Hikam*, chap. "*Kalimah Muhammadiyyah*".

of the very transparency of the feminine theophany;[9] and in the same order of ideas it is necessary to quote this *hadīth qudsī*: "I was a hidden treasure, and I wished to be known; therefore I created the world." The world—and with all the more reason Paradise, which is its luminous quintessence—represents in fact a knowledge of the Essence: God unfolds His possibilities in differentiated mode, and He created man in order to have a witness to this unfolding; in other words He projects Himself into Relativity in order to perceive Himself in relative mode. Moreover, this unfolding—on pain of being impossible—is prefigured *in divinis*, whence the distinction between the Essence and the Qualities, the second element pertaining in fact to Relativity or *Māyā*. Ordinary monotheistic theologies are scarcely capable of expressing this adequately because they operate only with the entirely insufficient alternative of "created" and "Uncreated": there is for them only God and the world, the Creator and the created, whereas in reality there is first of all the Absolute and the relative, and then within Relativity there is the creative Uncreated—not the Uncreated in itself—and all that is created.

Strictly speaking—and we have already alluded to this—the alternative could be transposed to the divine level, and thus the opposition between the "created" and the "Uncreated" could be replaced with that between the "personal God" and the "impersonal Divinity", hence between Being and Beyond-Being: Being in fact includes the diversity of the divine Qualities and existential Prototypes. In this perspective Beyond-Being would be the "Gardener", but He is in turn "Garden" by virtue of His Infinitude, the source of Being and thus of Existence.

---

[9] Since the human being is by definition a manifestation of God, each of the sexes manifests God additionally in a particular manner; man expresses more the Absolute and woman more the Infinite.

Atomism and Creation

Asharite unitarianism may be regarded as both an atomism and an occasionalism, depending on whether causality is conceived symbolically in spatial or temporal mode; in both cases the intention is to safeguard the absolute Unity and Omnipotence of God when confronted with the complexity of the hypostatic order. The starting point is plausible: to say that God alone is absolutely one, hence incomparable or "unassociable" (*lā sharīka lahu*), amounts to saying that He alone is absolutely simple, hence indivisible; as a result no created substance can be perfectly "dense": every substance must be as if "aerated" by the threat of nothingness, which Ashari expresses by saying that creation is recreated "at every moment"—and arbitrarily so, he thinks, since God "doeth what He will".

Indisputably, there is a basis of truth in Asharite atomism, and necessarily so since what is in question is a theology that *grosso modo* is orthodox. It has to be remembered that the word "atom", which is Greek, does not mean what is "unextended"—something inconceivable in the spatial order—but what is indivisible *de facto*, which is altogether different. The metaphysical reason that created things—and first of all the universal substance itself[1]—necessarily include an element of limitation and separativity is the gap between the Principle and Manifestation, God and the world, the Uncreated and the created; since the Principle alone is absolute Reality, it alone is situated beyond all trace of nothingness. Indeed all that exists necessarily includes this trace to some degree; this is why cosmic substance with its productions and cosmic energy with its effects must have a discontinuous character; it is precisely this discontinuity that marks the presence of the element of nothingness, which distinguishes the created from the Uncreated. Moreover this is why creation must be at once multiple and vibratory: the Unity of God not only requires that there be multiple worlds—since absolute Unity can belong only to God—but also that the worlds be repeated, as is taught by the Hindu doctrine of cosmic cycles; this means that the co-eternity of the world must be discontinuous, hence multiple, like cosmic existence itself. This prin-

---

[1] Of which ether is the reflection in the world of space and matter.

175

ciple of universal "porosity" and "vibration" applies to the principial order itself, and there is no contradiction here since the Principle prefigures within itself the scission between itself and its Manifestation: this is the well-known distinction between Being and Beyond-Being. It is with Being that the reign of *Māyā* begins, which by definition implies the presence of a trace of nothingness, hence of illusion;[2] therefore, only the Essence is absolutely the Principle, and in this lies the basis of the profound divergence between *gnosis* and theology.

The idea of a quasi-"historical" creation—despite the ineffectual precautions of Ghazzali—resulted in the Asharite image of a creation destroyed and renewed at every "moment"; this theological "atomism" nonetheless has the merit of being a symbol of relativity, which is woven of "yes" and "no". Thus it gave rise in Sufism to a valid theory, namely, the "renewing of creation at each breath" (*tajdīd al-khalq bil-anfas*), according to which the succession of "moments" is purely logical: in fact the immanence of the creative *Logos* in all things must have a quasi-"temporal" and dynamic aspect along with what we might call its "spatial" and static aspect; the divine immanence is not only a presence comparable to that of ether, *mutatis mutandis*, but also an incessant flow, pouring forth into the pre-existential "void". By definition all existence is existentiation because of the infinitude of the Principle: if the absoluteness of the Principle requires that things be, instead of not being, infinitude for its part requires that they be infinitely, as it were; in both cases outward and existential limitation must be compensated for by an inward and transcendent unlimitedness, or else this limitation would dissolve into nothingness. And all this contradicts neither the emanationism of the Hellenistic philosophers nor the causationism of the Mutazilites, whereas Ashari believed he had to reject both these doctrines.

The decisive error of Ashari—but ultimately it has its providential function and nothing happens by chance—is his total voluntarism: he attributes will to the Absolute whereas it is actualized only at the level of Being, and at the same time he practically reduces Being to will whereas will is only an aspect of Being. And if God projects possibili-

---

[2] But there is necessarily an essential difference between the "atomizing" contingency of the world and the restricting relativity that is found at the level of qualified and creative Being.

ties into the cosmic substance by existentiating them, He projects at the same time the homogeneity and coherence of their relationships, their existential laws if one will,[3] and this is precisely what Ashari believes he must deny in order to reserve the quality of cause, hence of "will", for God alone; furthermore, in practice he confuses will with arbitrariness since he cannot conceive of freedom otherwise. This amounts to saying that he fails to conceive of the quality of necessity, which he confuses with the theological notion of "servitude" (*'ibādah*) and which he therefore separates fanatically from God.

Ashari is primarily a theologian; if he is a philosopher, he is so in terms of theology. Theology on the whole is a philosophical commentary on Revelation—an "inspired" commentary in that it forestalls heresies properly so called, to the extent this is possible, while at the same time being psychologically and morally opportunistic.

The Mutazilites denied the divine qualities with the intention of keeping Unity intact; the Asharites reproach them for this—and not without reason—but *mutatis mutandis* they do exactly the same thing and with the same motivation in denying secondary causes, hence natural laws.[4] If one wished to apply the principle of exclusive Unity—as proclaimed by the Testimony of Faith—with an unsurpassable rigor, one would end up with *Advaita Vedānta*, where the personal God Himself is included in *Māyā*; Sufism has not avoided the dilemma that arises between the pure Absolute, which excludes the divine Person, and the divine Person, which precisely is not the pure Absolute. The solution to the problem, which we have expressed more than once, is the paradoxical but indispensable concept of the "relatively absolute": God is the Absolute in relation to the world but not in relation to His

---

[3] In the sense of the Sanskrit term *dharma*: the innate something that makes water flow and fire burn.

[4] In any case it is unjust to blame the Mutazilites, as the Asharites do, for subjecting faith to the authority of reason since for the Mutazilites reason always operates in connection with the givens of faith; this is why it is inappropriate to call the Mutazilites the "rationalists" of Islam.

Essence. This means that one must distinguish between a *Māyā* that is only cosmic and a *Māyā* that is universal and is *Māyā* as such: the first—cosmic *Māyā*—encompasses only the world, and in this case the Absolute is God-Creator as well as the Divinity-Essence, manifesting Being as well as nonmanifesting Beyond-Being; the second—universal *Māyā*—encompasses both the world and God-Creator, in which case the Absolute is only the Essence, Beyond-Being alone.

The Mutazilites did not see that their negation of the divine qualities would exclude creation, for a God without qualities would be exclusively static and would lack radiation; the Asharites for their part did not see that secondary causes in no way prevent the first Cause from having a direct effect on them nor that without the veil of secondary causes the first Cause would shatter the world. The Asharites are the first to admit that in order for the world to exist and subsist it must be separated from God by "veils" (*hujūb*), but this is precisely the role of the laws of nature.

Two errors result from this dilemma, which of course lies in the subject and not in the object: on the one hand attributing personal wills to the divine Essence on the pretext that "God wills" and on the other hand denying these wills to the divine Person by asserting that the Essence is beyond willing. And this leads us to the following explanation, which is fundamental and which we have provided more than once in various forms: if the Essence cannot have wills, it nonetheless does have a unique Will, from which are derived the diverse wills of the divine Person, and this is Radiation, hence the "desire" to communicate itself—or to be known from contingency as a starting point, which amounts to the same thing.

Leaving behind us the impasses of a certain theology, we would like to present in as concise a form as possible a metaphysical and cosmogonical picture of the "why" and "how" of creation; we do this without losing sight of the fact that a doctrinal outline can merely offer points of reference—if only for the simple reason that an expression is necessarily something other than the reality to be expressed. The identity between outline and reality is in any case as pointless as it is impossible, and this is precisely because a theory is able to furnish points of reference that are perfectly sufficient, for otherwise there would be no adequate and effective symbolism nor consequently any doctrine; most profane thinkers are incapable of understanding this because they wish to exhaust everything in words and imagine that one knows only what one expresses.

The whole problem of creation or universal manifestation has its root in the very nature of the divine Principle. The absolutely Real projects the world because its infinite nature requires that it be known starting from relativity and within it; to say that God "created" and not that He "creates" is a way of expressing the contingency or relativity of the world and of separating it from its transcendent Cause. God wishes to be seen—and the use of ellipsis in this turn of phrase does not imply any anthropomorphism—not only "starting" from the world and as He is in Himself "as such" but also "in" the world and "as" world, whether directly in qualities or indirectly and by contrast through their absence; and He wishes to be seen not only by man but also by the inferior creatures, who contemplate Him as if through their specific state itself, positively or in a privative way according to the species; but even privative consciousness is necessarily accompanied by—or subordinated to—a positive and participative existential consciousness, or it would not be consciousness at all.

Absolute, Infinite, Perfection: these are the first definitions of the divine Nature. Geometrically speaking, the Absolute is like a point, which excludes everything that is not it; the Infinite is like a cross or star or spiral, which prolongs the point and renders it as it were inclusive; and Perfection is like a circle or a system of concentric circles, which may be said to reflect a point within an expanse. The Absolute is ultimate Reality as such; the Infinite is its Possibility, hence also its Omnipotence; Perfection is Possibility to the extent that Possibility realizes a given potentiality of the absolutely Real. Creation or Manifestation is an effect of the divine Nature: God cannot prevent Himself from radiating, hence from manifesting Himself or creating, because He cannot prevent Himself from being infinite.

The divine Perfection is the sum or quintessence of all possible perfections, and we know this essentially from experience; these perfections are manifested thanks to the Infinite, which offers them existential space, or substance if one prefers, and which actualizes and projects them; and it is thanks to the Absolute that things exist inasmuch as they are distinguished from nothingness, if one may put it this way, or inasmuch as they are not "inexistent". The Absolute, which is imperceptible as such, makes itself visible through the existence of things; in a similar manner the Infinite reveals itself through their inexhaustible diversity; and similarly again Perfection manifests itself through the qualities of things, and in doing so it communicates both the rigor of the Absolute and the radiance of the Infinite, for things have their musicality as well as geometry.

On the Divine Will

The enigma of the expression "God doeth what He will" becomes clear with the help of the following argument: Exodus teaches us that "Pharaoh's heart was hardened" or that "Pharaoh hardened his heart"; but it also teaches on several occasions that "Yahweh hardened the heart of Pharaoh", and it places the following words in God's mouth: "I have hardened his heart, and the heart of his servants"; what this shows is that the two apparently contradictory expressions are in reality synonymous. Similarly the Koran: "God leadeth astray whom He will"; commentators specify that "God leadeth astray" by turning away from those who wish to go astray and thus by leaving them to the resources of their own darkness. The expressions "God leadeth astray" and "Yahweh hardened" are explained on the basis of their concern for reminding us that God is the cause of our light and therefore that the cause of our obscurities can only be the absence of God,[1] an absence provoked by a luciferian desire to be absent from Him or to be, more profoundly—like Pharaoh—wisdom and power outside the wisdom and power of God.

In the confrontation between Moses and Pharaoh, there is an opposition between the point of view of the moral alternative and—at least in principle—the point of view of intellectual and existential participation; but whereas in Moses the point of view of alternative is at its highest, the standpoint of participation is perfectly deviated and corrupted in Pharaoh, as it is with all the Mediterranean peoples of antiquity, with the exception of the esoterisms; it is deviated to the point of being contrary to the original intention, for the *Avatāra* could in no way be luciferian. Instead of participating in the divine qualities—of which the hero is a projection precisely—Pharaoh claims them for himself and thereby deprives himself of his "divine right".

"God leadeth astray", says the Koran, with typical Semitic ellipsism; now in going astray—and we have seen that God in this case is the cause only in an altogether indirect and nonacting manner—the initiative comes from man, which means that it manifests the funda-

---

[1] "Let no man say when he is tempted, I am tempted of God: for God cannot be tempted with evil, neither tempteth He any man" (James 1:13).

mental and global possibility personified by the man concerned, unless being led astray is only temporary, for in this case the possibility is only a secondary modality. The fundamental and characteristic possibility of the individual, what determines his ultimate destiny, is derived in the final analysis from universal Possibility and not from a decree of the creative Principle; with regard to individual possibilities, this Principle—the personal and legislating God—limits Himself to clothing them with concrete and cosmic existence, as Ibn Arabi has clearly explained; they are what they "want to be", as suggested by the Koranic passage in which the souls testify that God is their Lord before their projection into the cosmos. In other words the diverse possibilities, negative as well as positive, result indirectly from the Infinitude and Radiation of the divine Self: they are positive by their participation and negative by their distance.

—— .:. ——

Always full of obediential zeal, Ghazzali—with others—thinks on the one hand that no injustice can be attributed to God but on the other hand that God has no obligations in relation to anyone whatsoever; this is a flagrant contradiction, which is explained by the intention to testify in one and the same breath to the perfection of God and to the incommensurability between the Absolute and the contingent. But whatever the intention there is an element of metaphysical error in this reasoning: for from the moment He creates man "in His image", God in a sense "departs" from pure absoluteness and "enters" into an already relative absoluteness, which partakes of *Māyā.*[2] The very creation of man implies a certain obligation, which is freely and logically consented to by God and without which man would not be man and God would not be God.

Grosso modo, it would be inconceivable for God to create an animal or plant without at the same time creating what it needs to subsist, and this relationship between the creature and its vital surroundings marks an obligation on the part of the Creator, if one holds

---

[2] German mystics and theosophists have more than once expressed this interdependence, without fearing—rightly or wrongly—the ill-sounding formulations.

to expressing oneself in moral terms. God did not create an intelligent being so that it would grovel before the unintelligible; He created it in order to be known starting from contingency, and this is precisely why He made it intelligent. If God wished to owe nothing to man, He would not have created him.

In a general way the error of the partisans of an integral obedientialism consists in transferring—through an excess of zeal—the ontological "servitude" (*ubūdiyah*) of man onto the moral plane by inappropriately applying the ontological absoluteness of this subordination of the creature as such to man insofar as he is intelligent and free. Now the existential determination of man, which he shares with every pebble, is one thing, and his liberty is quite another, a liberty which he owes to his deiform personality and by which he participates in the divine Nature.[3]

"Verily, God faileth not to keep the tryst," says the Koran (*Sūrah* "The Family of Imran" [3]:9); this is the very formula of commitment, which results in any case from the divine Perfection, this Perfection excluding in God all injustice precisely. Only the pure Absolute, Beyond-Being, is beyond all commitment and reciprocity; it owes nothing to man, given that it asks nothing of him and could ask nothing of him.

All this leads us to the issue of the divine Subjectivity, which we have spoken about on other occasions and which one cannot address without leaving behind the impasses of an anthropomorphist and moralizing ontology. For to speak about the divine Subjectivity is to speak of what we might call the "gradation of the Self".

---

[3] The fact that in Muslim prayer the vertical positions alternate with prostrations expresses in its way the two aspects of man, that of "slave" (*'abd*) and that of "viceregent" (*khalīfah*); these are two aspects and also two relationships that must not be confused whenever there is a need to distinguish them. Obviously Islam knows this since it has the notions of intelligence, responsibility, and merit, but piety nonetheless seeks to reduce the viceregent to the slave, which is possible only in relation to ontological causality where the notion of "viceregency" itself does not arise.

First and fundamentally, the Divinity "wills" itself; there is no difference between its "Willing" and its Being; the word "willing" has no extrinsic meaning here but coincides simply with the Infinitude of the Absolute, which amounts to saying that it expresses the essence of what will be, within *Māyā*, the dynamic and cosmogonic dimension or function of the Principle: namely, the Radiation of the Sovereign Good (the Socratic or Platonic *Agathon*).

Second and more relatively, the divine Will has but one single object at the degree of this Radiation: to existentiate, that is, to project—and thus differentiate—the All-Possibility of the Infinite into contingency, relativity, Existence precisely; this is the second aspect of the divine Will.

Third, and on this basis or within this framework, the Divinity—now involved in the play of *Māyā*—wills to manifest its own Nature, which is the Good; therefore the personal, legislating, and saving God regulates human conduct: He orders virtue and forbids vice, and He rewards good and punishes evil. But His Will cannot extend, retrospectively as it were, to His own Root or Essence; He "must" accept and "wishes" to accept the fundamental and general cosmic consequences of the existentiating Radiation, for in order to be able to manifest the Good in a world it is necessary first that there be a world. The Will of Radiation, which precedes and conditions this manifestation, inevitably produces a movement away from the divine Source, and this movement—together with the diversifying, graduating, and contrasting deployment of possibilities—gives rise to the limited and transitory phenomenon we call "evil".

If we wish to explain the apparent contradictions of the divine Will, we must turn to the perspective just outlined, one that reveals three degrees of that Will, hence of the "Subjectivity" of the Principle. It is absurd to assume that one and the same subjectivity or will does not will sin on the one hand but wills a given sin on the other, or that one and the same subject orders obedience while creating a given disobedience or desires what it nonetheless hates. In this order of ideas the Christian *distinguo* between what God "wills" and what He "permits" is full of interest: God permits evil because He knows that evil is the ontologically inevitable shadow of an overall good and that every evil contributes in the final analysis to the good; in permitting evil God indirectly envisages the good of which this evil is like an infinitesimal, transitory, and necessary fragment, contingency requiring and provoking contrasts, fissures, or dissonances by its very nature. And it is in this sense alone that one can assert that everything is good because God wills it and that no possibility can be situated outside the divine Will.

In order to summarize we would say, first and fundamentally, that God wills Himself, His Will coinciding with His Being and conversely; second, that God wills Existence with all it requires and includes and that He wills it in order to manifest and communicate the treasures of His Nature; and third, that Existence having been given, God wishes to manifest the Good within it, hence the norm and the law. In other words the first Good is the Principle itself; then there is a second Good, which is Existence with all it entails; and finally a third Good, which is the totality of the reverberations of the Sovereign Good within Existence. But the very phenomenon of reverberation requires contrasts, whence the privative and subversive concomitance that is evil: now evil is evil only in relation to the particularity characterizing it and not in its existence; in the same way all the positive possibilities in evil, such as intelligence, strength, beauty, and the faculties of sensation and action, are good; there is no evil that is not woven existentially of good, and it is this that has allowed certain people to assert peremptorily that there is only good in the world and that evil is a matter of point of view.

On an ontologically higher level it could be said that Radiation includes a kind of evil since it projects the Real in the direction of nothingness and thus takes it away from the Essence; but here too, and indeed more than anywhere else, we must emphasize that this projection is "made of goodness", that of Radiation precisely, which is the principle and prime mover of Existence and hence of the existential unfolding of the divine Qualities—hence too of all the goods we know and can conceive, whether around us or within us. In the final analysis what we call evil—and what is so in its fragmentariness and on its own plane—is the price of relativity; and relativity, which coincides with contingency, cannot not be since the supreme Principle is infinite and since infinitude implies All-Possibility. The circle of *Māyā* is closed with the Vedantic truism that "everything is *Ātmā*"—or with the *Shahādah* when it is taken to mean: "There is no reality if not the sole Reality."

If the Asharites limited themselves to asserting that the Will of God is one in the same way as God is one, we would have nothing to say against them, and this is for the simple reason that the hypostatic modes of the divine Will do not preclude its essential unity. The divine Will that wills the good in the world is indeed only an application of the divine Will that wills existentiating Radiation or that wills the good as Radiation; and this initial Will in turn is only a projection of the intrinsic Will of the Essence, which has in view its own Being. The most "exterior" divine Will always contains in its very nature the hypostatic modes that precede it ontologically, if we may give the name "mode" to what is on the contrary pure Essence, at least at its summit; in other words the fact that the divine Will is necessarily one cannot prevent its being extrinsically diversified by virtue of its applications at different universal degrees.

Cosmic *Māyā*—and with all the more reason evil—is in the final analysis the possibility for Being not to be. By definition and on pain of contradiction All-Possibility must include its own impossibility; the Infinite must realize the finite, or else it is not really the Infinite. Regarding the "exhausting" of a possibility by its manifestation, we would say that in the world there is no absolute impossibility, and we shall give the following examples: it is impossible for black to be white or for a circle to be square, but since these impossibilities can only be relative, there is the possibility of gray and of a square with convex sides; or again, since two and two make neither three nor five, there is the possibility of doubled or divided unities, and so on. The indefinite multitude of paradoxical or absurd phenomena is explained—from the point of view in question here—by the requirements of All-Possibility; the exceptions and absurdities are produced because they cannot be impossible.

The reason for the existence of contingency is the manifestation of the Good in and by relativity, hence by combinations, gradations, and contrasts, and this entails or requires the privative and therefore existential phenomenon of evil; but evil would not be possible if this plane of relative Good were not remote and separated from the Principle on account of its very relativity. The Good wills to prolong or reflect itself in relativity in order to unfold all its possibilities and in this way exhaust them, but inexhaustibly since it is limitless.

APPENDIX

Selections from Letters and Other Previously Unpublished Writings

1

If we start with the idea that esoterism is fundamentally discernment between the Absolute and the contingent, the Real and the unreal, we can say that Christ personifies this discernment and that our participation in Christ is our integration into transcendent Truth, just as conversely our metaphysical discernment draws us to some degree into the nature of Christ. As for Islam, if we start with the idea that the object or content of esoterism is the Absolute, we can say that *Allāh* is this Absolute or the Absolute as such. But what I want to highlight above all is this Christian mystery: Christ is not only "manifestation" but also "discernment" of the Absolute or the Real; this specification is esoterically crucial because discernment is something direct, whereas manifestation is indirect.

Regarding myself personally, I shall say this: if I had entered Islam on the purely exoteric plane, I would be cut off from the sacramental graces I received in my childhood, but since I am an esoterist these graces remain in a living form in me, and I have not ceased being what I am as the result of these graces. Proof of this is the role the Holy Virgin plays in my life.

2

A true metaphysician cannot unreservedly identify himself with a religious *upāya* and take pleasure in it with a kind of nationalism, but obviously he must identify with what is essential—hence both universal and primordial—in the *upāya*, and this is "Islam" *a fortiori*. Needless to say, what is essential transcends the *upāya*.

I want to give two examples of religious limitation, although you already know what I shall talk about. For Christianity man is a "sinner"; this is the definition of man, and it entails the idea that the entire world is bad and that the only alternative is between the "flesh" and the "spirit"; it goes without saying that this perspective has a certain relative justification, but its disadvantage is that it presents itself as absolute. For Islam man is not totally corrupted by the fall—a total corruption would be contrary to the very definition of man—but he is totally a "servant" or "slave", which metaphysically is in fact an aspect of his nature but which could not sum up human nature as such; to believe the contrary is to deny the specifically human intelligence and dignity, and it is thus to deny what constitutes the very reason for the existence of *homo sapiens*. In the case of Islam as in that of Christianity, theology tends to push the respective dogmatic image to the point of absurdity, and most mystics identify *de facto* with these pious excesses, something a consistent metaphysician—hence one who is aware of the nature of things—would never do.

In Muslim thought the axiom "He hath no associate" gives rise to the most inappropriate conclusions in various domains, but in Christian thought it is hypostatic diversity—the Trinity—that functions as the absolute, and the absence of the idea of *Māyā* is particularly noticeable; now a true metaphysician could not possibly identify himself with such positions, and hence could not commit himself to what I call "religious nationalism". With good reason Guénon defined the "religious point of view"—the word "religious" having for him the meaning of "exoteric"—as a "sentimental attachment to an idea". And one should not forget all the secondary excesses—sometimes very troublesome—to which confessional sentimentalism gives rise.

Personally, I am very sensitive to the following argument: when you say you are a "Muslim" or a "Christian", you exclude an immense part of humanity; you separate yourself from it and reproach it for not being what you are; you proclaim before the entire world that only you have the truth, unless you speak with tacit Guénonian understandings that no one can presuppose *a priori*. Nothing of the kind is to be found with the American Indians: "The Great Spirit has given you your way of praying, and He has given us our way of praying"; and that is all.

3

If we situate ourselves within the framework of Islam, we nevertheless can find Christ in it; and if we situate ourselves within the framework of Christianity, we nevertheless can find Islam in it.

"Christ" in Islam is to see Jesus not as the only Savior but as the esoteric Genius of Inwardness (and not formalism or legalism).

"Islam" in Christianity is to see Christ not only as the saving Manifestation of the Absolute but also—and above all—as a Manifestation (among others) of the saving Absolute.

"Christ in Islam": essence and not form, substance and not accident, quality and not quantity.

"Islam in Christianity": the Absolute manifested and not an absolute Manifestation.

The question is not whether we choose Islam or Christianity, but whether we discern the Absolute in every religion and whether we understand that the Invocation of the Absolute contains all religious practice.

Christianity: "God became man that man might become God." The Absolute (Necessary Being) came to the contingent (possible being) that the contingent might return to the Absolute. Saving Manifestation.

Islam: "There is no divinity but the only Divinity." There is no absolute but the only Absolute. Saving Truth.

4

That a superficial and lukewarm Christian might change religions is something conceivable; one might always prefer one credo to another if only for purely sentimental reasons. But that a monk from Mount Athos would want to look for another path after several years of practice is inconceivable, and he would be a proud man and a wretch to do so. Likewise for Islam: it is possible for an exoterist Muslim to end up preferring another credo to his own, but it is not possible—this is not admissible under any circumstance—for a member of a Sufi brotherhood to seek a path other than Sufism. If he does so, he is an irresponsible person and an individualist, and in the final analysis a proud man and a wretch, because one does not invoke *Allāh*—for many years—for nothing!

5

In the first place we cannot but love the *Shahādah*, which is an unsurpassable formulation of metaphysical Truth; in a way it summarizes all the Koran. Next we cannot but love the moral and mystical personality of the Prophet, hence the second *Shahādah*, which is its symbol. Finally we cannot but love the *Dhikr*, by means of which we assimilate the mystery of the second *Shahādah* as well as that of the first. And it is impossible for us not to love the fundamental Laws of Islam, starting with canonical prayer, which are transparent and not in any way limitative in themselves. There is lastly the "liturgical" element in the broadest sense, namely Muslim art: calligraphy, architecture, the art of dress, and the arts and crafts; all of this is specifically Islamic, and spiritually speaking this is hardly insignificant.

But there is also theology—which interpenetrates Sufism to a very large extent—and the psychological style of average piety; we are now confronted with elements that cannot be likeable from our perspective, sharing as they do a close solidarity with what is most limitative in the "religious viewpoint"; and above all there are dogmatic elements: being unacceptable from the viewpoint of truth as such—while no doubt possessing a certain spiritually "therapeutic" function, but this is a completely different matter—they are thereby unacceptable for us, who are aware of the values these dogmas exclude.

What is the Gospel? "It is full of stupid things," a Maghrebi *faqīr* told me: the Apostles supposedly hid the true Gospel in a hollow tree, and a drunkard found it and wrote in it, and then the faithful found it and adopted it as it was; and there it is! Christ purportedly came not to establish a Church—and had he established it, it would have lasted for barely six centuries—but only to remind the Jews of what Abrahamic Islam was and to announce the coming of the Prophet, neither more nor less. Thus not only is the Gospel worthless, but Christ himself is obsolete and has been replaced by something better; the sacraments are nothing, and Christianity is a false religion leading one to hell. The Shaykh Darqawi narrates the story of a "great Christian saint" who converted to Islam and who, after becoming a Muslim, had to start from zero, at the level of the last of the Muhammadans.

Can we, or must we, who are Westerners "love" all of that? What must I think *a priori* of a Westerner who claims to have a "strong affinity with Islam"? Does this affinity include an ignorance of what Christ, the Gospel, the sacraments, and the ecclesiastical institution are? What interests me cannot be this "affinity" but the "wherefore" of such an affinity, not to mention its psychological style.

When Muslim books mention Christ, they attribute mostly commonplace attitudes to him or platitudes that are incompatible with his nature; for instance, it is said that he traveled constantly and that imitating him consists in this; or that he drank from a bowl, which he threw away when he saw a dog drink without a bowl—as a matter of fact, this is a confusion with Diogenes—which is ridiculous considering that we are dealing with the person of Jesus. Granted, Sayyidna Isa could never appear at the center of Islam since there is a difference in doctrinal and methodical perspective; nonetheless I do not "like" this way of casting him aside—no more, conversely, than I can "like" the Christian conviction that there is no salvation outside of the person of Jesus, or that the *Veda*s are not sacred Scriptures, and so on and so forth.

I shall perhaps be told that "everyone" knows all of this; no doubt, but not everyone draws the required conclusions; not everyone is aware of what, depending on circumstances, the relativity of the "religious point of view" implies.

6

I was glad to read in your letter your thoughts on the problem of Protestantism. Regarding this subject, I would like to specify further the intention of my opening paragraph—I am referring to the chapter in my book—with the help of the following image.

Imagine that two people with their child and a cat board a ferryboat to cross a river; it costs one franc per person, hence three francs total because it costs nothing for the cat. If the crossing were to cost one franc per "adult", the child would pay nothing; but it is per "person", and hence one must pay for the child; if it were per "creature", then one would also have to pay for the cat. Now in speaking of three "denominations", it is as if I were speaking of three "persons"; but this does not mean the child is an "adult" just because he is administratively a "person". Protestantism is the child; liberal Protestantism is the cat: a child is a "person"; a cat is not a person.

Hence, according to a certain relative aspect, I place Protestantism on the same plane as that of the two old Churches, but only according to this extrinsic aspect because I take care to add: "a Christian possibility, a limited one, no doubt, and excessive through certain of its features". Hence there is a difference in level. I depended completely on the words "a limited one, no doubt" to make the reader understand that even though there is a certain extrinsic equality, there is nonetheless a certain intrinsic inequality on another plane; but since Protestant piety is nonetheless a possible path—it is only liberal Protestantism that is not a path—I am obliged to take note of the existence of a third "denomination". I did not say that Catholicism is limited or that Orthodoxy is limited; I said that Lutheranism is so.

In any case, an Orthodox would tell me that the demonstration is not yet complete; I return now to the image of the ferryboat with the three persons. He would say that the two adults are of different sexes since they are the parents; if one supposed the child were a girl, then one would have a new division: only one person would be a male; the other two would be women. You see the conclusions that could be derived from this point of view with regard to the definition of the denominations: if the masculine sex symbolizes legitimacy, then only one denomination would be completely legitimate; the other two—despite the difference in age—would be more or less illegitimate, age representing here the denominational level, precisely. A Catholic could make the same argument against Orthodoxy, but I grant preeminence to the latter.

I fear I may have tired you with a demonstration that is perhaps quite useless, but after hesitating somewhat I allowed myself to do it because of the problem of my first paragraph. This is a mere question of emphasis, hence of dialectics.

7

In relation to Monotheism considered as such, Judaism stabilized but "confiscated" the Message; Christianity universalized but "altered" it; Islam in turn restored it by stabilizing and universalizing it.

The Christian perspective is essentially determined by divine Manifestation—a theophany that redounds upon the very conception of God—and this Manifestation gives rise to a mysticism of Sacrifice and Love. This anthropotheism, so to speak—together with the Trinitarianism resulting from it—is certainly one spiritual possibility among others, but it is not Monotheism in itself. Now Islam, which represents Monotheism in itself and nothing else, is logical in reproaching Christianity for not bringing out the full value of the Message of Monotheism and for replacing it with another Message, that of divine Manifestation. Islam is equally logical in reproaching Judaism for having unduly nationalized Monotheism and for having monopolized prophecy—for wanting God to belong to the Jews alone and for passionately opposing any prophecy outside Israel, even in the Abrahamic line as in the case of Islam. Certainly Mosaism and Christianity are intrinsically orthodox, but this is beside the point when it is a question of disengaging the essential Message of Monotheism, which is what Islam intends to do. This being said, it is important not to lose sight of the fact that it is God Himself who successively manifests different aspects of the one Truth, whatever men may do.

Christianity can be characterized by this paraphrase of a Patristic formula: the Interior became exterior in order that the exterior might become Interior. The One God of Monotheism as such—the God of Abraham—is in practice replaced by the Interior God, who exteriorizes Himself out of love while exteriorizing Himself already *in divinis*, whence the Trinity; and the divine Law concerning the exterior is abandoned and replaced by a Law of Inwardness, namely, the sacraments and evangelical counsels. In its intoxication with Inwardness—hence with nonexteriority—the newborn Church abandoned the advantages of the prudent and sagacious Mosaic Law along with its Pharisaic exaggerations, depriving itself thereby of many a factor of health and equilibrium; the premises of this attitude are to be met with already in the Gospel, where it is said that the disciples, in the name of the primacy of inward purity, did not wash their hands before meals, and other characteristics of this kind. The outward Law was replaced on its own plane by Roman Law and a few elements of Germanic Law; the consequences of this were grave. The universality of the Church abolished the world of Abraham; the universality of Islam, on the contrary, spreads it everywhere.

Islam thus reproaches Christianity for having conceived the Trinity to the detriment of Unity as such and for having renounced an outward Law of sacred character while assuming the function of an integral religion. And it reproaches Judaism for having rejected Jesus, a Jewish Prophet, and for having enclosed the One God within Israel, thus reducing Him to being the King of a people—He, the King of the Universe. The fact that these judgments are clothed with an imagery, sensibility, and logic that are more or less Bedouin takes nothing away from their profound significance; on the contrary it is a question here of the point of view of Monotheism as such and nothing else, for the intrinsic truth of the Mosaic and Christic perspectives is not at issue. The monotheistic Idea is that God is One and that being One He is Universal; He is not three-fold in His absoluteness, and He does not belong to any single people; it is according to this perspective alone that Islam judges the other religions.

All of this is in accordance with the "egocentric" logic—if one may so express it—of every religious crystallization.

8

Speaking of Jesus and Mary I said in one of my poems: *antumā 'l-hayātu fī dīni 'r-Rahmān*, which means: there is a certain complementarity of principles or qualities, or of means, in spiritual realization, and this complementarity is personified in Isa and Maryam. Indeed there are two essential elements in the invocatory method: *Dhikr* and *Faqr*—no *Dhikr* without *Faqr*, no *Faqr* without *Dhikr*. Now *faqr* is *illatī ahsanat farjahāh*, the word *farj* referring alchemically to the heart of the *faqīr*, which must be pure from concupiscence and worldliness. Maryam carried Isa in her womb just as *Faqr* envelops *Dhikr*, and Isa is the genius of *Dhikr* in the sense that he is the genius of Inwardness, for he said: "The kingdom of Heaven is within you", and also "but thou, when thou prayest, enter into thy closet, and when thou hast shut thy door, pray to thy Father which is in secret": now "thy closet" is the heart.

The Prophet is at once *'abd* and *ummī*, and he therefore personifies *Faqr*, but he is also *Dhikru'Llāh*, which means that he personifies the complementarity in question. Nonetheless the fact that the Koran mentions other Prophets traditionally allows for a mystical or devotional reference to one or another of them from the point of view of a specific element of contemplative alchemy. Even though each *Rasūl* realizes all the spiritual excellences, he appears at the same time more particularly as the "genius" of a specific excellence or specific element; and this is true not only of the Prophets but also of the Saints. For the Sufi the actualization of such a reference is a question of experience or grace.

9

If the Orthodox hold—as they do—that Catholicism and Protestantism are both heresies, that they are organically linked, that they are two virtually symmetrical abuses, that one does not go without the other, it is impossible to say they are completely wrong, esoterically speaking; their opinion is at the very least instructive.

In a word, where the Catholic phenomenon exists, there will also be the Protestant phenomenon. Why? Because ever since the Middle Ages there is something "not quite right" in Catholicism; a proof of this, and it is glaring, is to be found in its outward forms. Only Orthodoxy, which has always excluded change, innovation, and so-called progress, offers perfect equilibrium and perfect beauty.

I do not know whether you have ever visited an Orthodox country; true, there are the Copts in Egypt, but I do not think you went into their churches. The first time I went to Greece, I had this deeply moving impression: here at last is authentic Christianity—here at last are priests, churches, liturgies! For everything here reminds one of Christ, the Apostles, the early Church. What relationship is there in visual terms between a Catholic priest and the Christic *barakah*? None; the Catholic priest is for the most part a "civilized" man rather than a "primeval" man of religion; this mysterious and scandalous disparity must after all mean something. In the same vein of thought, when a false council and a false pope inverted the altars and falsified the Mass, the great majority of the Catholic world accepted it almost without flinching; this too must have a meaning as to the relativity of

Catholic orthodoxy. I am speaking as an esoterist and have in mind the overall orthodoxy of Catholicism, not the validity of the old rites, which is indisputable. But as the Shiite phenomenon in Islam proves, the question of "orthodoxy"—on the exoteric plane—is not as univocal or simple as one might think at first.

10

"But thou, when thou prayest, enter into thy closet, and when thou hast shut thy door, pray to thy Father which is in secret." This saying of Sayyidna Isa means that it is necessary to leave the world outside during the Invocation. It is necessary to shut the door of the heart.

Leave the world outside: not only the outer world but also the inner world; not only the accidents—preoccupations, enjoyments, or cares—coming from the world that surrounds us but also the accidents coming from the soul, from its tendencies and reactions. It is necessary to leave outside the accidents and enclose oneself in the Substance—in the *Ism*-sacrament, which is Substance manifested. The Substance has become accident that the accident might become Substance.

Shutting the door of the heart is an essential aspect of *Faqr*, and there is no perfect *Dhikr* without perfect *Faqr*.

The same meaning is found in two other sayings: "Let the dead bury their dead"; and likewise, "No man, having put his hand to the plough, and looking back, is fit for the kingdom of God."

Faqr must be sweet, satisfied, generous; a bitter or pretentious *Faqr* is satanic; it is inflation, not poverty.

To shut the door of the heart: not to be concerned with what remains outside; to entrust it to God; He will take care of it. To abandon the accidental to God, not to cling to it with disquiet.

The supreme Name means "there is no god but God." Now we cannot combine a reservation in the form of some care or other with this Truth; we cannot accept the Truth conditionally; we cannot put the accidental alongside the Substance. The *Shahādah*—hence the Name—extinguishes the accidents of the soul as well as those of the world. The Substance contains all that we love, and She is what we are.

The veil that separates Sayyidatna Maryam from the world is the shut door of the heart. In the *Shahādah* it is the *Nafy* that opens the way to the *Ithbāt*: without negation there is no affirmation. The Virginity of Mary is the condition for the divine Presence. "I am black, but beautiful": to pray "in secret".

11

You as a Catholic accuse the Protestants of being pretentious. I lived in the canton de Vaud for forty years, and I have now lived for two years in the state of Indiana, two Protestant lands, and I can say that I know the mentality of Protestantism, all the more so because I grew up among Protestants in Basel. Mediocrity exists everywhere, and obviously it can take on a different tone depending on the religion, but as for Lutheran or Calvinist piety I can assure you it is not at all pretentious in itself. For the danger of pretentiousness entailed by an emphasis on trust or faith is compensated for and neutralized among truly pious Protestants by a sincere humility, which is nurtured by the Augustinian awareness of our irremediable helplessness, the sole remedy being the grace of Christ, which we have access to by means of faith. This Christocentric faith is carried over into a morality that appears not as a merit but as a "categorical imperative", which is Biblical in its essence; quite simply, virtue enters into the logic of faith. This is an archetypal "argument" found also among Amidists or in the Vishnuite *prapatti*—as well as in Catholicism, more precariously, among the quietists. I have met some truly spiritual men among Protestants, especially pastors; they are not exactly analogous to pious Catholics in their *barakah*, but they attest unquestionably and quasi-existentially to a living dimension of the Gospel. That such a piety still survives four centuries after Luther means something after all.

It is in the nature of theology to over-accentuate and exclude, and this is why no theology is intellectually perfect, though there are certainly degrees in this. But there is not only the question of doctrine: there is also that of method, and a concern for method can determine a doctrinal formulation, as is basically the case with Luther, even though he himself was not aware of it.

I would have gladly preferred to spare myself from having to deal with the Protestant problem and from having to write my chapter on Lutheran Evangelicalism, but the Protestant phenomenon exists, and it is immense; sooner or later I was therefore obliged to address it. I would also just as gladly have preferred to spare myself from having to deal with Muslim theology—Lord knows how grating it can be—but I had no choice since Sufism is situated in parallel to this body of doctrine; it was a sacrifice for me because I am hardly enamored of exoterisms and would have preferred to deal only with pure metaphysics and the perennial religion, the *Sanātana Dharma*.

12

There are two ways of following the Prophet, one that is general and the other particular. The first is that of any man practicing Islam at one degree or another, if this practice is sincere: he who is in Islam follows the Prophet and cannot be situated outside of him. The second way is that of *fuqarā* who have a very particular devotion to the person of the Prophet: they know even the least incident in Muhammad's life and scrupulously follow the *Sunnah* while studying the *ahādīth* continuously; they are as if possessed by the avataric person of the Prophet. It is a kind of exclusive *bhakti* found in certain *turuq*.

Now in order to be able to follow the Prophet this way, it must be possible for one to follow the integral *Sunnah* in addition to having a providential vocation; and this is technically impossible for us, even vocationally so. But there is something else to consider: we are marked first by our intimate knowledge of other *Avatāra*s and their Laws and Wisdom and second by our awareness of the *Religio Perennis*. Moreover we are of Christian origin, and our point of departure is the *Vedānta*, and finally we live in a *kāfir* world. And given the world and times to which we belong, we are in any case under the regimen of Mercy. All these factors, and others still, enable us to understand better the significance Sayyidatna Maryam holds for us. And this cannot but please the Prophet, who knows our situation and needs and who in any case envelops us with his Presence.

The Holy Virgin is not only the link between Islam and Christianity—the summer and winter caravans in the *Sūrah* "Quraysh", according to a certain interpretation that came to my mind—but also the personification of the *Religio Perennis*, which is rooted in the Names *Rahmān* and *Rahīm* and in the *Basmalah*; there has never been a woman superior nor even equal to her in the Semitic world, and thus she alone has the plenary right to embody Layla for us.

13

On the one hand Christian morality sees the relative good represented by the preservation of the corporeal individual, and on the other hand it sees the abuse, namely gluttony; or on the one hand it sees the relative good represented by the preservation of the earthly species, and on the other hand it sees the abuse, namely lust; but unlike Islam it does not see a contemplative element between these two poles, an element transcending the relative good while in no way approaching the abuse corresponding to it. In the Koranic Paradise there is food and there are houris, even though there could be no question of any preservation of the corporeal individual or the earthly species. *Hadhā'l-ladhī razaqanā min qabl*: this verse—in its entirety—contains the whole doctrine of the metaphysical transparency of positive sensations.

14

The saving Manifestation of the Absolute is either Truth or Presence, but never exclusively one or the other, for as Truth it includes Presence, and as Presence it includes Truth. Such is the nature of all theophanies.

Islam is founded upon the axiom that the Truth saves; its exoteric limitation is the axiom that only the Truth saves, not Presence.

Christianity is founded upon the axiom that a particular Presence saves; its exoteric limitation is the axiom that only this particular Presence saves, not any other, and that only Presence saves, not Truth.

Islam: it is necessary to accept the Truth with Intelligence, Will, and Love, this being what constitutes Faith. In other words it is necessary to know the True, then to will it, then to love it; it is then that Truth saves us. For to accept sincerely—or really know—is also to will and love.

Christianity: it is necessary to accept the Presence with Love, therefore with Will, therefore also with Intelligence, this being what constitutes perfect Love of God. In other words it is necessary to love That which is Present, then to will it, then to know it; it is then that Presence saves us.

Truth: it is necessary to draw from it all the consequences; it is thus that we become what we are; for the True is not only transcendent; it is also immanent.

Presence: it is necessary to enter into its mold; it is thus that we become what we are; for That which is Present is not only immanent; it is also transcendent.

The element Truth in Christianity: to understand that the immanent Christ—the Heart that is Love and Intellect—is none other than God. To understand that Manifestation is none other than the Principle, whether in the Microcosm or the Macrocosm. It is this science of Identity that constitutes Christian *gnosis*.

The element Presence in Islam: to acknowledge that the Koran—and with it the Prophet—is none other than God; to enter through the *Sunnah* into the Muhammadan mold; sacramental reading of the Koran; the divine Name as Presence and Sacrament. The Heart is the immanent Koran or immanent Prophet.

Islam: the Truth is that the world is illusory, that God alone is real, the illusory or the contingent being prefigured in the Real or the Absolute and the Real or the Absolute being reflected in the contingent.

Christianity: the Presence is that of God in the world, of the Absolute in the contingent, of the Infinite in the finite.

Islam: the Presence is that of the Real in the illusory or the True in the false: the Koran, the Prophet, the *Sunnah*.

Christianity: the Truth is that the Manifestation of God—whether transcendent or immanent, macrocosmic or microcosmic—is none other than God Himself.

For Muslims only the Truth of the Absolute saves, whence their tendency to undervalue in Christianity the element Presence in all its aspects, whereas for Christians only Presence—or this particular Presence—saves, whence their tendency to underestimate all Platonism, that is, every perspective of saving Truth. But both spiritualities—or both esoterisms—rejoin each other in the Heart, which is at once immanent Truth and immanent Presence.

The invocation of the Name is the Way of the *Religio Perennis*: for in the Name, Truth is Presence, and Presence is Truth; the Name is at once Truth and Presence.

It could also be said that the doctrinal Enunciation—the *Shahādah*—refers more particularly to the element Truth and the divine Name to the element Presence. The Name is the Presence that gives the Truth, and the Enunciation is the Truth that gives the Presence.

15

In pure metaphysics exclusive accentuations—namely, "points of view" and "aspects"—are not admissible; seeing things through colored glass is not metaphysics. But in exoterism accentuations or colorations are not just allowed; they constitute the very principle of the exoteric outlook, and they inevitably assert themselves unsparingly and with vehemence. According to Islam the only sin that will certainly not be forgiven is that of associating partners with the One God; in this perspective of Unity, the Trinity appears almost as the worst of aberrations; and this perspective has its rights since exoterism does. According to Protestantism, it is the Mass that is an abomination since it seems to replace the unique Sacrifice of Calvary, given that the Mass is presented as a sacrifice; here too the accentuation of an exclusive point of view has its rights, those of exoterism precisely. For Christianity the worst of abominations is the rejection of Christ—not believing that Christ alone saves or thinking there could be other ways than his. For Judaism the ultimate blasphemy is to believe that the *Torah*, which is meant for all eternity, could actually be abolished and replaced by something else.

16

Since you have been baptized and received confirmation and have assimilated the one and universal metaphysics, there is no reason for you to fear that the Christian form does not contain a sufficient esoteric virtuality or to ask yourself what Christianity on the one hand and Islam on the other can give you; it is enough to practice the Invocation with sincerity and perseverance, and God will take care of the rest. There are only three things that matter: metaphysical discernment, invocatory practice, nobility of character.

There is nothing preventing a Christian from invoking God alone; Saint Teresa of Avila's confessor would repeat in Spanish the Name *Dios* for hours at a time; likewise, and obviously, Arab Christians—there are many in Lebanon and Syria—can repeat the Name *Allāh*, which does not belong exclusively to Islam when considered in this manner. Although you normally pronounce the avataric Names of Jesus and Mary, your intention is to go toward God; God knows your intention, and it is He who decides on our degrees and stations. When invoking God we must not analyze the degrees of the Absolute; we are addressing That which transcends us infinitely, and this is all. The fact that certain invocatory modes are less direct than others does not prevent the results from being the same, especially since recourse to Mercy is more necessary than ever. The real link between Christianity and Islam is the Holy Virgin; she personifies at once primordial Wisdom and Mercy. In her and through her we have the same religion. And there is only one God.

But you must get rid of the confused opinions expressed in your letter. There can be no question of esoteric Islam playing the role of a "spiritual coronation" in relation to a "Christian foundation". It is only too obvious that Muslim sages have something to offer Christians—and the reverse is true likewise—but Islam as such has nothing to add to Christianity; a traditional form is a closed system and is by definition perfect in its kind. Thus there is no possible "traditional complementarity" between the two religions; there can be no question of "grafting" the esoterism of Islam onto Christian practices. One must take great care to abstain from ambiguous speculations that risk compromising the efficacy of spiritual practices; and one must not needlessly complicate matters.

17

It is a fact that empirical Islam—exoterism, at any rate—is reticent about the question of the celestial intermediary, though without being able to be entirely consistent since Gabriel and the Prophet were both intermediaries; the Prophet spoke to Gabriel, and Muslims address litanies to the Prophet. Formerly, one could hear in Morocco—I was there in an epoch when you were not yet born and when the Maghreb was still in the full Middle Ages—beggars invoking "*yā Mūlanā Idrīs*" and "*yā Sīdī ʿAbd al-Qadr*", that is, names of saints. At Ephesus, in the Holy Virgin's house, there is a section reserved for Christians where the Mass is said and another section reserved for Muslims where the

Turks come to pray; when I was there, an old Turk next to me whispered prayers in which the name "Maryam" recurred over and over. On the Christian side there were ex-votos hanging near the altar in thanksgiving for miraculous healings obtained through the Virgin; on the Muslim side there were also some votive offerings—in the form of colored ribbons—which proves that the Turks address themselves also to this feminine Mediator and obtain the same graces as Christians; I have also been told that in India Muslim women pray to the Holy Virgin for their children.

18

By the very nature of things, man is connected with God in two ways, one that is direct and the other indirect; this follows from his very existence. It results in other words from the duality *Ātmā-Māyā*.

On the one hand the relationship between man and God is direct; man stands alone before God. On the other hand the relationship is indirect; man calls upon a heavenly interlocutor—a mediator—the *Logos*. In both cases it is God who hears and answers.

Islam and some other religions emphasize the first way of connection; Christianity and some other religions emphasize the second; but never in an exclusive manner. In Hinduism the two ways of connection are in balance.

There are Sufis who claim a mystical connection with a particular Prophet: they are *Ibrāhīmī, Mūsāwī, 'Īsāwī*, as may be seen from the *Fusūs al-Hikam* of Ibn Arabi. It is thus that the Shaykh of our *Tarīqah* is *Maryamī*—the Shaykh al-Alawi having been unquestionably *'Īsāwī*, whence his stress on inwardness and his detachment with respect to forms. The *Hikmah Maryamīyyah* coincides quite obviously with the *Hikmah 'Īsāwīyyah*, while adding to the latter an element of femininity, beauty, virginity, and maternity—an accentuation of sanctifying receptivity, adamantine purity, and appeasing and salvific goodness.

Every *Tarīqah* is by definition *Muhammadīyyah*; to say Islam is to say Muhammad.

19

It is not easy to situate the problem of the resurrection in a few words; it must be said first of all that it is a question of a cosmic event whose metaphysical cause is the state of fall or the disgrace of matter. All told it is a question of a return to the initial equilibrium: accursed or perverted matter must be replaced with a blessed or regenerate matter, and this change can take place only from within; a new matter will be as it were projected from the subtle state, and this is the resurrection. It may be impossible to imagine this, but it is no less real, and it is metaphysically necessary; every disequilibrium requires a return to equilibrium.

As for the question of the afterlife—or the eschatological destiny—of animals, Semitic and monotheistic theologies deal with this only from the outside and in passing; this means that the question does not interest them since they confine themselves essentially to a consideration of the human state, which begins with human birth and is prolonged in the Paradises or hells of the human species. It is easy to grasp that Paradise is eternal since it opens to Eternity; but what is the meaning of the "eternity" of hell? This expression does not mean that it is truly eternal, which would be metaphysically and morally absurd, but simply that the damned are definitively excluded from the human Paradise; this definitive character is expressed by the wholly symbolic notion of "eternity", which suggests something absolute or rather irreversible. In reality the damned will finally leave hell to enter into the lower transmigration, with the possibility in the end of being born into a state analogous to the human state, one that opens therefore to a Paradise analogous to the human Paradise; but the theologies are interested only in man and take into account only what concerns him. They are no more interested in animals than in the damned, or rather in their post-human destiny, to speak in theological terms; animals are "destroyed" just as damnation is "eternal"; "and let us be done with this question".

Now animals, not being central beings like man, actually continue through transmigration, though there is a possible exception here, that of noble animals that have lived in the ambiance of a saint or a sanctuary and that are absorbed upward after their death by the Paradise of this saint or the saints of the sanctuary; thus it is said that the cat of Jalal al-Din Rumi—filled with *barakah*—went to Paradise after his master.

20

All is well whenever we utter the Supreme Name with the right intention. As for the world and the life we leave behind us, they are in God's hands.

And this leads us to the following considerations. It is natural for a man to tell himself: "I want to be wherever Paradise is"—in other words where I feel happy, in surroundings that correspond to my nature. But it is much more perfect, or rather it already partakes of the supernatural, to express oneself thus: "Wherever I am, there is Paradise"—in other words to have understood that happiness is our relationship with God and that this relationship is "within you". The key to this relationship is prayer—"pray without ceasing"—and therefore also, and even above all, quintessential prayer: the universal and primordial sacrament of the Name. Wherever this Name is, there is the Presence of God; and wherever this Presence is, there is my Paradise. For to say "God" is to say "Sovereign Good": the unchangeable and inalienable Essence of all goods, all happiness, and all beatitude. "If there is a Paradise on earth, it is here, it is here, it is here": in the Supreme Name.

In the heavenly beyond the outward and inward coincide to a certain extent in the sense that one can see nothing without seeing God; this is why it is said—symbolically and not otherwise—that the houris are transparent. But in truth this is how it is already on this earth: for the spiritual man every positive phenomenon is transparent and archetypal, everything testifying to the Sovereign Good; nobility is to have a sense of the archetypes, hence of the divine Intentions.

21

To return to the questions discussed in my preceding letters, I will say this: the great religious happiness of a Muslim as such is Islam in all its extension; it is not *a priori* the Prophet or the Koran, but Islam; it is the happiness of plunging the individual will into all the ramifications of the Law—*shari'ah* and *sunnah*—which is itself the crystalliza-tion of the divine Will, and of accumulating supererogatory practices and merits. In a similar way the happiness of a Christian is Christ; the Church with the sacraments is the extension of Christ, who is everything. For a Muslim it is not the Prophet but Islam—and all it comprises—that is everything, for here what matters is totality, not the center; the Prophet is the personification of totality just as Christ is the center of the cosmos; the totality—the Koran—comes "before" the Prophet just as Christ comes "before" the cosmos.

If the happiness of an ordinary Muslim is zeal in the accomplish-ment of the *shari'ah* and *sunnah* and if the happiness of a Christian is in attachment to the saving divinity of Christ, where then is ours? It lies in what is common to all traditional forms: the metaphysical truth and the divine Name. Our "Islam" is conformity to the nature of things and to the divine Will manifested in it; our "Christ" is the salvific Name of God. Islam contains this Name since it contains everything that is for us in conformity to the divine Reality. Islam is surrendering oneself to the Name, and it is this Islam that encompasses our whole being. But this Islam is an essence rather than a form.

Christianity is like a dot that is red and warm, and Islam is like a surface that is green and fresh. From the point of view of *gnosis* and *tasawwuf* and *ma'rifah*, the color becomes white. But Islam also con-tains an element of warmth, which is *mahabbah*, and Christianity an element of freshness, which is *gnosis*.

The Spiritual Virtues according to
Saint Francis of Assisi

In his *Laudes*, Saint Francis of Assisi extols the virtues "with which the most holy Virgin was adorned and with which every holy soul must be adorned" (*Laude delle virtù delle quali fu adornata la Santissima Vergine, et deve esserne l'anima santa*). These two references, one to the Virgin and the other to the soul, have a profound and precise meaning, for the Virgin is the prototype of the perfect soul; she embodies the universal Soul in her purity, her receptivity toward God, her fecundity, and her beauty, these attributes being at the root of every angelic and human virtue, and even of every possible positive quality, such as the purity of snow or the incorruptibility and luminosity of crystal.

The first virtue Saint Francis salutes (*Dio vi salvi*) in the *Laudes* is "queen Wisdom", next to whom he places her "holy sister Pure Simplicity". This connection between wisdom and simplicity contains an essential truth: it allows us to see that simplicity is as it were the criterion of perfect wisdom—that it is a necessary dimension of wisdom and in a way its consummation. Simplicity is none other than "poverty of spirit", which the saint explains as follows in his *Beatitudes*: "Many persevere in prayers and offices and inflict numerous abstinences and sufferings on their bodies, but if any word appears to be an attack on their persons or they are deprived of something, they take offense and immediately become distressed. Such men are not poor in spirit, for those who are truly poor in spirit hate themselves"—that is, their egoism or the egocentric hardness of heart resulting from the fall—"and love those who persecute them and who strike them on the cheek", and this is because they love the reality that surrounds them insofar as it fulfills for them a divine function, that is, to the extent it opposes the "deifugal" and egocentric tendencies of fallen nature. Simplicity is therefore indifference toward the passional reactions of the soul, an imperturbable and calm concentration on the "one thing needful". To be complete, knowledge must in some way take possession of every aspect of man, and it must therefore be accompanied by indifference toward the passions, for in a certain respect these are privations of truth. Attachment to God goes hand in hand with detachment from the world; the "world" is not, however, the surrounding cosmos insofar as it reflects the truths and beauties of Heaven—Saint Francis was certainly capable of seeing God in nature, as is proven by his "Canticle of Brother Sun" among other things—but our passional connection with ephemeral things.

Finally, let us take note of the idea of "purity", which the saint associates with "simplicity" (*vostra santa sorella la pura semplicità*). The soul that is untroubled by passions is "pure", but this does not mean it is exempt from the natural conditions of the human microcosm, for a plane of existence cannot cease to be what it is by definition. While it is not absolutely impassive, such a soul is always fixed upon God, whence the exclusion of any pretentious, egoistic, and "worldly" movements, though it remains open to holy joy, holy sadness, and holy anger. The soul in a state of "pure simplicity" is a receptacle of the divine Presence and is neither determined nor sullied by anything beneath its nature; and this is why the Blessed Virgin is "pure" and "full of grace" and is prepared to receive the Word: she is thus the model of every holy soul, or rather she is as it were sanctity itself, without which there is neither divine revelation nor return to God.

After "queen Wisdom" and her "holy sister Pure Simplicity" come the "holy lady Poverty with your holy sister Humility", and then the "holy lady Charity with your sister holy Obedience".

Poverty, whether or not it takes the form of renunciation, is essentially detachment—from outward not inward things as in the case of simplicity; Saint Louis was just as detached—hence just as "poor"—as Saint Francis, but as king he could not materially renounce either his palace or family. The connection between this kind of poverty and humility is very important, for whoever is detached from things is also detached from himself, the one being impossible without the other.

Likewise for charity and obedience: whoever loves God more than anything in the world and, acting upon this love, loves his neighbor as himself also possesses obedience, that is, submission to the interest of others or, more precisely, to the divine will in one's neighbor. For love of one's neighbor is a criterion *sine qua non* for the love of God, which means that the second love determines and limits the first and that spiritual benefit takes precedence over temporal benefit to the extent such an alternative presents itself.

And now there follows an observation that is of the greatest importance for understanding this doctrine of the virtues: "There is no man on earth", Saint Francis continues, "who can possess one of you [that is, the virtues] without having first died [to himself]. Whoever possesses one of the virtues without offending against the others possesses them all; and whoever violates even one of them possesses none and violates them all."

The *Laudes* goes on to describe in further detail how the different virtues are to be understood: "And each one covers vices and sins with confusion. Holy wisdom confounds Satan and all his snares"—by striking evil at its very heart. "Pure and holy simplicity confounds all the wisdom of this world and the body"—that is, the "wisdom of the flesh" of which Saint Paul speaks: the blind reasoning of the ignorant and hardened mind, or a certain mental cleverness, or again rationalism and cunning. "Holy poverty confounds cupidity, avarice, and preoccupation with this world"—or rather the spirit of dissipation often involved in these sins. "Holy humility confounds pride and all worldly men"—by refusing to place itself on their level—"as well as all the things of this world"—by robbing them of their illusory value. "Holy charity confounds all the temptations of the demon and the flesh"—the first being active and subversive and the second passive and natural, corresponding to the difference between malice and weakness—"and all anxieties of the flesh"—that is, worldly fears, of which the subjective basis is the natural egoism of the soul. "Holy obedience confounds all corporal and fleshly desires"—that is, desires whose source is the earthly domain in the double respect of need and passion—"and maintains the body in a state of mortification"—the body having to participate in spiritual detachment from the world—"so that it obeys the spirit and its brother"—that is, God in one's neighbor, this neighbor being considered in his indirectly divine function of cosmic corrective—"and so that it is subjected and submissive toward everyone in the world: not only men but also all the animals, whether tamed or wild"—one's neighbor not being limited and obedience having become a universal attitude—"insofar as this is permitted them from above by the Lord" (*supernamente concesso dal Signore*)— for holy abandonment is compensated by divine protection.

In his aphorisms, entitled "Effects of the Virtues", Saint Francis says that "wherever true charity and true wisdom are found there is neither fear nor ignorance"; and with regard to poverty—which must be distinguished here from poverty of spirit, simplicity—he also says, "Wherever there is poverty with joy, there is neither cupidity nor avarice", nor (one might add) curiosity, pettiness, or any sort of greed, hence no passion causing dissipation or hardness of heart. Joy goes hand in hand with poverty because poverty is detachment, and release from limitations of any sort gives rise to joy.

In his commentary on the Lord's Prayer, Saint Francis defines the love of God thus: "Thy will be done on earth as it is in Heaven: so that we may love Thee with all our heart, by thinking unceasingly of Thee"—thought in this case not being a form of discursive ratiocination but a direct, intuitive, and synthetic recollection of the heart; "with all our soul, by desiring Thee always"—affective attitude; "with all our mind, by directing all our intentions toward Thee and seeking Thy honor in all things"—volitive attitude; "and with all our strength, by putting all the powers of the soul and the feelings [sensible faculties] of the body in the service of Thy love and nothing else"—synthesis of all possible human attitudes: "so that we may likewise love our neighbors as ourselves, drawing them all as far as we are able toward Thy love, rejoicing in the good they enjoy, having compassion in their misfortunes as if they were our own, and causing no offense whatsoever to anyone."

The definition of love of one's neighbor is very important here: to draw him as far as we are able—that is, according to our capacities and the vocation resulting from them—toward the love of God; all manifestations of charity are thus subordinated to this essential charity, which, without being opposed to any partial aspect, goes to the heart of things and touches what is divine in our neighbor with what is divine in ourselves.

As we have seen, love of the heart is "to think unceasingly of Thee": "Wherever there is repose and remembrance of God (*il riposo et il ricordo di Dio*)", says Saint Francis, "there is neither anxiety nor dissipation." This connection between calm and contemplation is very significant, for "peace" has always been associated with *gnosis*; the "holy silence" of the Hesychasts is none other than the "Intellect pacified in all its movements", according to the saying of a Greek Father; in other words the intelligence of the heart, purified of all passions and made fit to receive the immutable Light, imbues the soul with the serenity of things eternal.

EDITOR'S NOTES

Numbers in bold indicate pages in the text for which the following citations and explanations are provided.

On the Margin of Liturgical Improvisations

3: "God is a Spirit: and they that worship Him must worship Him *in spirit and in truth*" (John 4:24).

The *Desert Fathers* were Christian ascetics and hermits of the third, fourth, and fifth centuries who withdrew to the wilderness in Egypt, Syria, Palestine, and Arabia to lead lives of interior prayer.

Benedict of Nursia (c. 480-c. 550), known as the "patriarch of Western monasticism", drew upon the Desert Fathers and John Cassian in composing a short *Rule* for the communities of monks in his charge, a rule that came in time to define the spiritual practices of the Order associated with his name.

Note 1: "In vain they do worship me, teaching for doctrines the *commandments of men*" (Matt. 15:9; Mark 7:7).

The *other chapter of this book* is "The Question of Protestantism".

4: *The first Christians called themselves "saints"*: "Paul, an apostle of Jesus Christ by the will of God, and Timotheus our brother, to the saints and faithful brethren in Christ which are at Colose: Grace be unto you" (Col. 1:1-2; passim).

Note 2: On *the extreme complication of the rubrics*, see below "Alternations in Semitic Monotheism", p. 74, author's Note 14.

7: Gaius Julius *Caesar* (100-44 B.C.) was Roman Emperor from 49 B.C.; Marcus Tullius *Cicero* (106-43 B.C.) was a Roman statesman and philosopher and one of Rome's greatest orators and prose stylists.

Note 8: *Dante* Alighieri (1265-1321) was the author of the *Divine Comedy*, one of the summits of world literature.

Meister Eckhart (c. 1260-1327), regarded by the author as the greatest of Christian metaphysicians and esoterists, wrote his commentaries on Scripture in Latin but composed most of his sermons in his native German.

9: The "*Constantinian*" stage is in reference to Constantine the Great (d. 337), the first Christian Roman Emperor, whose defense and patronage of Christianity and involvement in the proceedings of the Council of Nicea created the precedent for a close connection between Church and State.

11: *Irenaeus* (c. 130-c. 200) was Bishop of Lyons and one of the most important of the early Church Fathers; the saying is taken from his most important work, *A Refutation and Overthrow of All Knowledge Falsely So Called*, also known as *Against Heresies*.

"Ye are come unto mount Sion, and unto the city of the living God, the *heavenly Jerusalem*, and to an innumerable company of angels" (Heb. 12:22).

The Enigma of the *Epiclesis*

13: The *epiclesis* in the Liturgy of Saint John Chrysostom, which is addressed to God the Father, reads as follows: "We offer unto Thee this reasonable and unbloody service, and beseech Thee and pray Thee and supplicate Thee: send down Thy Holy Spirit upon us and upon these gifts here spread forth: And make this bread the precious body of Thy Christ and that which is in this cup the precious blood of Thy Christ, changing them by Thy Holy Spirit."

The words of institution are the words Christ used at the Last, or Mystical, Supper: "Take, eat; this is my body, which is broken for you, for the remission of sins"; "Drink ye all of this; this is my blood of the new testament, which is shed for you and for many, for the remission of sins" (cf. Luke 22:19, 20; 1 Cor. 11:24, 25).

Ambrose (c. 339-97), Bishop of Milan, *John Chrysostom* (c. 347-407), Patriarch of Constantinople, and *Augustine* (354-430), Bishop of the North African city of Hippo, all wrote important works on the sacraments and are all recognized as Doctors of the Church.

Note 2: *Theodore of Melitene* (fl. c. 1350) was bishop of the Armenian city of Melitene; *Nicholas Cabasilas* (c. 1320-c. 1390) was a Byzantine theologian and mystical writer whose principal works are a set of seven discourses on *Life in Christ* and a *Commentary on the Divine Liturgy*.

14: *Pius V* (1504-72), Pope of Rome from 1566, attempted to standardize the Mass by making the 1570 edition of the Roman Missal mandatory throughout the Latin rite of the Catholic Church except where a Mass dating from before 1370 was already in use.

Basil the Great (c. 330-79), Bishop of Caesarea, was one of the Cappadocian Fathers and the first of the three Holy Hierarchs of the Eastern Orthodox Church; the *epiclesis* of his Liturgy reads as follows: "Presenting unto Thee the antitypes of the holy body and blood of Christ, we *pray* Thee and *implore*

Thee, O Holy of Holies, *by the favor of Thy goodness*, that Thy Holy Spirit may descend upon us and upon these gifts here spread forth, and bless them, and hallow them, and reveal this bread to be itself the precious body of our Lord, and God, and Savior, Jesus Christ, and this cup to be itself the precious blood of our Lord, and God, and Savior, Jesus Christ, which was shed for the life of the world and its salvation."

15: *The Eucharistic gift is fatal for the unworthy*: "But let a man examine himself, and so let him eat of that bread, and drink of that cup. For he that eateth and drinketh unworthily, eateth and drinketh damnation to himself, not discerning the Lord's body. For this cause many are weak and sickly among you, and many sleep [that is, are dead]" (1 Cor. 11:28-30).

The epicleses of Saint Basil and Saint John Chrysostom do not fail to take this fact into account: "Grant that no one of us may partake of the holy body and blood of Thy Christ unto judgment or unto condemnation" (Liturgy of Saint Basil); "Send down Thy Holy Spirit . . . that to those who partake [of the body and blood] they may be unto cleansing of soul . . . and not unto judgment or unto condemnation" (Liturgy of Saint John Chrysostom).

16: Note 6: "And God blessed them, and God said unto them, *Be fruitful and multiply*, and replenish the earth, and subdue it" (Gen. 1:28).

17: Note 7: *"Wisdom of the world" or "according to the flesh"*: "Where is the wise? where is the scribe? where is the disputer of this world? hath not God made foolish the wisdom of this world?" (1 Cor. 1:20); "I beseech you, that I may not be bold when I am present with that confidence, wherewith I think to be bold against some, which think of us as if we walked *according to the flesh*" (2 Cor. 10:2); "In simplicity and godly sincerity, not with fleshly wisdom, but by the grace of God, we have had our conversation in the world" (2 Cor. 1:12).

According to the Church Father *Justin Martyr* (c. 100-c. 165), "We have been taught that Christ is the *Logos*, of which every race of man partakes. Those who lived in accordance with the *Logos* are Christians, even though they were called godless, such as, among the Greeks, Socrates and Heraclitus and others like them" (*First Apology*, 46).

18: *The "spirit bloweth where it listeth"*: "The wind [Latin: *spiritus*] bloweth where it listeth, and thou hearest the sound thereof, but canst not tell whence it cometh, and whither it goeth: so is every one that is born of the Spirit" (John 3:8).

19: Note 9: Thomas De Vio *Cajetan* (1469-1534), Dominican theologian and Roman Catholic cardinal, was a prolific scholar and strong proponent of the works of Thomas Aquinas.

20: *The words of Christ to Peter.* "I say also unto thee, That thou art Peter, and upon this rock I will build my church; and the gates of hell shall not prevail against it. And I will give unto thee the keys of the kingdom of heaven: and whatsoever thou shalt bind on earth shall be bound in heaven, and whatsoever thou shalt loose on earth shall be loosed in heaven" (Matt. 16:18-19).

21: *Innocent III* (1160-1216) was Pope from 1198 and the author of a treatise concerning the Eucharistic sacrament, "On the Sacred Mystery of the Altar"; *Innocent IV* (d. 1254) was Pope from 1243.

The blessing mentioned in the Gospels: "As they were eating, Jesus took bread, and blessed it, and brake it, and gave it to the disciples, and said, Take, eat; this is my body" (Matt. 26:26; cf. Mark 14:22).

The Roman Catholic *Council of Trent* (1545-63), convened in response to the Reformation, was intended to eliminate abuses in the Church and promulgate a comprehensive system of Catholic doctrine and practice.

For *Meister Eckhart*, see editor's note "On the Margin of Liturgical Improvisations", p. 8, Note 8.

The Question of Protestantism

23: The word "Protestantism" has been used in the title and throughout this chapter in translating the French word *Évangélisme;* in the European context with which the author was most familiar, *Évangélisme* is used to refer primarily to the Lutheran, as distinct from the Calvinist, wing of the Reformation, then to the union of the Lutheran and Reformed churches, and finally to Protestant churches in general; in contemporary English usage, however, "Evangelicalism" has a very different, and much narrower, connotation.

Amidism is the Buddhist *Jōdo* or Pure Land sect, whose central spiritual practice is the invocation of the Name of Amida, the Buddha of "infinite light".

Nichiren (1222-82), a Japanese Buddhist monk, taught that enlightenment is available to all human beings through simple faith in the compassion and saving power of the Buddha as described in the *Lotus Sūtra*, a faith one expresses by invoking the *mantra:* "I take refuge in the Lotus of the wonderful law *Sūtra.*"

24: Note 2: *Arius of Alexandria* (c. 250-c. 336) taught that Christ, the Son of God, was the highest of all created beings (cf. Prov. 8:23) but not divine.

25: John *Wycliffe* (c. 1330-84), an English philosopher, theologian, and early reformer, taught that the Bible is the sole criterion of Christian doctrine, to which no ecclesiastical authority may rightly add; John *Huss* (c. 1372-1415) was a Czech preacher and outspoken critic of the papacy who was greatly influenced by the writings of Wycliffe.

"In vain they do worship me, teaching for doctrines the *commandments of men*" (Matt. 15:9; Mark 7:7).

26: Martin *Luther* (1483-1546), father of the German Reformation, is known for his insistence that justification is by faith alone.

"Then said the king to the servants, Bind him hand and foot, and take him away, and cast him into *outer darkness*; there shall be weeping and gnashing of teeth" (Matt. 22:13; cf. Matt. 8:12, 25:30).

27: *Dante* Alighieri (see editor's note for "On the Margin of Liturgical Improvisations", p. 7, Note 8) repeatedly condemned ecclesiastical corruption and denounced many of the Popes of his time, including Nicholas III, Boniface VIII, and Clement V; see the *Divine Comedy*, Canto 19.

Girolamo *Savonarola* (1452-98), a Dominican friar and apocalyptic preacher, was known for his prophetic condemnations of corruption among the clergy and specifically for his denunciation of Pope Alexander VI and his corrupt court.

Note 3: *Joseph de Maistre* (1753-1821), a French Ultramontanist, argued in his work *On the Papacy* that society should be based on monarchical authority, with spiritual authority being vested in the office of the Pope and temporal authority in that of kings.

28: According to *Augustine* (see editor's note for "The Enigma of the *Epiclesis*", p. 13), human history is the scene of a continuing conflict between the City of God, defined by its stress upon spiritual values, and the city of man, the earthly city or city of the devil, marked by its perversion and worldliness.

29: For the *Council of Trent*, see editor's note for "The Enigma of the *Epiclesis*", p. 21.

Note 6: John Henry *Newman* (1801-90) was an influential Anglican theologian and homilist and later, after his conversion, a Roman Catholic cardinal.

30: *Bernard* of Clairvaux (1090-1153), a Cistercian monk and author of numerous homilies on the Song of Songs, insisted that the churches of his Order should be plain and very simply appointed and that vestments and ornaments should not be made of precious materials.

"God is a Spirit: and they that worship Him must worship Him *in spirit and in truth*" (John 4:24).

"But when ye pray, use not *vain repetitions as the heathen do*" (Matt. 6:7).

Gregory VII (c. 1021-85) was Pope of Rome from 1073.

31: *The year of Wartburg*: in order to avoid arrest as a heretic, Luther lived *incognito* in Wartburg Castle at Eisenach for eleven months in 1521.

"But many that are *first shall be last*; and the last shall be first" (Matt. 19:30; cf. Matt. 20:16, Mark 9:35, 10:31, Luke 13:30).

Note 8: *Ramakrishna* (1834-86), a *bhakta* of the Hindu Goddess Kali, was one of the greatest Hindu saints of modern times. Elsewhere the author writes: "Ramakrishnian universality was a universality without prophecy. A deviation was inevitable the moment people sought to give this unique universalism a collective and quasi-religious expression; nothing could have been more contrary to the spirit of Ramakrishna. . . . He never pretended to be the founder of a religion, quite the contrary; at the same time he did not prevent such a thing from taking place in his name: his excessive independence with regard to orthodoxy was bound indirectly to bring about this error" (*Spiritual Perspectives and Human Facts: A New Translation with Selected Letters*, ed. James S. Cutsinger [Bloomington, Indiana: World Wisdom, 2007], 124, 127).

32: The three *Evangelical counsels* of poverty, chastity, and obedience, also known as the "counsels of perfection", gave rise to the traditional vows of the monk.

"And Jesus answered and said, Verily I say unto you, *There is no man that hath left house, or brethren, or sisters, or father, or mother, or wife, or children, or lands, for my sake, and the gospel's, but he shall receive an hundredfold* now in this time, houses, and brethren, and sisters, and mothers, and children, and lands, with persecutions; and in the world to come eternal life" (Mark 10:29-30).

"*Blessed are they which are persecuted for righteousness' sake: for theirs is the kingdom of heaven*" (Matt. 5:10).

Note 10: Luther composed the hymn *Ein feste Burg ist unser Gott*, "A Mighty Fortress is Our God", sometime between 1527 and 1529.

33: "There is therefore now no condemnation to them which are in Christ Jesus, who walk not *after the flesh*, but *after the Spirit*" (Rom. 8:1).

The ancient Greek philosopher *Aristotle* (384-322 B.C.) had a decisive influence on the teachings of Thomas Aquinas and other medieval *Scholastics*.

Note 12: Jean *de Labadie* (1610-74), a French Jesuit priest who became a Protestant in 1650, believed that the Bible could be understood only by the direct inspiration of the Holy Spirit; Philipp Jakob *Spener* (1635-1705), who was greatly influenced by the writings of de Labadie, is widely regarded as the father of German pietism; Gerhard *Tersteegen* (1697-1769), a German pietist writer, is best known for his "Spiritual Flower Garden for Ardent Souls", a collection of devotional hymns and lyric poetry.

Note 15: *Albert the Great* (c. 1200-1280) and Meister *Eckhart* (see editor's note for "On the Margin of Liturgical Improvisations", p. 7, Note 8) were both Germans, like Luther, and were also like him in being steeped in the Latin learning of their time.

34: *Jerome* (c. 342-420), the most important Biblical scholar of the early Church, is known for his passionate attacks against Arianism, Pelagianism, Origenism, and other heresies of his day.

"*Zeal for the house of the Lord*": "For the zeal of Thine house hath eaten me up; and the reproaches of them that reproached Thee are fallen upon me" (Ps. 69:9; cf. John 2:17).

Leo X (1475-1521) was Pope from 1513.

Note 16: *Nichiren* (see editor's note above for this chapter, p. 23) was adamantly opposed to the Pure Land practice of invoking *Amida*.

Note 17: *Johann Valentin Andrea* (1586-1642) was a Lutheran theologian, pastor, mathematician, and utopian writer; *Paul Gerhardt* (1607-76), also a Lutheran pastor, is widely regarded as Germany's greatest composer of hymns; *Novalis*—the pseudonym of Friederich Leopold Freiherr von Hardenberg (1772-1801)—was a German Romantic poet and the composer of *Spiritual Songs* and *Hymns to the Night*; the music of Johann Sebastian *Bach* (1685-1750) was originally composed for use in the Lutheran Church.

35: "And the angel came in unto her, and said, Hail, thou that art *full of grace*, the Lord is with thee: blessed art thou among women" (Luke 1:28); "And Mary said, My soul doth magnify the Lord, and my spirit hath rejoiced in God my savior. For he hath regarded the low estate of his handmaiden: for, behold, *all generations shall call me blessed*" (Luke 1:46-48).

Johann von *Staupitz* (c. 1460-1524), a Roman Catholic theologian and Vicar General of the Augustinian Order in Germany, having formerly served as Luther's confessor when the latter was still a monk, was assigned the task of representing the Catholic Church in discussions with Luther concerning the doctrine of the atonement and the means of sacramental grace.

36: Ulrich *Zwingli* (1484-1531) believed that the Eucharist was merely a memorial service and that Christ was not really present in the bread and wine.

Note 20: "*Give* not that which *is holy unto the dogs*, neither *cast* ye your *pearls before swine*, lest they trample them under their feet, and turn again and rend you" (Matt. 7:6).

37: Andreas Rudolf Bodenstein von *Karlstadt* (1486-1541) was a professor at the University of Wittenberg; Johannes *Oekolampad* (1482-1531) was principal of the Reformed Church in Basel.

Note 24: *Eleusis* was an important center of the ancient Greek mystery religions.

39: "Jesus saith unto him, Thomas, because thou hast seen me, thou hast believed: *blessed are they that have not seen, and yet have believed*" (John 20:29).

"*Love God with all our strength*": "And thou shalt love the Lord thy God with all thy heart, and with all thy soul, and with all thy mind, and with all thy strength: this is the first commandment" (Mark 12:30); "And he answering said, Thou shalt love the Lord thy God with all thy heart, and with all thy soul, and with all thy strength, and with all thy mind; and thy neighbor as thyself" (Luke 10:27).

Philipp *Melanchthon* (1497-1560), a close collaborator and friend of Luther, is credited with providing the first systematic exposition of Protestant doctrine.

42: *Shinran* (1173-1262), who was founder of the *Jōdo-Shinshū* or "true pure land school" of Japanese Buddhism, rejected all "ways of effort" and advocated complete reliance on the "power of the other" as manifest in the Name of the Buddha Amida, a single pronunciation of which is sufficient for rebirth in the Buddha's paradise, *Sukhāvatī*.

46: *The Saying of the Burning Bush*: "The Lord appeared unto [Moses] in a flame of fire out of the midst of a bush" (Exod. 3:2), and "God said unto Moses, I AM THAT I AM; and He said, Thus shalt thou say unto the children of Israel, I AM hath sent me unto you" (Exod. 3:14).

7

47: "*Though I speak with the tongues of men and of angels*, and have not love, I am become as sounding brass, or a tinkling cymbal. And though I have the gift of prophecy, and understand all mysteries, and all knowledge; and *though I have all faith, so that I could remove mountains, and have not love, I am nothing. . . . And now abideth faith, hope, love, these three; but the greatest of these is love*" (1 Cor. 13:1-2, 13).

Justification by faith: "Therefore we conclude that a man is justified by faith without the deeds of the law" (Rom. 3:28).

49: "One day when we were sitting with the Messenger of God there came unto us a man whose clothes were of exceeding whiteness and whose hair was of exceeding blackness; nor were there any signs of travel upon him, although none of us knew him. He sat down knee unto knee opposite the Prophet, upon whose thighs he placed the palms of his hands, saying: 'O Muhammad . . . Tell me what is spiritual excellence.' He answered: 'To serve *God as if thou sawest him, for if thou seest Him not, He nonetheless seeth thee*'" (*hadīth* of Gabriel).

"At that time Jesus went on the *sabbath* day through the corn; and his disciples were an hungered, and began to *pluck the ears of corn*, and to eat" (Matt. 12:1; cf. Mark 2:23, Luke 6:1).

Saint Paul suppressed "circumcision in the flesh" in the name of "circumcision in the spirit": "For he is not a Jew, which is one outwardly; neither is that circumcision, which is outward in the flesh: But he is a Jew, which is one inwardly; and circumcision is that of the heart, in the spirit, and not in the letter; whose praise is not of men, but of God" (Rom. 2:28-29; cf. Eph. 2:11, Col. 2:13).

"Jesus answered and said unto her, If thou knewest the gift of God, and who it is that saith to thee, Give me to drink; thou wouldest have asked of him, and he would have given thee *living water*" (John 4:10).

50: Note 27: *Jakob Boehme* (1575-1624), known as the "Teutonic Theosopher", was a German Lutheran, whose esoteric insights, often couched in Hermetic and alchemical language, can be found in such treatises as *Aurora*, *The Way to Christ*, and *Dialogue of the Supersensual Life*.

John Smith the Platonist (1618-52) was a mathematician and philosopher at Queens' College, Cambridge, and a founding member of the Cambridge Platonists.

William Law (1686-1761), greatly influenced in later life by the works of Boehme, is best known for his *Serious Call to a Devout and Holy Life* and a treatise *On Christian Perfection*.

Lilian Staveley (c. 1878-1928) was an Anglican laywoman whose anonymous writings, including the autobiographical *Prodigal Returns*, were much admired by the author.

52: *Eckhart* taught that *aliquid est in anima quod est* increatum et increabile: "There is something in the soul that is uncreated and uncreatable."

Note 28: *Paracelsus*—Theophrastus Bombastus von Hohenheim (1493-1541)—was learned in a vast array of subjects, including chemistry, alchemy, astrology, metallurgy, and above all medicine.

53: The sermons of John *Tauler* (c. 1300-1361), a Dominican theologian and popular preacher, were much admired by Luther; Henry *Suso* (c. 1295-1366), also a Dominican, was a student of Eckhart.

Note 30: *Kurzer Bericht von der Mystik* is German for "A Brief Account of a Mystic".

Note 31: *Angelus Silesius*, that is, the "Silesian Angel", was the penname of Johannes Scheffler (1624-77), whose mystical poetry was greatly influenced by Eckhart; the son of a Lutheran Polish nobleman, he converted to Catholicism and later became a priest.

Chaitanya (1486-1533), a Vaishnavite Hindu spiritual teacher and devotee of Krishna, was regarded by his followers as an *avatāra* of both Krishna and his consort Radha.

The Problem of Moral Divergences

57: "And [Jesus] answered and said unto them, What did Moses command you? And they said, Moses suffered to write a bill of divorcement, and to put her away. And Jesus answered and said unto them, For *the hardness of your heart* he wrote you this precept. But from the beginning of the creation God made them male and female. For this cause shall a man leave his father and mother, and cleave to his wife; and they twain shall be one flesh: so then they are no more twain, but one flesh. *What therefore God hath joined together, let not man put asunder*" (Mark 10:3-9).

58: "*My kingdom is not of this world*" (John 18:36).

59: "*No man can serve two masters*: for either he will hate the one, and love the other; or else he will hold to the one, and despise the other. Ye cannot serve God and mammon" (Matt. 6:24, Luke 16:13).

"*Not only the goods of the other world but also the goods of this world*": "There are some people who say, Our Lord, give to us in this world; such people will have no part in the Hereafter. And there are others who say, Our Lord, give to us in this world good, and good in the Hereafter, and guard us against the chastisement of the Fire. They shall have a portion from what they have earned; and God is swift at reckoning" (*Sūrah* "The Cow" [2]:200-202); "There is an hour during the night in which no Muslim will ask God for good in this world and the next (reciting 2:201 above) without His giving it to him. And this applies to every night" (*hadīth*).

60: According to *Meister Eckhart* (see editor's notes for "On the Margin of Liturgical Improvisations", p. 7, Note 8 and "The Question of Protestantism", p. 52) all food is Holy Communion for those who are pure of heart.

"*Man is made of desire*" (*Brihadāranyaka Upanishad*, 3.9.11).

"*But those things which proceed out of the mouth come forth from the heart; and they defile the man*" (Matt. 15:18).

"For laying aside the *commandment of God*, ye hold the *tradition of men*, as the washing of pots and cups: and many other such like things ye do" (Mark 7:8).

61: "*A new commandment I give unto you, that ye love one another*, as I have loved you, that ye also love one another" (John 13:34).

Alternations in Semitic Monotheism

65: *The "new law" of love*: "A new commandment I give unto you, that ye love one another; as I have loved you, that ye also love one another" (John 13:34).

66: "The *letter killeth*, but the spirit giveth life" (2 Cor. 3:6).

"*There is no change in the words of God*" (*Sūrah* "Jonah" [10]:64).

67: Note 3: "And in that day ye shall ask me nothing. Verily, verily, I say unto you, *Whatsoever ye shall ask the Father in my name, he will give it you*" (John 16:23).

The Father is "greater than the Son": "My Father is greater than I" (John 14:28).

68: Note 4: *The Queen of Sheba*: "The queen of the south shall rise up in the judgment with this generation, and shall condemn it: for she came from the uttermost parts of the earth to hear the wisdom of *Solomon*; and, behold, a greater than Solomon is here" (Matt. 12:42; cf. Luke 11:31).

"Consider the *lilies of the field*, how they grow; they toil not, neither do they spin; and yet I say unto you, that even *Solomon* in all his glory was not arrayed like one of these" (Matt. 6:28-29).

Note 5: "At that time Jesus answered and said, *I thank thee, O Father, Lord of heaven and earth, because thou hast hid these things from the wise and prudent, and hast revealed them unto babes*" (Matt. 11:25, Luke 10:21).

69: "*I am the light of the world*; he that followeth me shall not walk in darkness, but shall have the light of life" (John 8:12).

"He that loveth not knoweth not God; for *God is love*" (1 John 4:8).

For *aliquid increatum et increabile*, see editor's note for "The Question of Protestantism", p. 52.

"God *became man that man might become God*" is the formulation of Irenaeus (c. 130-c. 200) and Athanasius (c. 296-373), among other Church Fathers.

70: "I am the *door*. by me if any man enter in, he shall be saved, and shall go in and out, and find pasture" (John 10:9).

Shankara (788-820), one of the most influential sages in the history of India, was the pre-eminent spokesman for *Advaita Vedānta*, the Hindu perspective of "non-dualism".

Note 8: For *Arianism*, the doctrine of Arius, see editor's note for "The Question of Protestantism", p. 24, Note 2; *Sabellianism*, or modalism, was an ancient Trinitarian heresy, which claimed that each Person is merely a temporary mode or mask of an essentially unitarian Deity.

71: "Jesus said unto them, Verily, verily, I say unto you, *Before Abraham* was, I am" (John 8:58).

"Hear, O Israel: The Lord our *God is one* Lord" (Deut. 6:4).

"Go ye therefore, and teach all nations, *baptizing them in the name of the Father, and of the Son, and of the Holy Spirit*" (Matt. 28:19).

72: "Why callest thou me good? *There is none good but* one, that is, *God*" (Matt. 19:17, Mark 10:18; cf. Luke 18:19).

"Jesus saith unto her, Touch me not; for I am not yet ascended to my Father: but go to my brethren, and say unto them, *I ascend unto my Father, and your Father; and to my God, and your God*" (John 20:17).

73: "And have ye not read this scripture; *the stone which the builders rejected is become the head of the corner*" (Mark 12:10; cf. Matt. 21:42, Luke 20:17).

The promises made by God to Abraham and Hagar. "And God said unto Abraham, Let it not be grievous in thy sight because of the lad [Ishmael], and because of thy bondwoman [Hagar]; in all that Sarah hath said unto thee, hearken unto her voice; for in Isaac shall thy seed be called. And also of the son of the bondwoman will I make a nation, because he is thy seed" (Gen. 21:12-13); "And God heard the voice of the lad [Ishmael]; and the angel of God called to Hagar out of heaven, and said unto her, What aileth thee, Hagar? fear not; for God hath heard the voice of the lad where he is. Arise, lift up the lad, and hold him in thine hand; for I will make him a great nation" (Gen. 21:17-18).

Note 11: "So *the last shall be first, and the first last*: for many be called, but few chosen" (Matt. 20:16; cf. Matt. 19:30; cf. Mark 9:35, 10:31, Luke 13:30).

74: Note 12: "Think not that I am come to *destroy* the *law*, or the prophets: I am not come to destroy, but to *fulfill*" (Matt. 5:17).

Note 14: On *the disproportionate complication of the rubrics*, see above "On the Margin of Liturgical Improvisations", p. 4, author's Note 2.

The marriage of bishops: "A bishop then must be blameless, the husband of one wife, vigilant, sober, of good behavior, given to hospitality, apt to teach" (1 Tim. 3:2).

77: *Honorius I* (d. 638), Pope from 625, was condemned by the Fathers of the Seventh Ecumenical Council (Nicea, 787): "There shall be expelled from the Holy Church of God and anathematized Honorius, who was some time Pope of Old Rome."

78: Note 18: *Gregory of Nyssa* (c. 330-c. 395), one of the Cappadocian Fathers of the early Church, wrote an extensive commentary on the Biblical account of creation, including a treatise on the work of the sixth day, the formation of man.

Saint Paul writes in *Galatians 3:28*, "There is neither Jew nor Greek, there is neither bond nor free, there is neither male nor female: for ye are all one in Christ Jesus."

"*Multiply and fill the earth*": "And God blessed them, and God said unto them, Be fruitful, and multiply, and replenish the earth, and subdue it" (Gen. 1:28).

80: *Rejecting the prescriptions of the Pharisees*: "Ye hypocrites, well did *Isaiah* prophesy of you, saying, This people draweth nigh unto me with their mouth, and honoreth me with their lips; but their heart is far from me. But in vain they do worship me, teaching for doctrines the commandments of men" (Matt. 15:7-9; cf. Isa. 29:13).

Offer the left cheek: "Whosoever shall smite thee on thy right cheek, turn to him the other also" (Matt. 5:39).

"Then said Jesus unto him, Put up again thy sword into his place: for *all they that take the sword shall perish with the sword*" (Matt. 26:52).

81: Note 21: For *Meister Eckhart*, see "On the Margin of Liturgical Improvisations", p. 7, Note 8; "The Question of Protestantism", p. 33, Note 15 and p. 52; and "The Problem of Moral Divergences", p. 7.

"Now it came to pass, as they went, that [Jesus] entered into a certain village: and a certain woman named *Martha* received him into her house. And she had a sister called *Mary*, which also sat at Jesus' feet, and heard his word. But Martha was cumbered about with much serving, and came to him, and said, Lord, dost thou not care that my sister hath left me to serve alone? bid her therefore that she help me. And Jesus answered and said unto her, Martha, Martha, thou art careful and troubled about many things: But one thing is needful: and Mary hath chosen that good part, which shall not be taken from her" (Luke 10:38-42).

Muhyi al-Din *Ibn Arabi* (1165-1240), author of numerous works including *Meccan Revelations* and *Bezels of Wisdom*, was a prolific and profoundly influential Sufi mystic, known in tradition as the Shaykh al-Akbar, that is, the great master.

82: *Thomas* Aquinas (c. 1225-74), a giant among the medieval Scholastics and a Doctor of the Roman Catholic Church, followed Aristotle in teaching that "the principle of knowledge is in the senses" (*Summa Theologica*, Part 1, Quest. 84, Art. 6).

84: For *Aristotle*, see editor's note for "The Question of Protestantism", p. 33.

86: "I am *black, but beautiful*" (Song of Sol. 1:5).

Note 25: *The* Sūrah *"Purity"*: "Say: He is God, the One (*Ahad*)! God, the limitless and immutable (*Samad*). He begetteth not nor was begotten. And there is none comparable unto Him" (112:1-4); see below "The Idea of the 'Best' in Religions", p. 100, author's Note 9.

"Say: Call upon God, or call upon the Merciful: by whatever name ye call upon Him (it is well): for *to Him belong the most beautiful Names*" (*Sūrah* "The Children of Israel" [17]:110).

87: *Ecce enim regnum Dei intra vos est* is Latin for "For, behold, the kingdom of God is within you" (Luke 17:21).

Note 26: "My *yoke is easy*, and my *burden is light*" (Matt. 11:30).

Note 27: "And John answered and said, Master, we saw one casting out devils *in* thy *name*; and we forbad him, because he followeth not with us. And Jesus said unto him, Forbid him not: *for he that is not against us is for us*" (Luke 9:50; cf. Mark 9:40).

The Idea of the "Best" in Religions

94: "*Zeal for the house of the Lord*": "For the zeal of Thine house hath eaten me up; and the reproaches of them that reproached Thee are fallen upon me" (Ps. 69:9; cf. John 2:17).

Note 2: For *Ibn Arabi*, see editor's note for "Alternations in Semitic Mono-theism", p. 81, Note 21.

For *Bernard* of Clairvaux, see editor's note for "The Question of Protes-tantism", p. 30.

Etienne *Gilson* (1884-1978) was a French neo-Thomist and historian of medieval philosophy.

95: Note 4: The author's *L'ésotérisme comme principe et comme voie* was published in 1978 (Paris: Dervy-Livres); it appeared in English translation as *Esoterism as Principle and as Way* in 1981 (London: Perennial Books, trans. William Stoddart).

100: Note 9: *According to the Koran it is almost the equivalent of the name* Allāh: "Say: Call upon God [*Allāh*], or call upon the Merciful (*Rahmān*): by whatever name ye call upon Him (it is well): for to Him belong the most beautiful Names" (*Sūrah* "The Children of Israel" [17]:110); see above "Alternations in Semitic Monotheism", p. 86, author's Note 25.

Note 10: For *Dante* and *Savonarola*, see editor's notes for "The Question of Protestantism", p. 27.

101: *Abu Bakr* (d. 634) was among the Prophet Muhammad's foremost Com-panions and served after the Prophet's death as the first caliph of Islam.

Note 12: *Khadijah* was the first wife of the Prophet Muhammad.

Ali ibn Abi Talib (d. 661) was the cousin and son-in-law of the Prophet Muhammad and the fourth caliph of Islam.

Note 13: The *conversion* of *Saint Paul* (Saul of Tarsus) is described in Acts 9:1-22; *the denials of the apostle Peter* are related in Matthew 26:69-75, Mark 14:66-72, Luke 22:54-62, and John 18:25-27; "*Mary* called *Magdalene*, out of whom went seven devils", was among the women who "had been healed of evil spirits and infirmities" (Luke 8:2) by Christ.

104: *Our book on the unity of religions* is the author's *Transcendent Unity of Religions* (Wheaton, Illinois: The Theosophical Publishing House, 1984). Elsewhere he writes: "In Islam there is as it were no sanctity outside of esoterism; in Christianity there is no esoterism outside of sanctity", adding in a footnote, "These formulations have nothing absolute about them and mark in each case a kind of predominance rather than an exclusivity of mode; nonetheless they shine a clear light on certain fundamental differences between the two traditions in question" (*Spiritual Perspectives and Human Facts: A New Translation with Selected Letters*, ed. James S. Cutsinger [Bloomington, Indiana: World Wisdom, 2007], 87-88).

105: "*God became man that man might become God*": The essential teaching expressed by this formulation is common to many Church Fathers, including *Irenaeus* (see editor's note for "On the Margin of Liturgical Improvisations", p. 11), according to whom "the Son of God became the Son of man so that man, by entering into communion with the Word and thus receiving divine sonship, might become a son of God" (*Against Heresies*, 3:19).

Note 19: According to the Athanasian Creed, Christ is "*true God and true man*, of a reasonable soul and body, equal to the Father as touching his Godhead, and subordinate to the Father as touching his manhood".

106: "*Made in the image of God*": "God created man in His own image, in the image of God created He him; male and female created He them" (Gen. 1:27).

108: "*With My permission*": "God saith: O Jesus, son of Mary! Remember My favor unto thee and unto thy mother; how I strengthened thee with the holy Spirit, so that thou spakest unto mankind in the cradle as in maturity; and how I taught thee the Scripture and Wisdom and the Torah and the Gospel; and how thou didst shape of clay as it were the likeness of a bird *with My permission*, and didst blow upon it and it was a bird *with My permission*, and thou didst heal him who was born blind and the leper *with My permission*; and how thou didst raise the dead *with My permission*; and how I restrained the Children of Israel from (harming) thee when thou camest unto them with clear proofs, and those of them who disbelieved exclaimed: This is naught else than mere magic" (*Sūrah* "The Table Spread" [5]:110).

Note 20: The author's *Forme et substance dans les religions* was published in 1975 (Paris: Dervy-Livres); it appeared in English translation as *Form and Substance in the Religions* in 2002 (Bloomington, Indiana: World Wisdom, trans. Mark Perry and Jean-Pierre Lafouge). His book *Logique et transcendance* was published in 1970 (Paris: Éditions Traditionnelles); it appeared in English translation as *Logic and Transcendence* in 1975 (New York: Harper and Row; London: Perennial Books, trans. Peter N. Townsend).

109: *"My kingdom is not of this world"* (John 18:36).

111: "And *the light shineth in darkness; and the darkness comprehended it not*" (tenebrae eam non comprehenderunt)" (John 1:5).

112: *A holy war* (jihād) *that is "little" and another that is "great"*: "The Prophet Muhammad, returning from one of his military campaigns, said, You have come forth in the best way of coming forth: you have come from the little *jihād* to the great *jihād*. His companions asked, And what is the great *jihād*? He replied, The striving of God's servants against their idle desires" (*hadīth*).

113: Note 24: "But I say unto you, *Love* your *enemies*, bless them that curse you, do good to them that hate you, and pray for them which despitefully use you, and persecute you" (Matt. 5:44; cf. Luke 6:27).

114: *God alone is good*: "Why callest thou me good? There is none good but one, that is, God" (Matt. 19:17, Mark 10:18; cf. Luke 18:19).

Images of Islam

116: *Abu Sufyan* ibn Harb (d. 653) was a wealthy Qurayshite merchant who opposed the Prophet Muhammad before eventually converting to Islam.

Note 1: The *"Battle of the Camel"* took place at Basra, Iraq in 656 between forces allied to Ali (see editor's note for "The Idea of the 'Best' in Religions", p. 101, Note 12) and those allied to Aisha, daughter of Abu Bakr (see editor's note for "The Idea of the 'Best' in Religions", p. 101) and a wife of the Prophet Muhammad.

Clovis (c. 466-511), the first king to unite all the Frankish tribes under one ruler, and *Charlemagne* (c. 742-814), the first Emperor of the Holy Roman Empire, were alike in extending their lands through numerous conquests and wars.

117: *Umar* ibn al-Khattab (c. 581-684) was the second caliph of Islam; when offered the keys to the city of Jerusalem by the *Patriarch* Sophronius and invited to pray at the Church of the Holy Sepulcher, Umar declined in order not to endanger its status as a Christian temple.

Note 4: Salah al-Din—*Saladin* (1138-93)—was a Kurdish Muslim general who gained control of Jerusalem from the Crusaders in 1187 and successfully prevented Richard I—*Richard the Lion-Heart* (1157-99)—from retaking the city in 1192.

118: For *Constantine*, see editor's note for "On the Margin of Liturgical Improvisations", p. 9.

Fatimah, the daughter of the Prophet Muhammad and his first wife, Khadija, married the Prophet's cousin, Ali (see editor's note for "The Idea of the 'Best' in Religions", p. 101, Note 12); those who are privileged to claim membership in the "family of Muhammad" through descent from Fatimah are known as *sharīfs*.

119: For *Abu Bakr*, see editor's note for "The Idea of the 'Best' in Religions", p. 101. *Uthman* ibn Affan (d. 655) was the third caliph of Islam.

Moses broke the Tablets of the Law upon seeing the Golden Calf: "And it came to pass, as soon as he came nigh unto the camp, that he saw the calf, and the dancing: and Moses' anger waxed hot, and he cast the tables out of his hands, and brake them beneath the mount. And he took the calf which they had made, and burnt it in the fire, and ground it to powder, and strawed it upon the water, and made the children of Israel drink of it" (Exod. 32:19-20).

Karbala, Iraq is the site of a historic battle in which the Prophet Muhammad's grandson, Husayn ibn Ali, was killed while fighting against the vastly greater forces of the Umayyad caliph, Yazid I.

Al-*Hasan* ibn Ali (d. 669) and al-*Husayn* ibn Ali (626-80) were the two sons of Ali and Fatimah; *Aisha* (d. 678) was the daughter of Abu Bakr and a wife of the Prophet Muhammad.

121: *Rabiah Adawiyyah* (c. 713-801), one of the most renowned of Sufi saints, lived an extremely ascetical life, saying that there was no place in her heart for the desire of anything but God.

Note 10: *Yusuf ibn Ismail al-Nabahani* (1849-1932), author of *Al-Anwār al-Muhammadiyyah*, or "Muhammadan Light", was a Sufi poet, scholar of *hadīth*, and judge of the Shafii school of law.

Law of Love: "And thou shalt love the Lord thy God with all thine heart, and with all thy soul, and with all thy might" (Deut. 6:5); "Thou shalt love the Lord thy God with all thy heart, and with all thy soul, and with all thy mind, and with all thy strength" (Mark 12:30; cf. Luke 10:27).

122: *"And the light shineth in darkness; and the darkness comprehended it not"* (John 1:5); below the author also quotes this verse in Latin: *lux in tenebris lucet et tenebrae eam non comprehenderunt.*

123: *Lux in tenebris [lucet]* is Latin for "the light [shineth] in darkness" (see above).

Note 13: *Umar II* (682-720) was an Umayyad caliph who ruled from 717-720.

124: *Sita*, an incarnation of the goddess Lakshmi, was abducted by the demon king Ravana and taken from India to the island of Lanka, where she was eventually rescued by her husband, Rama, the seventh *Avatāra* of the Hindu god Vishnu; after rescuing her, however, Rama began to doubt her fidelity and ordered her banished to the forest and killed; spared by the executioner, she was finally able to convince Rama of her devotion, though her own heart was now broken.

Maya, the mother of Siddhartha, the historical Buddha, died shortly after giving birth to him; in Tibetan Buddhism, *Tara*, the "*Mother of all the Buddhas*" or "Mother of Compassion", is the female counterpart of the *bodhisattva* Avalokiteshvara.

125: Note 16: *Hasan al-Basri* (642-728), one of the earliest and most influential Sufis and a key figure in the transmission of many *ahādīth*, was noted for his outspoken criticism of the worldliness of the Umayyad rulers.

126: *The gopīs loved Krishna*: Hindu tradition tells of the youthful dalliance of the *Avatāra* Krishna, the eighth incarnation of the Hindu god Vishnu, with the adoring *gopīs*, or cowherd girls, of Vrindavan.

Note 18: *Muawiyah* ibn Abi-Sufyan (d. 680), founder of the Umayyad dynasty, rejected *Ali*'s claim to the caliphate and opposed him in the Battle of Siffin, the first Muslim *fitnah* or civil war.

Muhammad *Ibn Sirin* al-Ansari (653-728) was a noteworthy ascetic and interpreter of dreams.

127: Note 19: *Madhva* (1238-1317), founder of the Hindu Vishnuite school, opposed the advaitic or non-dual doctrine of *Shankara* (see editor's note for "Alternations in Semitic Monotheism", p. 70), asserting that there is an irreducible duality between *Brahma* and the soul.

130: *Jimmu Tenno* (660-585 B.C.), regarded in Shinto belief as a direct descendant of the sun goddess, Amaterasu, was in turn the ancestor of the Japanese emperors.

Note 28: The *Nusairis*, *Ali-Ilahis*, and *Bektashis* are heterodox Shiite sects.

132: "I say unto you, That *Elias is come* already, and they knew him not, but have done unto him whatsoever they listed. Likewise shall also the Son of Man suffer of them. Then the disciples understood that he spake unto them of *John the Baptist*" (Matt. 17:12-13; cf. Mark 9:13).

Dilemmas of Muslim Scholasticism

133: Abu al-Hasan al-*Ashari* (873-935), one of the most important theologians of early Islam, insisted that Koranic descriptions of God are to be understood literally, not metaphorically, but that it is impossible to know in exactly what way they pertain to God, who is utterly beyond human understanding.

Note 1: Ahmad *al-Alawi* (1869-1934), a famous Algerian Sufi *shaykh*, was the author's spiritual master.

134: Ahmad *Ibn Hanbal* (780-855) was the founder of the most conservative of the four orthodox schools of Islamic law, which accentuates a literal interpretation of the Koran and *sunnah*.

"*God doeth what He will*" (*Sūrah* "The Family of Imran" [3]:40, passim).

135: For *Ibn Arabi*, see editor's note for "Alternations in Semitic Monotheism", p. 81, Note 21.

136: The *Ten Commandments* are found in Exod. 20:2-17 and Deut. 5:6-21.

"God created man *in His* own *image*, in the image of God created He him; male and female created He them" (Gen. 1:27).

Note 3: "And when those who believe in Our revelations come unto thee, say: Peace be unto you! Your Lord hath *prescribed Mercy for Himself*, that whoso of you doeth evil and repenteth afterward thereof and doeth right, (for him) lo! God is Forgiving, Merciful" (*Sūrah* "Cattle" [6]:54; cf. 6:12).

138: The *Basmalah*, which is *placed at the head of each* sūrah, describes God as "*the Infinitely Good, the Ever Merciful*".

139: Abu Hamid Muhammad *al-Ghazzali* (1058-1111), often regarded as the greatest religious authority in Islam after the Prophet Muhammad, was a jurist and theologian before entering upon the Sufi path.

"And Our word unto a thing, when We intend it, is only that We say unto it: *Be*! and it is" (*Sūrah* "The Bee" [16]:40).

140: Note 5: Abu Nasr al-*Farabi* (870-950), a Muslim philosopher in the Neoplatonic tradition, wrote important works on mathematics, politics, medicine, and music.

Avicenna—Abu Ali Husayn ibn Sina (980-1037)—was a prodigious and highly influential authority on a wide array of subjects, including theology, philosophy, medicine, and natural science.

143: "Covet not the gifts by which God hath raised some of you above others. The men shall have a portion *according to their deserts*, and the women a portion *according to their deserts*. Of God, therefore, ask his gifts. Verily, God hath knowledge of all things" (*Sūrah* "Women" [4]:32).

He will reward the good far more than they deserve: "For those who do good is the best (reward) and more. Neither dust nor ignominy cometh near their faces. Such are rightful owners of the Garden; they will abide therein" (*Sūrah* "Jonah" [10]:27); "Whoso bringeth a good deed will receive tenfold the like thereof" (*Sūrah* "Cattle" [6]:160).

Note 6: *Abu Hanifah* (699-767), *Malik* ibn Anas (715-796), and Abu Abd Allah Muhammad al-*Shafii* (767-820), together with *Ibn Hanbal* (see note above, p. 134), were the founders of the four major schools of Islamic law.

144: "*God doeth what He will*" (*Sūrah* "The Family of Imran" [3]:40, passim).

Muhammad ibn al-Shafii al-*Fudali* (d. 1821) assembled a Muslim catechism, or "creed".

145: Ibn Hanbal (see editor's note above, p. 134) and other *partisans of tradition alone* accentuated a literal interpretation of the Koran and accepted anthropomorphic descriptions of God *bilā kayfa wa lā tashbīh*, that is, "without asking any questions [about how they apply to God] and without comparing [God to His creatures]".

147: "Thee (alone) we worship; Thee (alone) we ask for help. Show us the *straight path*, the path of those whom Thou hast favored; not (the path) of those who earn Thine anger nor of those who go astray" (*Sūrah* "The Opening" [1]:4-7).

147-48: "No man can say that Jesus is the Lord *except by the Holy Spirit*" (1 Cor. 12:3).

149: Note 11: "*All things are* Ātmā": "*Ātmā* was indeed *Brahma* in the beginning. It knew only that 'I am *Brahma*'. Therefore It became all. And whoever among the gods knew It also became That; and the same with sages and men. . . . And to this day whoever in like manner knows 'I am *Brahma*' becomes all this universe. Even the gods cannot prevail against him, for he becomes their *Ātmā*" (*Brihadāranyaka Upanishad*, 1.4.10).

150: Note 12: For *Thomas Aquinas*, see editor's note for "Alternations in Semitic Monotheism", p. 82.

151: *Averroes*—Ibn Rushd (1126-98)—was a philosopher, physician, and mathematician whose works were widely influential in the medieval West;

his *Tahāfut al-tahāfut*, or "Incoherence of the Incoherence", was written in response to Ghazzali's famous work *The Incoherence of the Philosophers* and includes a defense of the Aristotelian understanding of *secondary causes.*

155: The *Tao Te Ching*, traditionally ascribed to the ancient Chinese sage Lao-Tzu, is the fundamental sacred text of Taoism; the introductory sentence reads: "The *tao* that can be talked about is not the true *Tao; the name that can be named is not the true Name."*

For *Shankara*, see editor's notes for "Alternations in Semitic Monotheism", p. 70 and "Images of Islam", p. 127, Note 19.

For *Madhva*, see editor's note for "Images of Islam", p. 127, Note 19.

Ramanuja (1017-c. 1137) is widely regarded as the classic exponent of *Vishishta Advaita*, that is, the Hindu *darshana* or perspective of "qualified non-dualism", in which emphasis is placed on the personal nature of God.

157: *"Zeal for the house of the Lord"*: "For the zeal of Thine house hath eaten me up; and the reproaches of them that reproached Thee are fallen upon me" (Ps. 69:9; cf. John 2:17).

158: *"Divergence among the doctors of the Law is a blessing"* (*Ikhtilāf al-ʿulamāʾi rahmah*) (*hadīth*).

159: Note 17: Meister *Eckhart* (see editor's notes for "On the Margin of Liturgical Improvisations", p. 7, Note 8; "The Question of Protestantism", p. 52; and "The Problem of Moral Divergences", p. 7) distinguished between *Gott* or God, that is, the Divine insofar as it expresses itself as a person, and *Gottheit* or *Godhead*, which is the transpersonal divinity of the Absolute as such.

161: For al-*Hasan* ibn Ali, see editor's note for "Images of Islam", p. 119.

Abu Bakr al-*Kalabadhi* (d. 990 or 995) was the author of "The Book of Acquaintance with the Doctrine of the Sufis" (*Kitab al-taʿarruf li-madhhab ahl al-tasawwuf*), the first attempt to reconcile the teaching of Sufism with orthodox Islam.

Note 22: Abd al-Karim al-*Jili* (c. 1365-c. 1412) systematized the teachings of Ibn Arabi, notably in his most important work, *The Universal Man*, which is concerned with both cosmological and metaphysical questions.

162: Note 23: The *Jabriyyah* was a Muslim sect, eventually excluded from orthodox Islam, which emphasized the power or constraint (*jabar*) of God in such a way as to deny human free will.

Ashari (see editor's note above, p. 133) taught that all possibilities are created by God, but that man is responsibile for "acquiring" or "appropriating" actions from among these possibilities, thus becoming accountable for his choices and deeds.

164: *Dionysius the Areopagite* (dated c. 500 by many scholars) was a disciple of Saint Paul (Acts 17:34) and the greatest of all Christian masters of apophatic theology.

Palamite doctrine is the teaching of Gregory Palamas (c. 1296-1359), a monk of Mount Athos, known for his distinction between the Essence of God, which remains forever beyond every creature, and God's uncreated energies, in which the deified man comes to participate.

166: Note 26: *"Wisdom according to the flesh"*: "In simplicity and godly sincerity, not with fleshly wisdom, but by the grace of God, we have had our conversation in the world" (2 Cor. 1:12).

167: Note 28: *Origen* (185-252), the most prolific and influential of the early Church Fathers, is best known for his doctrine of the *apocatastasis* or universal salvation, esoterically linked with the recovery, through sleepless attention, of man's primordial unity in God.

Paradise as Theophany

169: *"Everything is* Ātmā": see editor's note for "Dilemmas of Muslim Scholasticism", p. 149, Note 11.

172: *"In my Father's house are many mansions:* if it were not so, I would have told you. I go to prepare a place for you" (John 14:2).

173: "Behold, the *kingdom* of God *is within you*" (Luke 17:21).

For *Ibn Arabi*, see editor's note for "Alternations in Semitic Monotheism", p. 81, Note 21.

Note 8: The *Fusūs al-Hikam*, or "Bezels of Wisdom", one of Ibn Arabi's most renowned works, consists of a series of mystical reflections on the wisdom embodied in the lives and characters of twenty-seven prophets; the *"Kalimah Muhammadiyyah"*, or "Muhammadan Word", is the twenty-seventh and final chapter.

Atomism and Creation

175: For *Ashari*, see editor's note for "Dilemmas of Muslim Scholasticism", p. 133.

"God *doeth what He will*" (*Sūrah* "The Family of Imran" [3]:40, passim).

176: For *Ghazzali*, see editor's note for "Dilemmas of Muslim Scholasticism", p. 139.

The *Mutazilites*, members of an early school of Islam that stressed human freedom and the justice of God, espoused the use of reason in finding a middle way between unbelief and fideism.

On the Divine Will

181: "*God doeth what He will*" (*Sūrah* "The Family of Imran" [3]:40, passim).

"*Pharaoh's heart was hardened*" (Exod. 7:22, 8:19; cf. Exod. 9:7, 35); "*Pharaoh hardened his heart*" (Exod. 8:32; cf. Exod. 8:15, 9:34); "Yahweh *hardened the heart of Pharaoh*" (Exod. 9:12; cf. Exod. 10:20, 11:10, 14:8); "*I have hardened his heart, and the heart of his servants*" (Exod. 10:1).

"*God leadeth astray whom He will*, and guideth whom He will. He is the Mighty, the Wise" (*Sūrah* "Abraham" [14]:4).

182: For *Ibn Arabi*, see editor's note for "Alternations in Semitic Monotheism", p. 81, Note 21.

The souls testify that God is their Lord: "And (remember) when thy Lord brought forth from the Children of Adam, from their reins, their seed, and made them testify of themselves, (saying): Am I not your Lord? They said: Yea, verily. We testify. (That was) lest ye should say at the Day of Resurrection: Lo! of this we were unaware" (*Sūrah* "The Heights" [7]:172).

For *Ghazzali*, see editor's note for "Dilemmas of Muslim Scholasticism", p. 139.

"God created man *in His* own *image*, in the image of God created He him; male and female created He them" (Gen. 1:27).

185: "*Everything is* Ātmā": see editor's note for "Dilemmas of Muslim Scholasticism", p. 149, Note 11.

Selections from Letters and Other Previously Unpublished Writings

189: Selection 1: Letter of 6 January 1984.

Selection 2: Letter of 18 November 1984.

189-90: "For when we were in the *flesh*, the motions of sin, which were by the law, did work in our members to bring forth fruit unto death. But now we are delivered from the law, that being dead wherein we were held; that we should serve in newness of *spirit*, and not in the oldness of the letter" (Rom. 7:5-6). "There is therefore now no condemnation to them which are in Christ Jesus, who walk not after the *flesh*, but after the *Spirit*" (Rom. 8:1).

190: "*He hath no associate*" (*Sūrah* "Cattle" [6]:164, passim).

René Guénon (1886-1951), a French metaphysician and prolific scholar of religions, was one of the formative authorities of the traditionalist or perennialist school; in Guénon's writings the term "religion" is reserved for the exoterism of the Abrahamic traditions, where salvation is understood to consist in the preservation or perpetuation of the human individual rather than in his final deliverance from individuality as such.

191: Selection 3: "The Book of Keys", No. 224, "Islam and Christianity".

"God *became man that man might become God*" is the formulation of Irenaeus (c. 130-c. 200) and Athanasius (c. 296-373), among other Church Fathers.

"*There is no divinity but the only Divinity*" is the first *Shahādah*, or "testimony", of Islam.

Selection 4: Letter of 31 July 1986.

192: Selection 5: Letter of 9 May 1982.

Abu Abdullah Muhammad al-Arabi al-*Darqawi* (1760-1823) was a Moroccan Sufi *shaykh* of the Shadhiliyyah lineage.

193: *Diogenes* of Sinope (c. 412-323 B.C.) was a Greek cynic philosopher.

Sayyidna Isa is "the Lord Jesus".

Selection 6: Letter of 25 May 1982.

The *opening paragraph* to which the author refers is the first paragraph of "The Question of Protestantism", p. 23.

195: Selection 7: "The Book of Keys", No. 535, "Foundation of the Islamic Argument".

The three *evangelical counsels* of poverty, chastity, and obedience, also known as the "counsels of perfection", gave rise to the traditional vows of the monk.

The disciples did not wash: "Then came to Jesus scribes and Pharisees, which were of Jerusalem, saying, Why do thy disciples transgress the tradition of the elders? for they wash not their hands when they eat bread" (Matt. 15:1-2; cf. editor's note for "The Problem of Moral Divergences", p. 60).

196: Selection 8: Letter of 31 October 1972.

Antumā 'l-hayātu fī dīni 'r-Rahmān is Arabic for: "They are the life in the religion of the All-Merciful."

Isa and *Maryam* are Jesus and Mary.

Illatī ahsanat farjahāh—"who kept her virginity intact"—is a phrase from the Koran: "And Mary, daughter of Imran, *who kept her virginity intact*, therefor We breathed therein something of Our Spirit" (*Sūrah* "The Banning" [66]:12).

"For, behold, *the kingdom of* God *is within you*" (Luke 17:21).

"*But thou, when thou prayest, enter into thy closet, and when thou hast shut thy door, pray to thy Father, which is in secret*" (Matt. 6:6).

197: Selection 9: Letter of 22 April 1982.

198: Selection 10: "The Book of Keys", No. 683, "The Shut Door".

"*But thou, when thou prayest, enter into thy closet, and when thou hast shut thy door, pray to thy Father, which is in secret*" (Matt. 6:6).

"Jesus said unto him, *Let the dead bury their dead*: but go thou and preach the kingdom of God" (Matt. 8:22, Luke 9:60). "And Jesus said unto him, *No man, having put his hand to the plough, and looking back, is fit for the kingdom of God*" (Luke 9:62).

"*There is no god but God*" is the first *Shahādah*, or "testimony", of Islam.

199: "*I am black, but beautiful*" (Song of Sol. 1:5).

"*Pray* to thy Father, which is *in secret*" (Matt. 6:6).

Selection 11: Letter of 2 July 1982.

For Martin *Luther*, see editor's note for "The Question of Protestantism", p. 26.

The author's *chapter on Lutheran Evangelicalism* is "The Question of Protestantism" in the present volume; see editor's note for that chapter, p. 23.

With regard to the *Protestant phenomenon*, the author writes elsewhere: "For Guénon the whole issue was simple, although I am not criticizing him for this because he had other preoccupations: Catholicism is orthodox; Protestantism is heterodox; Luther is the worst of heresiarchs. Yet faced with the immensity of the Protestant phenomenon, this is insufficient; the question is far too important. I could not write a whole book, but I thought I could cover the essential in one chapter; it contains all the indispensable elements, but it is possible that some of these will go unnoticed and that the reader will fail to make the applications they call for; once again it is difficult for me, given my mental structure, to put myself in the place of a given reader, or of all readers" (Letter of 22 April 1982).

200: Selection 12: Letter of 20 March 1967.

Sayyidatna Maryam is "the Lady Mary".

Summer and winter caravans: "For the taming of Quraysh, for their taming (We cause) the caravans to set forth in winter and summer" (*Sūrah* "Quraysh" [106]:1-2).

The story of Majnun and *Layla*, one of the best known in the Islamic world, tells of a young man nicknamed *majnun*, literally "mad-man", because of his love for a beautiful woman with hair as black as the "night" (*layla*); in Sufism Layla comes to stand for the divine Beloved, and more particularly for the dazzling darkness of the divine Essence.

201: Selection 13: Letter of 11 November 1971.

Hadhā'l-ladhī razaqanā min qabl—"This is what was given us aforetime"—comes from the following Koranic verse: "And give glad tidings (O Muhammad) unto those who believe and do good works; that theirs are Gardens underneath which rivers flow; as often as they are regaled with food of the fruit thereof, they say: This is what was given us aforetime; and it is given to them in resemblance. There for them are pure companions; there for ever they abide" (*Sūrah* "The Cow" [2]:25).

Selection 14: "The Book of Keys", No. 595, "Truth and Presence, Islam and Christianity".

203: Selection 15: Letter of 2 July 1982.

Selection 16: Letter of 28 January 1983.

Teresa of Avila (1515-82), a Spanish Carmelite nun and mystic, wrote extensively on the stages of the spiritual life and the levels of prayer.

204: Selection 17: Letter of 9 May 1982.

205: Selection 18: "The Book of Keys", No. 275, "The Two Ways of Connection".

Ibrāhīmī, Mūsāwī, ʿĪsāwī, and *Maryamī:* that is of Abraham, of Moses, of Jesus, and of Mary.

For the *Fusūs al-Hikam of Ibn Arabi,* see editor's note for "Paradise as Theophany", p. 173, Note 8.

The Shaykh of our Tarīqah *is* Maryamī: The author, who here refers to himself, was a Sufi master, and the *tarīqah* he founded and guided, a branch of the *Shādhilīyyah* lineage, is of a Marian provenance; known as the *Tarīqah Maryamīyyah,* it was blessed with the celestial patronage of the Virgin Mary—a patronage, Schuon explained, that was bestowed freely by Heaven and not by virtue of any initiative or intention of his own: "The coming of Sayyidatna Maryam did not depend upon my own will but upon the will of Heaven; it was a totally unexpected and unimaginable gift" (Letter of September 1981).

For the *Shaykh al-Alawi,* see editor's note for "Dilemmas of Muslim Scholasticism", p. 133, Note 1.

Hikmah Maryamīyyah is "Marian wisdom", and *Hikmah ʿĪsāwīyyah* is "the wisdom of Jesus"; *Muhammadīyyah* means "Muhammadan".

206: Selection 19: Letter of 19 April 1973.

207: *Jalal al-Din Rumi* (1207-73), a Sufi mystic and poet, was the founder of the Mevlevi order.

Selection 20: "The Book of Keys", No. 274, "Where is Paradise?".

"For, behold, the kingdom of God is *within you*" (Luke 17:21).

"*Pray without ceasing*" (1 Thess. 5:17).

"*If there is a Paradise on earth, it is here, it is here, it is here*": The Mogul emperor Jahangir (1569-1626), quoting a Persian poet's famous description of the Peacock Throne, is said to have uttered these words upon his completion of the Shalimar Gardens.

Selection 21: Letter of 4 April 1956.

The Spiritual Virtues according to Saint Francis of Assisi

209: "*The Spiritual Virtues according to Saint Francis of Assisi*" was first published under the title "Les vertus spirituelles selon Saint François d'Assise" in the journal *Études traditionnelles* (April-May, 1953); an English translation of the article appeared in the journal *Studies in Comparative Religion* (Vol. 4, No. 3 [1970]) and was reprinted in the 1985 World Wisdom Books edition of the present volume, *Christianity/Islam: Essays on Esoteric Ecumenicism*, trans. Gustavo Polit (Bloomington, Indiana).

Francis of Assisi (1181-1226), founder of the Order of Friars Minor, or Franciscans, took the admonition of Christ to abandon all for his sake (Matt. 10:7-19) as a personal call to poverty and holiness and was noted for bearing the stigmata of Christ.

In this article the author quotes several passages from an Italian collection of the saint's meditations, though on this page he cites Latin titles: *Laudes*, or "Praises", and *Beatitudes*, or "Beatitudes".

"*Poverty of spirit*": "Blessed are the *poor in spirit*: for theirs is the kingdom of heaven" (Matt. 5:3).

Hate themselves: "If any man come to me, and hate not his father, and mother, and wife, and children, and brethren, and sisters, yea, and his own life also, he cannot be my disciple" (Luke 14:26).

Love those who persecute them: "Love your enemies, bless them that curse you, do good to them that hate you, and pray for them which despitefully use you, and persecute you" (Matt. 5:44).

Strike them on the cheek: "Unto him that smiteth thee on the one cheek offer also the other" (Luke 6:29; cf. Matt. 5:39).

"*One thing* is *needful*" (Luke 10:42).

210: The "*Canticle of Brother Sun*", the most famous of Francis's works, consists in a litany of praises offered to "my Lord, with all your creatures", including "Sister Moon and the Stars", "Brother Wind", "Sister Water", "Brother Fire", "Mother Earth", and "especially Sir Brother Sun".

The Roman Catholic Rosary includes the words: "Hail Mary, *full of grace*, the Lord is with thee; blessed art thou amongst women, and blessed is the fruit of thy womb, Jesus" (cf. Luke 1:28, 42).

Louis IX (1214-70), King of France from 1226, is said to have fed beggars from his table, eaten their leavings, and washed their feet.

211: *Wisdom of the flesh*: "In simplicity and godly sincerity, not with fleshly wisdom, but by the grace of God, we have had our conversation in the world" (2 Cor. 1:12).

212: *Hesychasts* are monks of the Eastern Christian tradition whose aim is to attain a state of *hesychia*, that is, inner stillness or "*holy silence*", through the practice of the Jesus Prayer or other prayer of the heart.

GLOSSARY OF FOREIGN TERMS AND PHRASES

'*Abd* (Arabic): "servant" or "slave"; as used in Islam, the servant or worshiper of God in His aspect of *Rabb* or "Lord".

Ab extra (Latin): "from outside"; proceeding from something extrinsic or external.

Ad majorem Dei gloriam (Latin): "for the greater glory of God".

Advaita (Sanskrit): "non-dualist" interpretation of the *Vedānta*; Hindu doctrine according to which the seeming multiplicity of things is the product of ignorance, the only true reality being *Brahma*, the One, the Absolute, the Infinite, which is the unchanging ground of appearance.

Agathon (Greek): "the Good"; in Platonism, a name for the Supreme Reality.

Ahādīth (Arabic): see *hadīth*.

Allāh (Arabic): "the (one and only) God".

Ānanda (Sanskrit): "bliss, beatitude, joy"; one of the three essential aspects of *Apara-Brahma*, together with *Sat*, "being", and *Chit*, "consciousness".

Anaphora (Greek): "offering, oblation"; the central prayer of the Eastern Orthodox Liturgy, which begins with the words, "Let us stand aright; let us stand with fear; let us attend, that we may offer the holy oblation (*anaphora*) in peace."

Apara-Brahma (Sanskrit): the "non-supreme" or penultimate *Brahma*, also called *Brahma saguna*; in the author's teaching, the "relative Absolute".

Apocatastasis (Greek): "restitution, restoration"; among certain Christian theologians, including Clement of Alexandria, Origen, and Gregory of Nyssa, the doctrine that all creatures will finally be saved.

Ascesis (Greek): "exercise, practice, training", as of an athlete; a regimen of self-denial, especially one involving fasting, prostrations, and other bodily disciplines.

Ātmā or *Ātman* (Sanskrit): the real or true "Self", underlying the ego and its manifestations; in the perspective of *Advaita Vedānta*, identical with *Brahma*.

Avatāra (Sanskrit): the earthly "descent", incarnation, or manifestation of God, especially of Vishnu in the Hindu tradition.

Ayāh (Arabic, plural *ayāt*): "sign, mark"; in Islam, a sign of God's power, especially a miracle; a verse of the Koran.

Barakah (Arabic): "blessing", grace; in Islam, a spiritual influence or energy emanating originally from God, but often attached to sacred objects and spiritual persons.

Basmalah (Arabic): traditional Muslim formula of blessing, found at the beginning of all but one of the *sūrahs* of the Koran, consisting of the words *Bismi 'Llāhi 'r-Rahmāni 'r-Rahīm*, "In the Name of God, the Clement (*Rahmān*), the Merciful (*Rahīm*)".

Bhakta (Sanskrit): a follower of the spiritual path of *bhakti*; a person whose relationship with God is based primarily on adoration and love.

Bhakti, bhakti-mārga (Sanskrit): the spiritual "path" (*mārga*) of "love" (*bhakti*) and devotion; see *jnāna* and *karma*.

Bodhi (Sanskrit, Pali): "awakened, enlightened"; in Buddhism, the attainment of perfect clarity of mind, in which things are seen as they truly are.

Bodhisattva (Sanskrit, Pali): literally, "enlightenment-being"; in *Mahāyāna* Buddhism, one who postpones his own final enlightenment and entry into *Nirvāna* in order to aid all other sentient beings in their quest for Buddha-hood.

Brahma or *Brahman* (Sanskrit): the Supreme Reality, the Absolute.

Brahma nirguna (Sanskrit): *Brahma* considered as transcending all "qualities", attributes, or predicates; God as He is in Himself; also called *Para-Brahma*.

Brahma saguna (Sanskrit): *Brahma* "qualified" by attributes and predicates; God insofar as He can be known by man; also called *Apara-Brahma*.

Buddha (Sanskrit, Pali): "one who has awakened"; in *Mahāyāna* Buddhism, one in a series of enlightened beings who come into the world at various moments of history to re-establish the *dharma*.

Buddhi (Sanskrit): "Intellect"; the highest faculty of knowledge, distinct from *manas*, that is, mind or reason.

Calix sanguis mei (Latin): "the cup, or chalice, of my blood"; from the words of institution in the canon of the Tridentine Mass.

Chit (Sanskrit): "consciousness"; one of the three essential aspects of *Apara-Brahma*, together with *Sat*, "being", and *Ānanda*, "bliss, beatitude, joy".

Civitas Dei (Latin): "city of God".

Civitas diaboli (Latin): "city of the devil".

Civitas terrena (Latin): "earthly city".

Creatio ex nihilo (Latin): "creation out of nothing"; the doctrine that God Himself is the sufficient cause of the universe, needing nothing else; often set in contrast to emanationist cosmogonies.

Darshana (Sanskrit): a spiritual "perspective", point of view, or school of thought; also the "viewing" of a holy person, object, or place, together with the resulting blessing or merit.

Deificatio (Latin): "deification", participation in the nature of God (cf. 2 Pet. 1:4); in Eastern Christian theology, the supreme goal of human life; see *theosis*.

Deo juvante (Latin): literally, "God helping"; with God's help.

Deo volente (Latin): "God willing"; by or with God's will.

Dharma (Sanskrit): in Hinduism, the underlying "law" or "order" of the cosmos as expressed in sacred rites and in actions appropriate to various social relationships and human vocations; in Buddhism, the practice and realization of Truth.

Dhikr (Arabic): "remembrance" of God, based upon the repeated invocation of His Name; central to Sufi practice, where the remembrance is often supported by the single word *Allāh*.

Dhikru 'Llāh (Arabic): "remembrance, or invocation, of God".

Dios (Spanish): "God".

Distinguo (Latin): literally, "I mark or set off, differentiate", often used in the dialectic of the medieval Scholastics; any philosophical distinction.

Domine non sum dignus (Latin): "Lord, I am not worthy [that Thou shouldest come under my roof; but speak the word only and my soul shall be healed]"; spoken by the priest during the Tridentine Mass before communicating and before giving Communion to the people; cf. Matt. 8:8.

Epiclesis (Greek): "invocation"; in the Eastern Orthodox Liturgy, a petition addressed to God the Father, asking that He send the Holy Spirit upon the

247

bread and wine of the Eucharist to make them, or reveal them to be, the body and blood of Christ.

Ex cathedra (Latin): literally, "from the throne"; in Roman Catholicism, authoritative teaching promulgated by the Pope and regarded as infallible.

Ex nihilo (Latin): "out of nothing"; see *creatio ex nihilo*.

Ex opere operato (Latin): literally, "from the work performed"; Christian teaching that divine grace is mediated through the sacraments by virtue of the corresponding rites themselves and independently of the merits or intentions of those by whom the rites are performed; in contrast to *ex opere operantis*, "from the work of the one working".

Fanā (Arabic): "extinction, annihilation, evanescence"; in Sufism, the spiritual station or degree of realization in which all individual attributes and limitations are extinguished in union with God; see *Nirvāna*.

Faqīr (Arabic, plural *fuqarā*): literally, the "poor one"; in Sufism, a follower of the spiritual Path, whose "indigence" or "poverty" (*faqr*) testifies to complete dependence on God and a desire to be filled by Him alone.

Faqr (Arabic): "indigence, spiritual poverty"; see *faqīr*.

Filioque (Latin): "and (from) the Son"; a term added to the Nicene Creed by the Western Church to express the "double procession" of the Holy Spirit from the Father "and the Son"; rejected by the Eastern Orthodox Church.

Fitrah (Arabic): in Islam, the natural predisposition of man, as created by God, to act in accordance with the will of Heaven; the original uprightness of humanity (cf. *Sūrah* "The Romans" [30]:30); in the author's usage, the primordial norm or "nature of things".

Flabella (Latin): "fans"; liturgical fans made of leather, silk, feathers, or precious metals, used as a mark of honor for bishops and princes; two such fans flank the *sedia gestatoria* whenever the Pope is carried in state.

Fuqarā (Arabic): see *faqīr*.

Gnosis (Greek): "knowledge"; spiritual insight, principial comprehension, divine wisdom.

Gopi (Sanskrit): literally, "keeper of the cows"; in Hindu tradition, one of the cowherd girls involved with Krishna in the love affairs of his youth, symbolic of the soul's devotion to God.

Guru (Sanskrit): literally, "weighty", grave, venerable; in Hinduism, a spiritual master; one who gives initiation and instruction in the spiritual path and in whom is embodied the supreme goal of realization or perfection.

Hadīth (Arabic, plural *ahādīth*): "saying, narrative"; an account of the words or deeds of the Prophet Muhammad, transmitted through a traditional chain of known intermediaries.

Hadīth qudsī (Arabic): "divine, holy narrative"; a saying in which God Himself speaks through the mouth of the Prophet Muhammad.

Hoc facite in meam commemorationem (Latin): "Do this in remembrance of me"; from Christ's words of institution in the Mass or Liturgy.

Hypostasis (Greek, plural *hypostases*): literally, "substance"; in Eastern Christian theology, a technical term for one of the three "Persons" of the Trinity; the Father, the Son, and the Holy Spirit are distinct *hypostases* sharing a single *ousia*, or essence.

Ihsān (Arabic): "excellence, perfection"; in Islam, virtuous or beautiful action; spiritual excellence.

Ijtihād (Arabic): literally, "exertion"; in Islamic law, an independent judgment concerning a legal or theological question involving a reinterpretation of the Koran or *Sunnah*.

Īmān (Arabic): "trust"; in Islam, faith and trust in God and in the Prophet Muhammad, hence in the content of his message.

In divinis (Latin): literally, "in or among divine things"; within the divine Principle; the plural form is used insofar as the Principle comprises both *Para-Brahma*, Beyond-Being or the Absolute, and *Apara-Brahma*, Being or the relative Absolute.

In persona Christi (Latin): "in the person of Christ"; used in reference to the sacramental words and actions of the consecrating priest in a Christian liturgy.

Īshvara (Sanskrit): literally, "possessing power", hence master; God understood as a personal being, as Creator and Lord.

Islām (Arabic): "submission, peace"; in Islam, the peace that comes from submission or surrender to God.

Ism (Arabic): "name"; in Sufism, the Name of God.

Ithbāt (Arabic): literally, "affirmation"; in Islam, used in reference to the second part of the first *Shahādah*, consisting of the words *illā 'Llāh*, "but [except] God"; see *nafy*.

Japa (Sanskrit): "repetition" of a *mantra* or sacred formula, often containing one of the Names of God; see *dhikr*.

Jejunium (Latin): "fasting, abstinence from food".

Jiriki (Japanese): literally, "power of the self"; a Buddhist term for spiritual methods that emphasize one's own efforts in reaching the goal of liberation or salvation, as for example in Zen; in contrast to *tariki*.

Jīvan-mukta (Sanskrit): one who is "liberated" while still in this "life"; a person who has attained a state of spiritual perfection or self-realization before death; in contrast to *videha-mukta*, one who is liberated at the moment of death.

Jnāna or *jnāna-mārga* (Sanskrit): the spiritual "path" (*mārga*) of "knowledge" (*jnāna*) and intellection; see *bhakti* and *karma*.

Jōdo or *Jōdo-Shinshū* (Japanese): "pure land" or "true pure land school"; a sect of Japanese Buddhism founded by Shinran, based on faith in the power of the Buddha Amida to bring his devotees to his untainted, transcendent realm and characterized by use of the *nembutsu*.

Kāfir (Arabic): literally, one who "covers" or "conceals"; in Islam, the person who deliberately covers the truth and is thus in fundamental opposition to God and in danger of damnation.

Kalām (Arabic): literally, "discourse, speech"; in Islam, the science of theology, based upon a reasoned exposition of the Koran and *sunnah*.

Karma, karma-mārga, karma-yoga (Sanskrit): the spiritual "path" (*mārga*) or method of "union" (*yoga*) based upon right "action, work" (*karma*); see *bhakti* and *jnāna*; in Hinduism and Buddhism, the law of consequence, in which the present is explained in relation to the nature and quality of one's past actions.

Logos (Greek): "word, reason"; in Christian theology, the divine, uncreated Word of God (cf. John 1:1); the transcendent Principle of creation and revelation.

Magnificat (Latin): literally, "doth magnify"; the song of praise sung by the Blessed Virgin Mary (Luke 1:46-55) when her cousin Elizabeth had greeted her as the mother of the Lord, so named from the opening word in the Vulgate: *Magnificat anima mea Dominum*, "My soul doth magnify the Lord."

Mahabbah (Arabic): "love"; in Sufism, the spiritual way based upon love and devotion, analogous to the Hindu *bhakti mārga*; see *ma'rifah*.

Mahāyāna (Sanskrit): "great vehicle"; a form of Buddhism, including such traditions as Zen and *Jōdo-Shinshū*, regarded by its followers as the fullest or most adequate expression of the Buddha's teaching; distinguished by the idea that *Nirvāna* is not other than *samsāra* truly seen as it is.

Mahdi (Arabic): "the guided one"; in Islam, an eschatological figure who will arise at the end of the world to restore the observance of Islam after a period of decline; identified in Shiism with the twelfth, or hidden, imam.

Majlis (Arabic): literally, "a place of sitting"; a session or meeting; in Sufism, a gathering of *fuqarā* for recitation or chanting of *dhikr*.

Mantra (Sanskrit): literally, "instrument of thought"; a word or phrase of divine origin, often including a Name of God, repeated by those initiated into its proper use as a means of salvation or liberation; see *japa*.

Ma'rifah (Arabic): "knowledge"; in Sufism, the spiritual way based upon knowledge or *gnosis*, analogous to the Hindu *jnāna-mārga*; see *mahabbah*.

Māyā (Sanskrit): "artifice, illusion"; in *Advaita Vedānta*, the beguiling concealment of *Brahma* in the form or under the appearance of a lower reality.

Nafy (Arabic): literally, "negation"; in Islam, used in reference to the first part of the first *Shahādah*, consisting of the words *Lā ilāha*, "there is no god"; see *ithbāt*.

Nembutsu (Japanese): "remembrance or mindfulness of the Buddha", based upon the repeated invocation of his Name.

Nemo bonus nisi solus Deus (Latin): "None is good but God alone" (cf. Matt. 19:17, Mark 10:18).

Nirvāna (Sanskrit): "blowing out, extinction"; in Indian traditions, especially Buddhism, the extinction of the fires of passion and the resulting, supremely blissful state of liberation from egoism and attachment; see *fanā*.

Nolite dare sanctum canibus (Latin): "Give not that which is holy unto the dogs" (Matt. 7:6).

Oratio (Latin): literally, "language, speech"; in Christian usage, words addressed to God; prayer.

Para-Brahma (Sanskrit): the "supreme" or ultimate *Brahma*, also called *Brahma nirguna*; the Absolute as such.

Paramātmā or *Paramātman* (Sanskrit): the "supreme Self".

Parousia (Greek): literally, "presence, arrival"; in Christian doctrine, the Second Coming of Christ.

Pax Romana (Latin): "Roman peace"; period from the end of the civil war under Augustus Caesar in 27 B.C. to the death of Marcus Aurelius in 180 A.D. during which the Roman Empire experienced its greatest peace and stability.

Pontifex (Latin): "bridge-maker"; man as the link between heaven and earth.

Prapatti (Sanskrit): "seeking refuge"; pious resignation and devotion to God.

Pratyeka Buddha (Sanskrit): "solitary Buddha"; in Buddhism, one who attains enlightenment without a teacher and who makes no attempt to instruct disciples.

Primus inter pares (Latin): "first among equals"; a phrase acknowledging the primacy of honor traditionally accorded to the Bishop of Rome (Pope) in relation to the patriarchs of the other ancient sees of the Church.

Pro domo (Latin): literally, "for (one's own) home or house"; serving the interests of a given perspective or for the benefit of a given group.

Purusha (Sanskrit): "man"; the informing or shaping principle of creation; the "masculine" demiurge or fashioner of the universe, whose sacrifice gave rise to all creation.

Quod absit (Latin): literally, "which is absent from, opposed to, or inconsistent with"; a phrase commonly used by the medieval Scholastics to call attention to an idea that is absurdly inconsistent with accepted principles.

Rahīm (Arabic): see *Basmalah*.

Rahmah (Arabic): "compassion, mercy"; in Islam, one of the Names of God, who is supreme Compassion, Mercy, and Clemency; see *Basmalah*.

Rahmān (Arabic): see *Basmalah*.

Rashidūn (Arabic): "rightly guided", orthodox; in Sunni Islam, used in reference to the first four caliphs: Abu Bakr, Umar, Uthman, and Ali.

Rasūl (Arabic): "messenger, apostle"; in Islam, one whom God sends with a message for a particular people.

Religio perennis (Latin): "perennial religion".

Risālah (Arabic): "message, epistle"; in Islam, the message brought from God for a particular people.

Rishi (Sanskrit): "seer"; in Hinduism, one of the ancient sages whose visions and auditions of Truth are transcribed in the *Veda*s.

Rūh (Arabic): "breath, spirit"; in the Koran (*Sūrah "Al-Hijr"* [15]:29), the breath breathed into human beings by God to bring them to life.

Samsāra (Sanskrit): literally, "wandering"; in Hinduism and Buddhism, transmigration or the cycle of birth, death, and rebirth; also the world of apparent flux and change.

Sanātana Dharma (Sanskrit): "eternal law"; in Hinduism, the universal or absolute law or truth underlying specific and relative laws and truths.

Sat (Sanskrit): "being"; one of the three essential aspects of *Apara-Brahma*, together with *Chit*, "consciousness", and *Ānanda*, "bliss, beatitude, joy".

Sedia gestatoria (Italian): literally, "portable chair"; the throne on which the Pope was traditionally carried in procession.

Shahādah (Arabic): the fundamental "profession" or "testimony" of faith in Islam, consisting of the words *Lā ilāha illā 'Llāh, Muhammadan rasūlu 'Llāh*: "There is no god but God; Muhammad is the messenger of God."

Shakti (Sanskrit): creative "power", expressed in Hinduism in the form of divine femininity.

Sharī'ah (Arabic): "path"; in Islam, the proper mode and norm of life, the path or way willed and marked out by God for man's return to Him; Muslim law or exoterism.

Sharīf (Arabic): "noble"; in Islam, a title of honor for those descended from the Prophet Muhammad.

Shūdra (Sanskrit): a member of the lowest of the four Hindu castes; a laborer.

Solve et coagula (Latin): literally, "dissolve and solidify"; the formula of the alchemical work, in which a reduction to constituent elements precedes an establishment on a new foundation.

Sophia perennis (Greek): "perennial wisdom"; the eternal, non-formal Truth at the heart of all orthodox religious traditions.

Sunnah (Arabic): "custom, way of acting"; in Islam, the norm established by the Prophet Muhammad, including his actions and sayings (see *hadīth*) and serving as a precedent and standard for the behavior of Muslims.

Sūrah (Arabic): one of the one hundred fourteen divisions, or chapters, of the Koran.

Sūtra (Sanskrit): literally, "thread"; a Hindu or Buddhist sacred text; in Hinduism, any short, aphoristic verse or collection of verses, often elliptical in style; in Buddhism, a collection of the discourses of the Buddha.

Tanzīh (Arabic): "remove, declare to be incomparable"; in Islam, the assertion that God is pure and free of all imperfections, hence utterly unlike His creatures; a perspective stressing divine distance and rigor.

Tao (Chinese): literally, "way"; in Taoism, the ultimate Source of all things, from which they come and to which they return; the Way of the universe and the sage.

Tariki (Japanese): literally, "power of the other"; a Buddhist term for forms of spirituality that emphasize the importance of grace or celestial assistance, especially that of the Buddha Amida, as in the Pure Land schools; in contrast to *jiriki*.

Tarīqah (Arabic, plural *turuq*): "path"; in exoteric Islam, a virtual synonym for *sharī'ah*, equivalent to the "straight path" mentioned in the *Fātihah*; in Sufism, the mystical path leading from observance of the *sharī'ah* to self-realization in God; also a Sufi brotherhood.

Tasawwuf (Arabic): a term of disputed etymology, though perhaps from *sūf* for "wool", after the garment worn by many early Sufis; traditional Muslim word for Sufism.

Tashbīh (Arabic): "compare, assimilate"; in Islam, the assertion that God must have some similarity to His creatures, anthropomorphic descriptions of Him in the Koran being analogically accurate; a perspective stressing divine nearness and mercy.

Theosis (Greek): "deification", participation in the nature of God (cf. 2 Pet. 1:4); in Eastern Christian theology, the supreme goal of human life; see *deificatio*.

Torah (Hebrew): "instruction, teaching"; in Judaism, the law of God, as revealed to Moses on Sinai and embodied in the Pentateuch (Genesis, Exodus, Leviticus, Numbers, Deuteronomy).

Turuq (Arabic): see *tarīqah*.

Ummī (Arabic): "unlettered"; a term used in the Koran (*Sūrah* "The Heights" [7]:157-58) to describe the Prophet Muhammad, who is traditionally thought to have been unable to read or write.

Upanishad (Sanskrit): literally, "to sit close by"; hence, any esoteric doctrine requiring direct transmission from master to disciple; in Hinduism, the genre of sacred texts that end or complete the *Veda*s; see *Vedānta*.

Upāya (Sanskrit): "means, expedient, method"; in Buddhist tradition, the adaptation of spiritual teaching to a form suited to the level of one's audience.

Veda (Sanskrit): "knowledge"; in Hinduism, the body of sacred knowledge held to be the basis of orthodoxy and right practice.

Vedānta (Sanskrit): "end or culmination of the *Veda*s"; one of the major schools of traditional Hindu philosophy, based in part on the *Upanishads*, esoteric treatises found at the conclusion of the Vedic scriptures; see *advaita*.

Yin-Yang (Chinese): in Chinese tradition, two opposite but complementary forces or qualities, from whose interpenetration the universe and all its diverse forms emerge; *yin* corresponds to the feminine, the yielding, the moon, and liquidity; *yang* corresponds to the masculine, the resisting, the sun, and solidity.

For a glossary of all key foreign words used in books published by World Wisdom, including metaphysical terms in English, consult:
www.DictionaryofSpiritualTerms.org.
This on-line Dictionary of Spiritual Terms provides extensive definitions, examples, and related terms in other languages.

INDEX

Darqawi, Shaykh, 192, 239
darshana, 23, 236
de Labadie, Jean, 33n, 221
deificatio, 104, 114
Deism, 106
de Maistre, Joseph, 27n, 219
democracy, 6n, 28
Desert Fathers, 3, 215
detachment, 69, 109, 117n, 126,
  205, 210-12
dharma, 177n, 200
Dhāt, 134, 161n
dhikr, 80, 192, 196, 198
Dhikru'Llāh, 197
Diogenes, 193, 239
Dionysius the Areopagite, 164, 237
Dios, 203
dissipation, 211-12
divorce, 57-58, 58n, 59
dvaitavāda, 155
dyotheletism, 76-77

Eckhart, Meister, 7n, 21, 33n, 49,
  52, 60, 81n, 82, 159n, 215, 218,
  221, 224-25, 228, 236
"Effects of the Virtues", 212
Eleusis, 37n, 222
Elias, 132, 233
emperor, 26, 28, 215-16, 231, 242
Enoch, 97
epiclesis, 13, 13n, 14, 14n, 15, 15n,
  16, 16n, 17-18, 18n, 19-21, 216,
  219
Epistle to the Corinthians, 47
Epistle to the Romans, 38, 47, 48n
equilibrium, 31, 38, 43, 58, 61, 63,
  67, 72, 74, 77-79, 107, 109, 111-
  13, 115, 128, 138, 154, 158, 195,
  197, 206
esoterism, 25, 41, 47, 53n, 60-61,
  63, 65, 69, 72, 91, 93, 94n, 95n,
  104, 112-13, 122-23, 128, 129n,
  131n, 189, 204, 229-30
Essence, 69, 72, 82n, 83n, 94, 100,
  103, 134-35, 151, 155, 159,
  161n, 162, 167n, 173-74, 176,

178, 184-86, 237, 241
Eucharist, 4n, 15, 18, 36, 69n, 222.
  See also Communion
Europeans, 74n, 111, 166
Evangelical counsels, 32, 195, 220,
  239
Evangelicalism, 23, 199, 218, 240
exoterism, 25, 52-53, 60-61, 65, 77,
  92, 98n, 104n, 113, 123, 127-28,
  147, 152, 154-55, 160, 165, 203-
  4, 239

Fadak Oasis, 123
Fall (the), 22, 38, 52n, 59, 68, 70,
  78n, 80, 101n, 190, 206, 209
faqr, 81, 196-98
faqīr, 115, 121n, 192, 196
al-Farabi 141n, 234
fasting, 69, 78
Fatimah, 118, 118n, 119-20, 120n,
  122-23, 123n, 124, 124n, 130,
  232
fear, 38n, 40-41, 79, 81, 87, 92, 119-
  20, 120n, 121, 134, 143n, 172n,
  194, 203, 212, 227
femininity, 205
fitrah, 80, 109, 112
flabella, 31
flesh, 28, 33, 37, 49-50, 59, 94-95,
  107, 189, 211, 217, 221, 223-24,
  237-39, 243
formalism, 28, 82, 95, 191
Francis of Assisi, 209, 242-43
friends of God, 53
al-Fudali, 144, 235
fuqarā, 115, 200
Fusūs al-Hikam, 175n, 205, 237,
  242

Gabriel, 204, 223
generosity, 81, 107-8, 113n, 117,
  117n, 137, 143
Gerhardt, Paul 34n, 221
Germanic soul, 7, 23-24, 28, 75n
Germans, 10, 28, 29n, 74n, 221
al-Ghazzali, 139-40, 142n, 143n,

BIOGRAPHICAL NOTES

Frithjof Schuon

Born in Basle, Switzerland in 1907, Frithjof Schuon was the twentieth century's pre-eminent spokesman for the perennialist school of comparative religious thought.

The leitmotif of Schuon's work was foreshadowed in an encounter during his youth with a marabout who had accompanied some members of his Senegalese village to Basle for the purpose of demonstrating their African culture. When Schuon talked with him, the venerable old man drew a circle with radii on the ground and explained: "God is the center; all paths lead to Him." Until his later years Schuon traveled widely, from India and the Middle East to America, experiencing traditional cultures and establishing lifelong friendships with Hindu, Buddhist, Christian, Muslim, and American Indian spiritual leaders.

A philosopher in the tradition of Plato, Shankara, and Eckhart, Schuon was a gifted artist and poet as well as the author of over twenty books on religion, metaphysics, sacred art, and the spiritual path. Describing his first book, *The Transcendent Unity of Religions*, T. S. Eliot wrote, "I have met with no more impressive work in the comparative study of Oriental and Occidental religion", and world-renowned religion scholar Huston Smith said of Schuon, "The man is a living wonder; intellectually apropos religion, equally in depth and breadth, the paragon of our time". Schuon's books have been translated into over a dozen languages and are respected by academic and religious authorities alike.

More than a scholar and writer, Schuon was a spiritual guide for seekers from a wide variety of religions and backgrounds throughout the world. He died in 1998.

James S. Cutsinger (Ph.D., Harvard) is Professor of Theology and Religious Thought at the University of South Carolina.

A widely recognized writer on the *sophia perennis* and the perennialist school, Professor Cutsinger is also an authority on the theology and spirituality of the Christian East. His publications include *Advice to the Serious Seeker: Meditations on the Teaching of Frithjof Schuon, Not of This World: A Treasury of Christian Mysticism, Paths to the Heart: Sufism and the Christian East, The Fullness of God: Frithjof Schuon on Christianity*, and *Prayer Fashions Man: Frithjof Schuon on the Spiritual Life.*